LOEB CLASSICAL LIBRARY

FOUNDED BY JAMES LOEB 1911

EDITED BY

JEFFREY HENDERSON

CICERO

XVa

LCL 189

CICERO

PHILIPPICS
1–6

EDITED AND TRANSLATED BY

D. R. SHACKLETON BAILEY

REVISED BY

JOHN T. RAMSEY
AND
GESINE MANUWALD

HARVARD UNIVERSITY PRESS
CAMBRIDGE, MASSACHUSETTS
LONDON, ENGLAND
2009

50 B|kw|. ²/₁₀   24.10

First published 2009

LOEB CLASSICAL LIBRARY® is a registered trademark
of the President and Fellows of Harvard College

Library of Congress Control Number 2009930988
CIP data available from the Library of Congress

ISBN 978-0-674-99634-2

*Composed in ZephGreek and ZephText by
Technologies 'N Typography, Merrimac, Massachusetts.
Printed on acid-free paper and bound by
The Maple-Vail Book Manufacturing Group*

CONTENTS

LIST OF CICERO'S WORKS   vii

PREFACE   xi

PREFACE TO THE ORIGINAL EDITION   xv

INTRODUCTION   xvii

INTRODUCTION TO THE ORIGINAL EDITION   xxxiii

NOTE ON MANUSCRIPTS AND EDITIONS   xxxvii

DIVERGENCES FROM SHACKLETON BAILEY   xxxix

ABBREVIATIONS   xlv

BIBLIOGRAPHY   xlvii

CHRONOLOGY   lix

MAPS   lxviii

PHILIPPIC 1   1

CONTENTS

PHILIPPIC 2   47

PHILIPPIC 3   173

PHILIPPIC 4   219

PHILIPPIC 5   239

PHILIPPIC 6   299

LIST OF CICERO'S WORKS
SHOWING ARRANGEMENT
IN THIS EDITION

RHETORICAL TREATISES. 5 VOLUMES

VOLUME

   I. [Cicero], Rhetorica ad Herennium

  II. De Inventione.   De Optimo Genere Oratorum.   Topica

 III. De Oratore, Books I–II

 IV. De Oratore, Book III.   De Fato.   Paradoxa Stoicorum.   De Partitione Oratoria

  V. Brutus.   Orator

ORATIONS.   10 VOLUMES

  VI. Pro Quinctio.   Pro Roscio Amerino.   Pro Roscio Comoedo.   De Lege Agraria Contra Rullum

 VII. The Verrine Orations I: In Q. Caecilium. In C. Verrem Actio I.   In C. Verrem Actio II, Books I–II

VIII. The Verrine Orations II: In C. Verrem Actio II, Books III–V

LIST OF CICERO'S WORKS

IX. De Imperio Cn. Pompei (Pro Lege Manilia). Pro Caecina. Pro Cluentio. Pro Rabirio Perduellionis Reo

X. In Catilinam. Pro Murena. Pro Sulla. Pro Flacco

XI. Pro Archia. Post Reditum in Senatu. Post Reditum ad Quirites. De Domo Sua. De Haruspicum Responsis. Pro Cn. Plancio

XII. Pro Sestio. In Vatinium

XIII. Pro Caelio. De Provinciis Consularibus. Pro Balbo

XIV. Pro Milone. In Pisonem. Pro Scauro. Pro Fonteio. Pro Rabirio Postumo. Pro Marcello. Pro Ligario. Pro Rege Deiotaro

XVa. Philippics 1–6

XVb. Philippics 7–14

PHILOSOPHICAL TREATISES. 6 VOLUMES

XVI. De Re Publica. De Legibus

XVII. De Finibus Bonorum et Malorum

XVIII. Tusculan Disputations

XIX. De Natura Deorum. Academica

XX. Cato Maior de Senectute. Laelius de Amicitia. De Divinatione

XXI. De Officiis

LIST OF CICERO'S WORKS

LETTERS.   8 VOLUMES

XXII.   Letters to Atticus, Letters 1–89

XXIII.   Letters to Atticus, Letters 90–165A

XXIV.   Letters to Atticus, Letters 166–281

XXIX.   Letters to Atticus, Letters 282–426

XXV.   Letters to Friends, Letters 1–113

XXVI.   Letters to Friends, Letters 114–280

XXVII.   Letters to Friends, Letters 281–435

XXVIII.   Letters to Quintus and Brutus.   Letter Fragments.   Letter to Octavian.   Invectives. Handbook of Electioneering

PREFACE

D. R. Shackleton Bailey (1917–2005) is well known as an editor and translator, and in both these capacities he is particularly renowned for his work on Cicero's writings and as a contributor to the Loeb Classical Library. So the two present editors, John T. Ramsey and Gesine Manuwald, were very honored and delighted when they were invited to revise for the Loeb series Shackleton Bailey's bilingual edition of Cicero's *Philippics* (1986). We hope that this replacement for the previous Loeb edition by Walter C. A. Ker (1926) will provide a fitting conclusion to Shackleton Bailey's long association with the series and will at the same time honor his memory.

The project only became possible when the University of North Carolina Press reassigned rights to the 1986 edition (now out of print) to Shackleton Bailey's estate, to which the present editors owe a debt of gratitude. Warmest thanks are due especially to Kristine Baseley, D. R. Shackleton Bailey's widow, and to Richard F. Thomas, D. R. Shackleton Bailey's literary executor and Trustee of the Loeb Classical Library Foundation, for making possible this new edition. And finally, Jennifer Snodgrass and

Sharmila Sen of Harvard University Press and their editorial staff have been most supportive and helpful throughout.

To Shackleton Bailey's very brief general introduction to the 1986 edition, we have added a new one that seeks to provide a concise summary of information relevant to understanding how Cicero's *Philippics* came into being and what their aim was. For more detailed treatments, we refer the reader to our commentaries (see Bibliography), and we thank one of our publishers, Walter de Gruyter, for permission to reuse material in the introduction and notes to the present edition. The general introduction is supplemented by a chronology, a sketch of the manuscript tradition, maps, and a bibliography. Each speech is also prefaced by a short introduction setting the speech in its historical context and providing an outline of its structure. In keeping with the format of the series, references to secondary literature have been kept to a minimum; for suggestions for further reading, the reader is referred to the Bibliography. An annotated index (in the second volume of this edition), which includes all proper names occurring in the *Philippics*, should permit the reader to identify every individual and place mentioned in these speeches.

In preparing the Latin text and English translation, we soon discovered that the revision of another author's work presents unique challenges, especially if one is seeking to preserve the flavor of the original. While we tried to remain faithful to Shackleton Bailey's admirable edition, we nonetheless felt the need to revise his text and translation quite considerably in places. In particular, we have removed some of his most audacious conjectures from the Latin text, and we have tried to make the English translation follow more closely Cicero's mode of expression without violating idiomatic English usage. The footnotes to the Latin text chiefly report significant departures from the manuscript traditions; divergences from Shackleton Bailey's text are listed in the Note on Manuscripts and Editions.

The translation of some words in particular provided a challenge, notably highly charged terms such as *res publica* or *patria* or *boni*. In the case of those three words, after consultation with friends and colleagues whom we thank for their generous advice (especially, M. Alexander, D. Berry, J. Briscoe, R. Kaster, A. Lintott, J. D. Morgan, M. Winterbottom, and A. Woodman), we eventually settled on "Republic" (in preference to Shackleton Bailey's "Commonwealth"), "native land" (in preference to "fatherland"), and "decent men" (instead of "honest men"). Our aim has been to convey the meaning of the Latin words without evoking unwanted associations for a modern reader, and we have adopted a similar policy for other expressions.

In carrying out this work, we initially divided the task roughly in half: J. T. Ramsey revising *Philippics* 1–2 and 12–14, and G. Manuwald *Philippics* 3–11. We then subjected our respective versions to each other's critical judgment, and we have had lengthy and fruitful discussions on all major issues. We take joint responsibility for all other material, and we thank the friends and colleagues enumerated above for generously responding to queries on points of detail. We also want to express our inevitable indebtedness to translators of the *Philippics* who have gone before us and not infrequently provided us with an ideal turn of phrase. Especially helpful was the excellent translation of the *Second Philippic* by D. H. Berry (2006). Work on this project by J. T. Ramsey was supported by a fellowship from the National Endowment for the Humanities (2007–08) and by a visiting Smithies Fellowship at Balliol College, Oxford (Hilary Term 2008).

J. T. R. / G. M.
Chicago / London, July 2008

PREFACE TO THE
ORIGINAL EDITION

For all their importance as a historical source and their considerable merit as literature Cicero's *Philippics* remain a comparatively neglected area. P. Fedeli in his Teubner edition of 1982 has provided a comprehensive apparatus criticus and bibliography, but not, in my opinion, a really critical text. There exists no satisfactory English translation and no adequate commentary. The latter desideratum should one day be met by a historian and expert on Roman political institutions, and one of the two principal purposes I have had in mind was to provide such a commentator with a textual and interpretative foundation on which to build. The other is to make the speeches more accessible to students and others interested. The introductions and explanatory notes aim only at providing a necessary minimum. For detailed historical background there are plenty of places to go: standard histories of Rome, R. Syme's *The Roman Revolution* (Oxford, 1939), and recent Ciceronian biographies such as D. Stockton's *Cicero: A Political Biography* (Oxford, 1971) and E. Rawson's *Cicero* (London, 1975).

The textual appendix and references to my earlier textual articles are naturally for specialists and provide explanations or justifications of readings adopted or advanced, particularly conjectures of my own. But I have practiced brevity and deliberately refrained from comment where I feel that none ought to be needed.

I desire to thank the University of North Carolina Press and especially Laura Oaks, who has spared no pains.

[D.R.S.B.]
Cambridge, Massachusetts
January 1985

INTRODUCTION

Title

The title *Philippics* (*orationes Philippicae*) for a corpus of political speeches composed by Cicero during the conflict with Mark Antony in 44–43 B.C. was inspired by a group of speeches delivered by the Greek orator Demosthenes (384–322).[1] Demosthenes' *Philippic Orations* took their name from king Philip II of Macedon, against whom Demosthenes tried to rouse his fellow Athenians to defend their freedom and ward off the threat of Macedonian domination in the period 351 to 341.

Apparently, Cicero himself tentatively described his speeches against Antony as "Philippics" when he sent copies of some of them to Marcus Brutus in the spring of 43, and Brutus wrote back from Greece with approval, having read the *Fifth* and the *Tenth Philippics* (*Ad Brut.* 2.3.4 [trans. SB]): "I am now willing to let them be called by the proud name of 'Philippics,' as you jestingly suggested in one of your letters." (*Iam concedo, ut vel Philippici vocentur, quod tu quadam epistula iocans scripsisti.*)

Cicero seems to have employed jocular language to test the waters and to learn whether this title would find favor

---

[1] All dates are B.C. unless otherwise indicated.

in the eyes of Brutus, who admired Demosthenes and adhered to a style of oratory that aimed at recalling the Attic
orators of the fifth and fourth centuries B.C. (e.g., *Att.*
15.1a.2; *Orat.* 105; 110). In a subsequent letter to Brutus,
Cicero used without qualification the term Brutus had
approved (*Ad Brut.* 2.4.2, of 12 April [trans. SB]): "The
speech (*Phil.* 11) will be sent to you, since I see you enjoy
my 'Philippics.'" (*Haec ad te oratio perferetur, quoniam te
video delectari Philippicis nostris.*)

Since the description is employed in the plural by both
Brutus and Cicero, it was obviously intended to be applied to a group of self-contained, yet thematically connected speeches. The title *Philippicae (orationes)* is am-
ply attested by later authors (e.g., Quint. *Inst.* 3.8.46; Juv.
10.125–126; cf. Plut. *Cic.* 24.6; 48.6), but those same
speeches also are sometimes referred to as (*orationes*)
Antonianae (Gell. *NA* 1.22.17; 6.11.3; 13.1.1; 13.22.6) or
(*orationes*) *in Antonium* (Gell. *NA* 1.16.5; Sen. *Suas.* 6.15;
Macrob. *Sat.* 1.5.5), taking their name, that is, from their
subject matter.

Formation of the Corpus

Cicero's *Philippics* comprise the largest extant collection
of his speeches under a single title. Since other speeches
delivered by Cicero in his struggle with Antony are attested, speeches that have not been preserved and were
not, apparently, included in the collection of *Philippics*
(e.g., a speech before a public meeting, falling between
Phil. 11 and 12: *Fam.* 12.7.1), a particular aim is likely to
have governed the formation of the corpus. The speeches
that were not included in the collection all seem to have

been less relevant to conveying Cicero's assessment of the various protagonists and to portraying his own political stance. By contrast, the actual *Philippics* consistently present Cicero's policy in relation to important events, and they picture Cicero as being incessantly active for the public welfare in his pursuit of the "right" goal. They cover the important stages in the conflict with Mark Antony and maintain a consistency and cohesion in their paradigmatic presentation of Cicero's position.

For the purposes of trying to determine how many speeches were intended to be included in the corpus of *Philippics*, an instructive possible parallel is furnished by a collection of Cicero's consular speeches of 63 that he outlined in 60 (*Att.* 2.1.3). In that instance, too, Cicero did not include all his speeches delivered during a given period, but rather made a selection of twelve speeches. Since in his letter to Atticus he explicitly likens this collection of his consular speeches to Demosthenes' *Philippic Orations*, the number twelve may well have been chosen to recall the number of works in ancient editions of Demosthenes that were assigned to his clash with Philip.

If that was Cicero's intent, there is good reason for surmising that the collection bearing the title *"Philippics"* was intended to comprise twelve, not fourteen speeches as we have it today, even though, in this case, Cicero nowhere enumerates the speeches covered by that name or explains principles of selection. Furthermore, there are good grounds for arguing that the *Third* to the *Fourteenth Philippics* in the modern numbering scheme are the twelve speeches to which Cicero intended to give the title *Philippics*.

To begin with, a fundamental change in the political

landscape occurred between the *Second* and the *Third Philippics*, and that change caused Cicero to alter radically his approach. A key factor in the *First* and the *Second Philippics* is the physical presence of Antony in Rome. The *Third* to the *Fourteenth Philippics*, by contrast, were delivered after Antony had departed for Gaul in late November 44. Therefore, those twelve speeches are cast as indirect invectives against a physically absent enemy (Antony), thereby inviting comparison with Demosthenes' struggle against the physically remote enemy Philip, king of Macedon. Furthermore, the *Third* to the *Fourteenth Philippics* of Cicero share with their Demosthenic counterparts the role of giving advice to the populace—and, in Cicero's case, to the senate—in the interests of maintaining freedom and putting up a stout resistance to the threat of tyranny.

Moreover, the *Third Philippic* is the unmistakable starting point in Cicero's fight against Antony and outlines his overall strategy. It is the first speech to sound the battle cry (3.1–2) and to urge that vigorous measures be taken to crush Antony before his military operations can be turned against Rome. In this way too, it is reminiscent of the situation that faced the Athenians when Demosthenes urged them to take timely and vigorous action against the growing threat of Philip of Macedon before it was too late. Cicero's *Third Philippic* is also the first speech in the cycle to issue the often repeated call for Antony to be regarded as a "public enemy" and a dire threat to the Republic (3.14). The *Third Philippic* and subsequent speeches consistently employ such disjunctive pairs as "hero vs. traitor," "consul vs. enemy," "war vs. peace," "Republic vs. tyranny," or "liberty vs. slavery." Tellingly, the final speech in the series of twelve running from the *Third* to the *Four-teenth Philippics* takes the day of the *Third* and the *Fourth Philippics* (20 Dec.) as the starting point in offering a retrospective account of Cicero's activities in the conflict with Antony (14.20).

On the grounds of internal structure as well, a corpus comprising the *Third* to the *Fourteenth Philippics* makes sense. If the *First* and the *Second Philippics* are set aside as being later additions to the intended core corpus, the resulting group of twelve orations can be neatly divided into 2 + 5 + 5 speeches. The two opening orations on the same day (20 Dec. 44) and on the same topic (*Phil.* 3–4) are followed by two blocks or mini-cycles, symmetrically constructed in themselves, and belonging to 43. The first group (*Phil.* 5–9) concerns the (first) embassy to Antony, while the second one (*Phil.* 10–14) focuses on events in the East and the military conflict with Antony.

The last of the twelve speeches, the *Fourteenth Philippic*, was delivered on the very day of the victory over Antony near Mutina (21 April 43), which was regarded as assuring a swift conclusion to the war. However, at the time of the speech Cicero and his audience were not yet aware of that battle and its outcome. By choosing to make the *Fourteenth Philippic* round out the cycle, Cicero contrives to end on a note of expectation, rather than on a celebration of a great victory, which became known in Rome about a week after the delivery of the *Fourteenth Philippic*. If he had done otherwise, the character of his *Philippics*, which sought to emulate Demosthenes' speeches, would have been compromised.

Of course, plans for an eventual corpus of twelve speeches (of which no publication details are known) did

not preclude the circulation of individual speeches soon
after their delivery (as the correspondence with Brutus
shows), and this practice may help make sense of testimonia pointing to further *Philippic* speeches beyond the
fourteen that go by that title today. Arusianus Messius, a
grammarian of the fourth century A.D., quotes a single
short sentence from purportedly a *Sixteenth* and a *Seven-
teenth Philippic* (frr. 3–4), and there are three additional
phrases specifically attributed to Cicero's *Philippics* but
not found in any of the fourteen extant speeches (frr. 1–2,
5). Presumably, these late notices represent traces of other
speeches in the struggle with Antony, copies of which were
made and distributed soon after their delivery, but which
Cicero chose not to include in the core collection of twelve
speeches. Inevitably, these further Antonian speeches
were connected with the intended corpus of twelve (which
may have affected the numbering), just as the later inclu-
sion of the *First* and *Second Philippic* caused the number
of extant speeches to swell from twelve to fourteen.

Demosthenes and Cicero

The choice of the name *Philippics* indicates that Cicero
was inviting comparison between himself and the great
Athenian orator Demosthenes, and thereby aspiring to be
viewed as Demosthenes' Roman counterpart (cf. Quint.
Inst. 10.1.105, and Plutarch's pairing of the two orators in
his parallel lives). Cicero had doubtless been familiar with
Demosthenes' works since the beginning of his rhetorical
training, but the earliest explicit mention of Demosthenes
by Cicero is in the letter to Atticus in 60 (*Att.* 2.1.3) that

has been discussed above. That letter reveals that Demosthenes' *Philippic Orations* were in Cicero's mind when he formed a selection of his own consular speeches; this fact suggests that Cicero was already thinking about modeling the image of himself after the paradigm of Demosthenes, on both a rhetorical and a political level. However, it was not until the last decade of Cicero's life that he particularly focused his attention on Demosthenes. He even set about producing a Latin translation of one of the most celebrated speeches of Demosthenes, *On the Crown* (a model for Cicero's *Second Philippic*), and of Aeschines' *Oration against Ctesiphon*, the companion piece by Demosthenes' opponent (*Opt. Gen.* 14).

Cicero's renewed interest in Demosthenes is to be explained, in part, as a reaction to the so-called Neo-Attic movement in Roman oratory, a leading figure of which was C. Licinius Macer Calvus (*c.* 88–54). Cicero found his own style coming under attack by a younger generation of orators who characterized it as "Asiatic" (i.e., florid and luxuriant). Although Cicero eschewed the extremes practiced by the "Atticists," especially their fondness for an overly plain and jejune mode of expression intended to recall the simplicity of the Greek orator Lysias, he laid claim to be himself in the best tradition of Attic oratory as he interpreted it (*Att.* 15.1a.2). And what better way to make his point than to produce a collection of speeches whose title recalled Demosthenes, who was regarded in antiquity as the preeminent Attic orator (Quint. *Inst.* 10.1.76). In his later speeches, therefore, and especially in his *Philippics*, Cicero sought to achieve passion and a robustness of expression, while at the same time aiming for a restrained

"Attic" style, one that he felt captured the vigor and compactness of Demosthenes' language (cf. *Brut.* 289; *Orat.* 23–24; 28–29).

Although direct imitation of Demosthenes in Cicero's *Philippics* is rare, there are obvious analogies between Demosthenes' speeches against Philip of Macedon and those of Cicero against Antony. Both orators professed to believe that the liberty and the very fabric of their respective political systems had been brought into danger by a hostile individual striving for domination. Each tried to motivate an often divided or hesitant audience to take swift and decisive action by waging war energetically against the enemy. Demosthenes and Cicero both assert repeatedly that their countrymen must decide between self-government and tyranny, between *true* peace and illusory peace that is peace in name only, between liberty and slavery. They both describe the present situation as a singularly favorable one demanding an immediate response to ward off threatened danger. In both Demosthenes and Cicero, the enemy and the consequences of that enemy's victory are sharply contrasted with the advantages of the political system being defended by the orators.

On the other hand, Philip and Antony most certainly did not occupy the same position vis-à-vis the respective audiences of Demosthenes and Cicero. One was a foreign monarch, the father of Alexander the Great; the other a Roman (ex-)consul and scion of a noble Roman family. Cicero, however, presents Antony in terms that recall Athens' great fight. He adopts Demosthenes' characterization of Philip and makes Antony out to be a public enemy, a tyrant, an un-Roman and in-human barbarian.

All the time, however, Cicero had to work against a

historical backdrop that was different from the one that existed in Athens of the fourth century. For example, in Demosthenes' case, a state of war between Athens and Philip did, in fact, exist on and off, even if that war was not being prosecuted as resolutely as the orator wished. Cicero, by contrast, had to call repeatedly for a formal declaration of war against Antony and chose to describe the current situation as a state of war. At the same time, Cicero's political opponents just as strenuously rejected the use of such a harsh term to describe actions being taken against Antony. Demosthenes could point out that Philip had broken the peace and could thus justify his proposals. Antony's position was quite different because (in 43) he was a proconsular governor possessing *imperium* conferred by legislation. This made it difficult for Cicero to form a united front of his fellow citizens against one of their own foremost magistrates.

Strategies and Aims

Cicero's professed aim in the *Philippics* is to defend the Republic and the liberty of the Roman people against those who were striving for sole rule and violating basic Republican principles. The true Republic, in Cicero's view, was in need of recovery because it had been lost as a consequence of the tyrannical governments of Caesar and Antony (e.g., *Fam.* 10.1.1; *Off.* 1.35; 2.29). This stance causes Cicero to direct his attack against Mark Antony and portray him as the sole cause of all public evils. Cicero characterizes the struggle as a conflict between the whole Republic on the one hand and a single "public enemy" on the other (e.g., *Phil.* 5.32; 7.7–8; 13.38–39, 45–47; *Ad Brut.*

1.15.6). In this way, he turns the conflict into a defense of the traditional political system against one individual who is endangering it (e.g., *Phil.* 13.39, 45) and so deserves to be treated as a *hostis*, a "public enemy" (e.g., *Phil.* 3.1; 4.14–15). To justify this view Cicero argues that Antony himself had forfeited all right to be regarded as a legitimate consul or proconsul by setting himself and his army against the Republic (e.g., *Phil.* 10.12; cf. 3.6, 21; 4.6).

This sophistical construct permits Cicero to assert that illegal actions on the part of Octavian, for instance, in raising a private army in October 44, or of Decimus Brutus in refusing to hand over his province of Cisalpine Gaul to Antony as his successor in December 44, were wholly justified. Cicero defends such claims by arguing that all activities of the protagonists in the conflict are to be judged against the overarching goal of promoting the best interests of the Republic (esp. *Phil.* 11.27–28). In other words, the end justifies the means, and a desirable outcome (achieved according to the law of nature) trumps traditional law. Therefore, according to Cicero, the actions of the defenders of the Republic, even if they were not sanctioned by formal law or a decree of the senate, were nevertheless deserving of being regarded as legitimate, since they adhered to a higher and more important divine law. Indeed, to wait for official sanction might in some cases be impossible, Cicero argues, because without bold initiatives on the part of its supporters there would be no Republic left to defend (e.g., *Phil.* 8.5; *Fam.* 10.16.2; 11.7.2–3).

As a practical counterweight to Antony's considerable military might, Cicero backed Octavian (the future emperor Augustus and Julius Caesar's great-nephew and chief heir). Cicero hoped to be able to influence the young man, who had just recently turned nineteen (in Sept. 44), and to gain through an alliance with him sufficient military strength to defend the Republic and crush Antony. Before Antony's seemingly unassailable position showed signs of cracking in November 44 when two legions deserted Antony and went over to Octavian, Cicero was stymied. As he wrote to Gaius Cassius, one of Caesar's assassins, in October 44, nothing could be done against force without a counterforce (*Fam.* 12.3.1). And as he put it in a letter to another correspondent, Cornificius, at about the same time, all that Cicero had at his disposal to oppose Antony's weapons were words (*Fam.* 12.22.1), which were quite useless in the defense of peace and liberty (*Ad Brut.* 2.5.1) because Antony's weapons had taken the place of civil power (*Phil.* 2.20). Late in 44, however, Cicero began to see a way of gaining access to more practical means for opposing Antony thanks to the success of Octavian in winning over part of Antony's army and thanks to Decimus Brutus' refusal to hand over his army and province to Antony, his designated successor.

In the *Philippics*, Cicero presents Octavian as a heaven-sent, effective, and reliable defender of the Republic; he praises the youth for raising troops on his own initiative and using them to thwart Antony's dire plans for butchering his opponents in Rome (e.g., *Phil.* 3.3–5; 4.2–5; 5.42–52). Cicero prods an irresolute senate to place in Octavian hope for salvation and to confer approval on his actions by granting him rewards for his deeds and a military command so that he can help prosecute war against Antony (*Phil.* 5.45–46, 53; 13.22; 14.6). This wholly positive and heroic portrayal of Octavian is absent, however, from Cicero's letters, where he characterizes Octavian as the lesser of two evils in comparison with Antony and values the young man merely as a temporary expedient to offset Antony's military power; it is reasonably clear that Cicero intended his collaboration with Octavian to be short-lived and purpose-driven (e.g., *Att.* 15.12.2; 16.9; 16.14.1; cf. *Fam.* 11.20.1).

In the course of the struggle, Cicero became firmly convinced that the only way to resolve the conflict with Antony was by means of a military victory, not through negotiation. He regarded the elimination of Antony and his supporters as essential for the preservation of any vestige of the Republic and the avoidance of slavery under the guise of a false peace (*Ad Brut.* 1.15.10). In Cicero's view, Antony posed a threat to the very survival of the Republic, and so war was both justified and necessary for self-defense (*Phil.* 13.35).

Rhetoric and Style

Since Cicero did not hold political office or command military forces in 44 and 43, he had to rely upon his status as a senior consular to provide him with a pulpit from which to lead the opposition to Mark Antony. He used this position and the influence he could hence exert by the clever use of language on two fronts: in Rome, in the senate and before the people in public meetings in the Forum, he delivered stirring and persuasive speeches. At the same time, through the frequent exchange of letters with key provincial governors, such as Pollio in Farther Spain (e.g., *Fam.* 10.31–33), Lepidus in Nearer Spain and Narbonese Gaul (e.g., *Fam.* 10.27, 34–35), and Plancus in Outer Gaul (e.g., *Fam.* 10.3–24), Cicero tried to remain in constant touch with potential allies who controlled significant military forces close to the theater of action against Antony in northern Italy. Often in his speeches, to win support for his political goals, Cicero had to rely more on rhetoric than substance because the official standing of Cicero's enemy Antony as a consul and later ex-consul and provincial governor made it difficult for Cicero to advance an argument based solely on the facts. Instead, he tended to play upon his audience's emotions and to motivate them by a suggestive presentation with the consequent psychological impact supporting the policy favored by him; thus he directly engaged with his audience and presented his view as compelling.

For instance, Cicero heaps abuse on Antony and Antony's supporters, painting their character in the most lurid terms (e.g., *Phil.* 2.44–114; 3.15–27; 4.14–15; 5.6–25; 13.26–28). He places his own idiosyncratic interpretation upon frequently repeated keywords such as "Republic," "liberty," or "consul." He treats facts selectively and presents details to suit his purposes, such as in relating the measures taken by Antony in October 44 to suppress an attempted mutiny in his army. As Cicero tells the story, the ringleaders of the discontent whom Antony executed were valiant, patriotic citizens, even heroes; they were victims of Antony's savagery and lust for blood (*Phil.* 3.4, 10; 5.22; 13.18). To make their deaths more pitiable, Cicero presents a picture of the soldiers' "innocent" blood being splashed on the garments of Antony's wife Fulvia (*Phil.* 3.4), who was accompanying her husband at the time.

The orator continually strives to move his audience and win their assent by taking it for granted that they were already hostile to Antony: the senate because, according to

Cicero, Antony had marked it down for a bloody purge verging on annihilation, which only the timely intervention of Octavian had forestalled (e.g., *Phil.* 3.4, cf. 13.23, 47); the Roman people, because they had come to loath the excessive power lately exercised in Rome by Antony and by his equally power-hungry brothers, especially Lucius, who had overseen an ambitious land allotment scheme in the latter half of 44 (cf. *Phil.* 6.12–15).

The style of the *Philippics* exemplifies a shift in Cicero's later speeches to a more transparent and simpler form of expression in response to the popularity of the concise Attic mode of expression. Rhetorical abundance is limited; rhetorical ornament is curtailed; clarity, exactness, and impact are the chief aims. Leading ideas are phrased succinctly and memorably and are frequently repeated (with variations). A good example of this technique is furnished by the *exordium* of the *Third Philippic* (§§1–2). After beginning with the simple statement that the senate has met at last but later than circumstances demanded, Cicero goes on to develop this idea, first by observing that he had repeatedly called for such a meeting and next by stating his reasons why (viz. the sinister activity of Antony and the immediate danger posed thereby). Then, he fires off a rapid succession of key contrasts in relatively short, pointed sentences: the senate delays, Antony does not; the delay is brief, but even a brief delay can produce disaster; setting a future date is appropriate for performing a sacrifice to the gods but not for making plans when faced with a full-blown crisis; if there had been no delay, there would be no war. He ends by linking victory and speed as the two objects of his desire.

The distinctive features that are to be found in the *Phi-*

lippics may be subsumed under the term "rhetoric of crisis." The "crisis," of course, is not simply produced by external circumstances, but it is, in part, brought into being by Cicero's portrayal of certain events as threatening and calling for an immediate response. This "rhetoric of crisis" is characterized by a vivid depiction of an impending or already present danger through emotive language (e.g., by exaggerations, illustrative comparisons, graphic descriptions). It places an incessant emphasis on the need for timely action, which is conveyed by means of short, clipped sentences, rhetorical questions, and the repetition of important keywords of the sort that has just been pointed out above in the *exordium* to the *Third Philippic*.

Of course, within the corpus, there are naturally some differences in language and complexity of argument between speeches addressed to the populace (*Phil.* 4, 6) and those delivered in the senate (all the rest, *Phil.* 2 excepted). And occasionally the "rhetoric of crisis" is subdued, such as in the *Ninth Philippic*, which proposes honors in memory of Cicero's friend Servius Sulpicius Rufus, who died of illness while serving on a peace mission to Antony in January 43.

INTRODUCTION TO THE
ORIGINAL EDITION

The victory of C. Julius Caesar over Pompey and his republican allies at Pharsalia in August 48 B.C. put Rome and her empire, apart from some pockets of resistance, under the control of one man. That had happened once before, nearly forty years previously, when Sulla defeated the opposition in Italy. Sulla's object was to restore a republican constitution of the kind he approved of; having done that, he retired and Rome lived with his constitution, more or less, until civil war broke out again in 49. Whether Caesar began that war with any definite political intentions is open to conjecture. What seems certain is that during his few years of supreme power, much of them spent fighting resurgent republicans overseas, he arrived at no political solution except his personal autocracy. Hence in the main the conspiracy which struck him down on the Ides of March 44, as he was on the point of setting out for one more war, against distant Parthia.

The leading conspirators, M. Brutus (more formally Q. Servilius Caepio Brutus) and C. Cassius Longinus, both former Pompeians who had been pardoned and advanced by Caesar, and D. Brutus Albinus, Caesar's former lieutenant and close friend, had apparently looked no further than the act. With Caesar gone they seem to have expected

the wheels of the Republic to begin turning again automatically. Caesar's foremost adherent and colleague in the
consulship of the year, M. Antonius (Mark Antony), had
not been harmed. He fled into hiding, but presently re-
emerged to negotiate with the assassins, or liberators, on
the Capitol. At a meeting of the Senate two days after the
killing (17 March) a compromise took shape. On Cicero's
motion the Senate decreed an amnesty and at the same
time confirmed all Caesar's measures and appointments
(*acta*).

The story of the following months has often been told.
In summary, Antony and his new colleague as consul, P.
Cornelius Dolabella (formerly Cicero's son-in-law), at first
took a conciliatory line with the Senate, which seems for
the most part to have been eager for a restored republic, especially in the lower echelons and despite the fact
that most of the members were of Caesar's creation. But
M. Brutus and Cassius, both praetors for the year whose
official duties lay in Rome, were soon driven out by hostile
mobs, leaving Antony in control of the situation. Caesar's
widow had given him her husband's papers, and with the
assistance of Caesar's secretary he forged orders as con-
venient and passed them off as Caesar's memoranda, valid
with the rest of Caesar's *acta*. In June, not without intimidation exercised through Caesar's old soldiers, he provided for his future with a law which gave him Cisalpine
Gaul for a term of five years in place of the existing governor, D. Brutus, who had gone there under Caesar's appointment. With the province went command of four legions which had been assembled in Macedonia by Caesar
for the Parthian war. There was one complication. Caesar's
eighteen-year-old great-nephew, C. Octavius, was with

these legions. Under Caesar's will he became Caesar's heir and adopted son. Arriving in Italy in April, he became Antony's rival for the loyalty of the pro-Caesarian Roman populace and, more important, the veteran soldiers who had been settled in large numbers on the land in Campania.

Cicero, now in his sixty-third year, had no advance knowledge of Caesar's assassination but wholeheartedly applauded it. The results, however, disappointed him, and on 5 April he left Rome for his villas in Campania. Later he decided to visit his son, who was studying in Athens, and actually got as far as Syracuse, on 1 August. That same day in Rome the Senate heard an attack upon Antony's political conduct from a senior consular, none other than Caesar's father-in-law and Cicero's old enemy, L. Calpurnius Piso Caesoninus, not normally hostile to Antony and later on almost his partisan. Nobody backed him up.

As Cicero explained to his friend Atticus in a contemporary letter (*Att.* 16.7) and subsequently to the Senate, hopeful news from Rome reached him on 7 August, while he was waiting for a fair wind to continue his journey. It looked as though Antony and the "liberators" were about to settle their differences. That prospect was to prove delusive, but Cicero promptly reversed course and set out on the way back to Rome. He reentered the city on the last day of the month,[1] and on 2 September delivered in the Senate, Antony not present, the challenge which in its published form became the *First Philippic*.

---

[1] The date of 1 Sept. is to be preferred; see introduction to *Phil*. 1, n. 2 [note added by revisers].

We shall never know after what private hesitations
Cicero set foot on the fatal ladder. Perhaps this time
he did not hesitate at all. The mortifications and dis-
appointments of his later career and the calamities
of his private life had only sharpened his urge for
primacy—not power such as Caesar had had and
Pompey had been suspected of wanting, but in the
words of his speech, "equality in freedom, primacy
in esteem." Much in his record that looked like ti-
midity was really an incapacity or reluctance to seize
the essential in a complex moral problem. But the
case of the Republic against Antony in 44 held no
complexities for Cicero. Conscience chimed with
ambition, striking his hour.[2]

The fourteen *Philippics* were delivered between 2 September 44 and 21 April 43, except for the second, which
was not delivered at all. The name, taken from Demosthenes' orations against Philip of Macedon, was Cicero's
own coinage, originally a sort of joke.[3] Brutus wrote from
Dyrrachium on 1 April of having read the fifth and tenth,
spoken on 1 January and in mid-February.[4] Hence it appears that the speeches were edited by Cicero and circulated soon after delivery. Quotations show that at least
three more *Philippics* existed in antiquity.

[2] D. R. Shackleton Bailey, *Cicero* (London, 1971) 246–47.
[3] Cic. *Ad M. Brutum* 3 (2.3).4.
[4] Ibid.

[Sections on Suggested Reading, Primary Historical Sources,
Manuscripts and Editions, and Sigla have not been reprinted here
but replaced by the revisers.]

NOTE ON MANUSCRIPTS
AND EDITIONS

The text of Cicero's *Philippics* is based on the following manuscripts (*sigla* taken from Fedeli 1982 / 1986, XXVII):

V	=	cod. tabularii Basilicae Vaticanae H 25, saec. IX
b	=	cod. Bernensis 104, saec. XIII–XIV
c	=	familia Colotiana, i.e. codicum Paris. Lat. 5802 (saec. XIII), Paris. Lat. 6602 (saec. XIII), Berolin. Phill. 1794 (olim 201, saec. XII) consensus
n	=	cod. Vossianus Lat. O 2, saec. X–XI
s	=	cod. Vaticanus Lat. 3228, saec. X
t	=	cod. Monacensis 18787 (olim Tegernseensis 787), saec. XI
v	=	cod. Vaticanus Lat. 3227, saec. XII
D	=	codicum *bcnstv* consensus
Cus.	=	cod. Nicolai Cusani, saec. XII, excerpta continens
ς	=	codd. deteriores

The textual tradition of the *Philippics* is represented by two branches (*V* and the *D* family) that go back ultimately to a single archetype (not surviving). *V*, the oldest extant manuscript, was written by an ignorant scribe, who faithfully copied whatever he found in the text that he was transcribing, even if it made no sense. In addition to the hand of the original scribe, who also corrected himself (V^1), further additions and corrections were made by a number of other hands (V^2).[1] Although for the most part V is the best witness to the text because it is free of interpolations and conjectures of the sort found in D, it is not always to be preferred to D, since it contains numerous (scribal) errors.

At times D offers readings differing from V's that are almost certainly genuine, and editors must depend entirely on D in the following places where V does not preserve the text: *Phil.* 11.22b–40, *Phil.* 12.1–12a and 23b–30, most of *Phil.* 13 (10b–50), and all of *Phil.* 14. Elsewhere, it is D that has lacunae, and the establishment of the text therefore must rely on V: the lacunae in D comprise one brief gap in *Phil.* 2 (93b–96), another in *Phil.* 10 (8b–10a), and a much larger one beginning more than half way through *Phil.* 5 and extending through all but less than the last half page of *Phil.* 6 (i.e. 5.31b–6.18a).

The first printed editions of the *Philippics* appeared in 1471: *Editio Romae typis impressa a. 1471 (ed. Romana)*, cur. Io. Andreas Aleriensis, and *Editio Venetiis typis impresa a. 1471 (ed. Veneta)*, cur. Ludovicus Carbo. More recent critical editions include those by A. C. Clark (Oxford Classical Text, 1901; 2nd ed., 1918), A. Boulanger and P. Wuilleumier (Budé, 1959–60; rev. ed., 1972–73), P. Fedeli (Teubner, 1982; 2nd ed., 1986), D. R. Shackleton

[1] Magnaldi (2008) proposes further distinctions between those; but for the purposes of this edition a distinction between the original hand (V^1) and later additions (V^2) will be sufficient.

Bailey (1986), and G. Magnaldi (2008). For a more comprehensive conspectus of editions and a discussion of the individual manuscripts, see the introductions by Fedeli (pp. V–XXVII) and Magnaldi (pp. IX–XLI, LXIII–LXV) in the editions just mentioned. Both editors also provide a full critical apparatus.

DIVERGENCES FROM SHACKLETON BAILEY

The present edition has taken as its starting point the text established by D. R. Shackleton Bailey for his bilingual edition. The *siglum* "SB" in the notes to the Latin text identifies textual choices made by him and his contributions to the text, many of which are argued for in either the apparatus and textual appendix to his edition, or his articles in *HSPh* and *Philologus* (see Bibliography). Modifications to Shackleton Bailey's text have been kept to a minimum, and for this reason the text printed here differs occasionally from those found in the revisors' commentaries. Some changes, however, have been deemed desirable, especially when Shackleton Bailey's choices seemed unnecessarily conjectural. Departures from his text are listed below.

Phil.	Loeb edition	SB
1.3	post Idus Martias	post Idus †Martias†
1.13	usquam	nusquam
1.21	rogari	†manere†
1.30	adfectis, ‹urbe incendio et caedis metu liberata›	adfectis

Phil.	Loeb edition	SB
1.36	⟨At⟩ populi	populi
2.21	oportebat	opportebat
2.41	filium praeterit,	filium praeterit;
2.41	amicissimi;	amicissimi,
2.41	ne nominat quidem	ne nomen quidem
2.45	ut se	ut te
2.56	Licinium Denticulum	Licinium Lenticulam
2.64	servientibusque animis	servientibusque †animis†
2.71	Pharsalica; ante-signanus	Pharsalica ante-signanus;
2.75	Tu vero quid es?	tu vero quid ais?
2.88	redeamus, de quibus [rebus]	redeamus; de quibus rebus
2.91	post Idus Martias	post Idus †Martias†
2.92	dissimilis esse?	esse dissimilis?
2.93a	Ubi . . . desisti? *post §96*	[ubi . . . desisti?] *in situ*
2.96	auctorem odimus	a[u]ctorem odimus
2.118	aliquando rem publicam	aliquando †rem publicam†
3.4	nobis	bonis
3.19	Sed quid fecit ipse? Cum tot edicta ⟨pro⟩-posuisset, edixit ut adesset senatus frequens a.d. VIII Kalendas Decembris:	⟨At⟩ cum tot edicta ⟨pro⟩posuisset, edixit ut adesset senatus frequens a.d. VIII Kalendas Decembris. sed quid fecit ipse?

Phil.	Loeb edition	SB
3.25	carere metu et periculo	metu et periculo carere
3.25	[nullam se habere provinciam,]	nullam se habere provinciam,
3.38	optimorum et fortissimorum virorum	optimorum et fortissimorum
3.39	L. Egnatuleio duce, quaestore optimo, civi egregio	duce L. Egnatuleio quaestore, civi egregio
4.1	spem recuperandae	spem ‹libertatis› recuperandae
4.10	appropinquet	appropinqu‹are vid›eat‹ur›
4.13	Nam cum . . . sint	[quamquam] . . . sunt
5.7	de auspiciis	de auspiciis ‹silet›
5.13	‹en› Cydam	‹sedentem videre› Cydam
5.15	cogitavisset	‹relinquere› cogitavisset
5.27	iussi erant	iussi sunt
5.45	Itaque illa	itaque ‹ne› illa
5.46	pro praetore	[pro praetore]
5.46	pro praetore	[pro praetore]
5.46	pro praetore	pro praetore ‹eo iure quo qui optimo et›
5.51	profecto ‹pro alio›	profecto
5.51	in maxima re periculosam opinionem	in maxima re ‹et› periculosa opinionem

Phil.	Loeb edition	SB
6.7	operam exhibere nullam	horam eximere unam
6.10	illos Africanus	illos ⟨Laelius, ille⟩ Africanus
6.10	Plancus. Videte quantum exsiluerit adulescens nobilis! Plancum, qui	Plancus, quam †tum exiluerit† adulescens nobilis. Plancum quidem, qui
7.3	Macedoniam. Suam	Macedoniam, ⟨quam⟩ suam
7.4	statu	statu, ⟨casu⟩
7.12	Quid igitur? Profectus est vir fortissimus, meus collega et familiaris, A. Hirtius consul: at qua imbecillitate, qua macie!	ad id igitur profectus est vir fortissimus, meus collega et familiaris, A. Hirtius consul. at qua imbecillitate, qua macie!
7.25	ipse	ipsi
7.26	fuerit et in senatus	fuerit in senatus
8.7	an etiam	an est
8.7	faciebat: ⟨contendebat⟩ Sulla	faciebat. Sulla
8.20	Quasi	quid si
8.26	chirographorum sua et commentariorum	[chirographorum et commentariorum] sua non vult
8.27	mavolt	non vult
8.29	maximum	maxime

Phil.	Loeb edition	SB
8.30	alicuius constantiae, qui labori, qui eius perpetuam	alicui, ⟨qui ei⟩us constantiam, qui laborem, qui perpetuam
8.33	Idus Martias primas	Idus Martias proximas
9.16	quod is . . . obierit, eamque causam in basi inscribi	eamque causam in basi inscribi quod is . . . obierit
10.7	regni nomen	regnum omnino
10.11	extrusimus	elusi sumus
10.18	igitur	[igitur]
10.25	exercitus	auxilia
11.6	ex hoc	ex hac
11.7	[si evenerit] . . . si cvenerit	si evenerit . . . [si evenerit]
11.23	omissa omni	omissa ⟨alia⟩ omni
11.27	conversione ⟨et⟩ per-turbation⟨e omni⟩um rerum	conversione et con-cursatione perturbatarum rerum
13.3	Melam Pontium	Melam, Pontium
13.9	quod silentio bellum	quod sine ⟨caede atque fe⟩rro bellum
13.12	Atque illud	itaque illud
13.24	genus	†genus†
13.29	senatus. Utrum	senatus. *** utrum
13.37	[cum]	cum
13.39	Potius Treboni	potiusne Treboni
14.9	qui hostis	qui ⟨hos⟩ hostis

NOTE ON MANUSCRIPTS AND EDITIONS

Phil.	Loeb edition	SB
14.17	dixerim	dicerem
14.38	exstet . . . divina virtus	testetur . . . divinam virtutem

ABBREVIATIONS

Works by Cicero are referred to by title only, except in instances where confusion might arise. In the notes and introductions, where it is clear that references by speech number and section are to the *Philippics*, "*Phil.*" is generally omitted. Titles and names of ancient authors are abbreviated as in *OCD*[3].

The following abbreviations of modern works are employed in the introductions to the speeches and in the notes:

CIL	*Corpus Inscriptionum Latinarum*
ILS	Dessau, H., ed. (1892–1916) *Inscriptiones Latinae Selectae*. Berlin.
MRR	Broughton, T. R. S. (1951–2, 1986) *The Magistrates of the Roman Republic*. 3 vols. Atlanta.
ORF	Malcovati, H., ed. (1976) *Oratorum Romanorum Fragmenta Liberae Rei Publicae*. 4th ed. Turin.
RE	Pauly, A. F. and Wissowa, G., edd. (1893–1980) *Real-Encyclopädie der klassischen Altertumswissenschaft*. Stuttgart.
SB, *Two Studies*[2]	Shackleton Bailey, D. R. (1991) *Two Studies in Roman Nomenclature*. 2nd ed. Atlanta.

BIBLIOGRAPHY

EDITIONS, COMMENTARIES, AND TRANSLATIONS

Bellardi, G. *Le Orazioni di M. Tullio Cicerone. Volume quarto, dal 46 al 43 a. C.*, Turin 1978 (Classici latini 31/4).

Berry, D. H. *Cicero's Political Speeches,* Oxford 2006 (includes: translation of *Second Philippic*).

Boulanger, A., and P. Wuilleumier. *Cicéron. Discours. Tome XIX. Philippiques I à IV. Texte établi et traduit*, Paris 1959, 2ème éd., 1963 (revu et corrigé), 3ème éd., 1966, 4ème éd., 1972 (revu et corrigé) (CUF).

Wuilleumier, P. *Cicéron. Discours. Tome XX. Philippiques V à XIV. Texte établi et traduit*, Paris 1960, 2ème éd., 1963, 3ème tirage, 1973 (CUF).

Clark, A. C. *M. Tulli Ciceronis orationes. Vol. II. Pro Milone, pro Marcello, pro Ligario, pro rege Deiotaro, Philippicae I–XIV, recognovit brevique adnotatione critica instruxit*, Oxford 1901, 2nd ed., 1918 (repr.).

Cristofoli, R. *Cicerone e la II Filippica. Circostanze, stile e ideologia di un'orazione mai pronunciata*, Rome 2004.

Denniston, J. D. *M. Tulli Ciceronis in M. Antonium orationes Philippicae prima et secunda. Edited, with Introduction, Notes (mainly historical) and Appendices*, Oxford 1926 (repr.).

Fedeli, P. *M. Tulli Ciceronis scripta quae manserunt omnia. Fasc. 28. In M. Antonium orationes Philippicae XIV, edidit*, Leipzig 1982, 2nd ed., 1986.

Halm, K., and G. Laubmann. *Ciceros ausgewählte Reden. Sechster Band. Die erste und zweite Philippische Rede*, 8th ed., Berlin 1905.

King, J. R. *The Philippic Orations of M. Tullius Cicero. With English notes*, Oxford 1868, 2nd ed., 1878 (Clarendon Press Series).

Lacey, W. K. *Cicero: Second Philippic oration. Edited with translation and notes*, Warminster 1986.

Long, G. *M. Tullii Ciceronis orationes. With a Commentary*. Vol. IV, London 1858 (Bibliotheca Classica).

Magnaldi, G. *Le Filippiche di Cicerone. Edizione critica*, Alessandria 2008 (Minima Philologica, Serie latina 5).

Manuwald, G. *Cicero, Philippics 3–9. Edited with Introduction, Translation and Commentary. Vol. 1: Introduction, Text and Translation, References and Indexes; Vol. 2: Commentary*, Berlin / New York 2007 (Texte und Kommentare 30).

Monteleone, C. *La «Terza Filippica» di Cicerone. Retorica e regolamento del Senato, legalità e rapporti di forza*, Fasano 2003 (Biblioteca della ricerca, Philologica 4).

———. *Prassi assembleare e retorica libertaria. La* Quarta Filippica *di Cicerone*, Bari 2005 (Palomar athenaeum 48).

Novielli, C. *La retorica del consenso. Commento alla tredecesima Filippica di M. Tullio Cicerone*, Bari 2001 (Scrinia 19).

Ramsey, J. T. *Cicero. Philippics I–II. Edited*, Cambridge 2003 (Cambridge Greek and Latin Classics).

BIBLIOGRAPHY

Saner, P. *Von den Iden des Maerz 44 bis zur dritten Philippica Ciceros (mit einem historischen Kommentar zur dritten Philippica Ciceros)*, Diss. Bern, Luzern 1988.

Shackleton Bailey, D. R. *Cicero. Philippics. Edited and translated*, Chapel Hill / London 1986.

Sternkopf, W. *Ciceros ausgewählte Reden. Fortsetzung der Halmschen Sammlung. Achter Band. Die dritte, vierte, fünfte und sechste Philippische Rede*, Berlin 1912.

———. *Ciceros ausgewählte Reden. Fortsetzung der Halmschen Sammlung. Neunter Band. Die siebente, achte, neunte und zehnte Philippische Rede*, Berlin 1913.

SECONDARY LITERATURE

Text and Transmission

Clark, A. C. *The descent of manuscripts*, Oxford 1918 (repr. 1969).

Magnaldi, G. *La forza dei segni. Parole-spia nella tradizione manoscritta dei prosatori latini*, Amsterdam 2000 (Lexis Research Tools I).

———. "Lezioni genuine e glosse nelle *Filippiche* di Cicerone," *Lexis* 20, 2002, 61–78.

———. *Parola d'autore, parola di copista. Usi correttivi ed esercizi di scuola nei codici di Cic. Phil. 1.1 – 13.10*, Alessandria 2004 (Minima Philologica, Serie latina 2).

Reeve, M. D., R. H. Rouse, M. Winterbottom, J. G. F. Powell, L. D. Reynolds. "Cicero," in: L. D. Reynolds (ed.), *Texts and Transmission. A Survey of the Latin*

Classics, Oxford 1983 (corr. repr. 1986; 1990, repr. 1998), 54–142.

Schöll, F. *Über die Haupthandschrift von Ciceros Philippiken nebst Bemerkungen zu Stellen dieser Reden*, Heidelberg 1918 (Sitzungsberichte der Heidelberger Akademie der Wissenschaften, Philosophisch-historische Klasse, Jahrgang 1918, 4. Abhandlung).

Shackleton Bailey, D. R. "On Cicero's Speeches," *HSPh* 83, 1979, 237–285.

———. "Notes on Cicero's *Philippics*," *Philologus* 126, 1982, 217–226.

Criticism

Cerutti, S. "Further Discussion on the Delivery and Publication of Cicero's Second Philippic," *CB* 70, 1994, 23–28.

Delaunois, M. "Statistiques des idées dans le cadre du plan oratoire des *Philippiques* de Cicéron," *LEC* 34, 1966, 3–34; partly reprinted (pp. 3–15, 27–34) in German translation: "Ciceros 'Philippika': Statistische Zählungen der Gedanken innerhalb der einzelnen Reden," in: B. Kytzler (ed.), *Ciceros literarische Leistung*, Darmstadt 1973 (WdF CCXL), 345–371.

Hall, J. "The *Philippics*," in: J. M. May (ed.), *Brill's Companion to Cicero. Oratory and Rhetoric*, Leiden / Boston / Cologne 2002, 273–304.

Manuwald, G. "Performance in Cicero's *Philippics*," *Antichthon* 38, 2004 [2006], 53–71.

———. "Ciceros Attacke gegen die Provinzverlosung unter Antonius (zu Cic. *Phil*. 3,24–26)," *Klio* 88, 2006, 167–180.

Monteleone, C. ""Adsum igitur". Adunanza senatoria e discorso-testo della "Terza Filippica" ciceroniana," *AFLB* 41, 1998, 215–334.

Newbound, B. P. *Rhetoric and reality in Cicero's Philippics: a study of Philippics 3–14*, Diss. University of Oxford, Oxford 1986.

Orlandini, A. "Pour une approche pragmatique de l'ironie (Cicéron, *Philippiques*, livres I–2)," *Pallas* 59, 2002 (Mélanges Jean Soubiran), 209–224 (419: summary in Engl.).

Palmieri, R. "*Laudatio* e *vituperatio* nell'*exordium* dell' XI *Filippica* di Cicerone," *Euphrosyne* 24, 1996, 199–204.

Pinkernell-Kreidt, S. "Das Erkennen des καιρός in Ciceros dritter Philippischer Rede," in: B. Czapla / T. Lehmann / S. Liell (edd.), *Vir bonus dicendi peritus. Festschrift für A. Weische zum 65. Geburtstag*, Wiesbaden 1997, 331–344.

Schäublin, C. "Ciceros demosthenische Redezyklen: ein Nachtrag," *MH* 45, 1988, 60–61.

Stevenson, T., and M. Wilson, (edd.) *Cicero's Philippics: History, Rhetoric and Ideology, Prudentia* 37–38, 2008 [2009].

Stroh, W. "Die Nachahmung des Demosthenes in Ciceros Philippiken," in: W. Ludwig (ed.), *Éloquence et Rhétorique chez Cicéron. Sept exposés suivis de discussions*, Vandœuvres – Geneva 1982 (Entretiens sur l'antiquité classique, Tome XXVIII), 1–31 (discussion: 32–40).

———. "Ciceros demosthenische Redezyklen," *MH* 40, 1983, 35–50.

———. "Ciceros Philippische Reden. Politischer Kampf und literarische Imitation," in: M. Hose (ed.), *Meister-*

werke der antiken Literatur. Von Homer bis Boethius, Munich 2000, 76–102 (beck'sche Reihe).

Taddeo, D. J. *Signs of Demosthenes in Cicero's* Philippics, Diss. Stanford University, Stanford 1971.

Wooten, C. W. "Cicero's Reactions to Demosthenes: A clarification," *CJ* 73, 1977, 37–43.

———. "Démosthène, le mode satirique et la Cinquième Philippique de Cicéron," *LEC* 50, 1982, 193–200.

———. *Cicero's* Philippics *and Their Demosthenic Model. The Rhetoric of Crisis*, Chapel Hill / London 1983.

Life, Oratory, and Rhetoric

Classen, C. J. *Recht – Rhetorik – Politik. Untersuchungen zu Ciceros rhetorischer Strategie,* Darmstadt 1985; Italian translation (by P. Landi): *Diritto, retorica, politica. La strategia retorica di Cicerone,* Bologna 1998 (Collezione di Testi e di Studi, Linguistica e critica letteraria).

Everitt, A. *Cicero. A Turbulent Life,* London 2001.

Fogel, J. *Cicero and the "Ancestral Constitution": A Study of Cicero's* Contio *Speeches,* Diss. Columbia University, New York 1994.

Frisch, H. *Ciceros Kamp for Republiken. Den historiske Baggrund for Ciceros filippiske Taler,* Copenhagen 1942; English translation (by N. Haislund): *Cicero's fight for the republic. The historical background of Cicero's Philippics,* Copenhagen 1946 (Humanitas 1).

Fuhrmann, M. *Cicero und die römische Republik. Eine Biographie,* Munich / Zurich 1989, 2. durchges. Aufl., 1990, 3. durchges. u. erw. Aufl., 1991, 4. durchges. und bibliogr. erw. Aufl., 1997; English translation (by W. E.

Yuill): *Cicero and the Roman Republic,* Oxford / Cambridge (MA) 1992 (translation of the 1990 edition).

Gelzer, M., W. Kroll, R. Philippson, K. Büchner. "Tullius (29): M. Tullius Cicero," *RE* VII A 1 (1939), 827–1274.

Habicht, C. *Cicero der Politiker,* Munich 1990; English version: *Cicero the Politician,* Baltimore / London 1990 (Ancient Society and History).

Hall, J., and R. Bond. "Performative Elements in Cicero's Orations: an Experimental Approach," *Prudentia* 34.2, 2002, 187–228.

Lintott, A. *Cicero as Evidence. A Historian's Companion,* Oxford 2008.

Marinone, N. *Cronologia ciceroniana,* Rome / Bologna 1997, Seconda edizione aggiornata e corretta con nuova versione interattiva in Cd Rom a cura di E. Malaspino, Rome / Bologna 2004 (Collana di studi ciceroniani VI).

May, J. M. (ed.) *Brill's Companion to Cicero. Oratory and Rhetoric,* Leiden / Boston / Cologne 2002 [includes bibliography].

Mitchell, T. N. *Cicero. The senior statesman,* New Haven / London 1991.

Rawson, E. *Cicero. A Portrait,* London 1975 (repr.).

Shackleton Bailey, D. R. *Cicero,* London 1971.

Steel, C. *Reading Cicero. Genre and Performance in Late Republican Rome,* London 2005 (Duckworth Classical Essays).

———. *Roman oratory,* Cambridge 2006 (Greece & Rome, New Surveys in the Classics No. 36).

Stockton, D. *Cicero. A Political Biography,* Oxford 1971.

Stroh, W. *Cicero. Redner, Staatsmann, Philosoph,* Munich 2008 (C.H. Beck Wissen).

BIBLIOGRAPHY

Weische, A. *Ciceros Nachahmung der attischen Redner,* Heidelberg 1972 (Bibliothek der klassischen Altertumswissenschaften, Neue Folge, 2. Reihe, Bd. 45).

Wiedemann, T. *Cicero and the End of the Roman Republic,* London 1994 (Classical World series).

Historical and Political Background

The Cambridge Ancient History. Second Edition. Volume IX. The Last Age of the Roman Republic, 146–43 B.C., ed. by J. A. Crook, A. Lintott, E. Rawson, Cambridge 1994.

Arena, V. "Invocation to liberty and invective of *dominatus* at the end of the Roman republic," *BICS* 50, 2007, 49–73.

van der Blom, H. *"Officium and Res Publica:* Cicero's Political Role after the Ides of March," *C&M* 54, 2003, 287–319.

Botermann, H. *Die Soldaten und die römische Politik in der Zeit von Caesars Tod bis zur Begründung des Zweiten Triumvirats,* Munich 1968 (Zetemata 46).

Brunt, P. A. *The Fall of the Roman Republic and Related Essays,* Oxford 1988 (repr. 1999).

Ehrenwirth, U. *Kritisch-chronologische Untersuchungen für die Zeit vom 1. Juni bis zum 9. Oktober 44 v. Chr.,* Munich 1971.

Gotter, U. *Der Diktator ist tot! Politik zwischen den Iden des März und der Begründung des zweiten Triumvirats,* Stuttgart 1996 (Historia, Einzelschriften 100).

Morstein-Marx, R. *Mass Oratory and Political Power in the Late Roman Republic,* Cambridge 2004.

Ortmann, U. *Cicero, Brutus und Octavian – Republikaner*

und Caesarianer. Ihr gegenseitiges Verhältnis im Krisenjahr 44/43 v. Chr., Bonn 1988 (Habelts Dissertationsdrucke, Reihe Alte Geschichte, Heft 25).

Ramsey, J. T. "The senate, Mark Antony, and Caesar's legislative legacy," *CQ* 44, 1994, 130–145.

———. "Did Mark Antony Contemplate an Alliance with His Political Enemies in July 44 B.C.E.?," *CPh* 96, 2001, 253–268.

———. "Did Julius Caesar temporarily banish Mark Antony from his inner circle?" *CQ* 54, 2004, 161–173.

———. "Mark Antony's Judiciary Reform and its Revival under the Triumvirs," *JRS* 95, 2005, 20–37.

———. "At What Hour did the Murderers of Julius Caesar Gather on the Ides of March 44 B.C." in: S. Heilen et al. (edd.), *In Pursuit of Wissenschaft. Festschrift für William M. Calder III zum 75. Geburtstag,* Hildesheim 2008 (Spudasmata 119), 351–363.

———. "Debate at a Distance: A Unique Rhetorical Strategy in Cicero's *Thirteenth Philippic*" in: D. H. Berry and A. Erskine (edd.), *Form and Function in Roman Oratory,* Cambridge (forthcoming).

Toher, M. "Octavian's arrival in Rome, 44 B.C.," *CQ* 54, 2004, 174–184.

Welch, K. E. "Antony, Fulvia and the Ghost of Clodius in 47 B.C." *G&R* 42, 1995, 182–201.

Brief Survey of Scholarship

The scholarly history of Cicero's *Philippics* starts, as it were, with the first printed editions in 1471 and the first edition with commentary in 1488. Editions and commentaries have continued to appear ever since, but general scholarly interest has been varied and almost non-existent or exclusively focused on textual matters for significant periods.

Hence the commentary by G. Long (London 1858), part of an annotated edition of all Ciceronian speeches, and that by J. R. King (Oxford 1868 / 2nd ed., 1878) are still the most recent commentaries on the whole corpus. The German commentary by K. Halm, G. Laubmann and W. Sternkopf (Berlin 1905; 1912; 1913) came out slightly later and seems to have been intended as a comprehensive work as well, but covers only *Philippics 1–10*.

Since about the middle of the twentieth century historical studies have appeared in greater numbers, which use the *Philippics* (as well as other ancient texts) as sources of information on Roman political institutions, on the decisive transitional phase from the Roman Republic to the Empire or on the individuals involved in the events of this period.

And finally, since the last decades of the twentieth century interest in the *Philippics* as texts and works of literature in their own right seems to have increased (as is also the case for other Ciceronian speeches); thus various critical and / or bilingual editions and translations have been produced. Several of the speeches have been equipped with modern commentaries or been the focus of monographs (*Phil*. 1–2: J. T. Ramsey 2003; *Phil*. 2: W. K. Lacey 1986 and R. Cristofoli 2004; *Phil*. 3: C. Monteleone 2003; *Phil*. 4: C. Monteleone 2005; *Phil*. 3–9: G. Manuwald 2007; *Phil*. 13: C. Novielli 2001). Besides there now exist the overview by J. Hall (2002), the studies by C. W. Wooten (1983) and W. Stroh (1982; 1983; 2000) as well as the collection of essays edited by T. Stevenson and M. Wilson (2008). And scholarly work on Cicero's *Philippics* continues.

The last bibliographical survey of literature on Cicero's speeches and his rhetorical works by C. P. Craig (in May 2002, 503–599) provides a comprehensive overview of the relevant works on individual Ciceronian speeches.

CHRONOLOGY

44 B.C.

consuls: M. Antonius and C. Iulius Caesar (V); after Caesar's death: P. Cornelius Dolabella

15 Feb.	Festival of *Lupercalia*: Antony tries to crown Caesar with a diadem
15 Mar	Ides: assassination of Caesar
17 Mar.	Senate meets in Temple of Tellus: amnesty for assassins, ratification of Caesar's acts, Dolabella recognized as suffect consul
late Mar./ early Apr.	A number of conspirators withdraw from Rome
Apr. to Nov.	Antony's "urban consulship," exploiting Caesar's papers to sell and confer favors
3/4 Apr.	Consuls receive provinces Macedonia and Syria for 43
7 Apr.	Cicero leaves Rome and withdraws to his rural estates
c. 25 Apr.	Antony leaves Rome to win support of veterans in Campania
c. 8/9 May	Octavian arrives in Rome via southern Italy and presents himself as Caesar's heir
c. 18 May	Antony returns to Rome with armed supporters

1 Jun.	Antony summons the senate to Temple of Concord; many senators do not attend out of fear; no action taken
c. 2 Jun.	Antony and Dolabella given five-year proconsular commands by popular assembly; probably on the same occasion Antony receives the two Gauls in place of Macedonia
3 Jun.	Cicero appointed legate by Dolabella
5 Jun.	Senate assigns an overseas grain commission to the praetors M. Iunius Brutus and C. Cassius Longinus (later in the summer they are given new provinces)
6–13 Jul.	C. Antonius holds the *Ludi Apollinares* in place of the city praetor M. Brutus
17 Jul.	Cicero sets out for Greece
1 Aug.	L. Calpurnius Piso Caesoninus delivers a courageous speech against Antony in the senate
2 Aug.	Piso does not attend senate meeting because he received no support on the previous day
7 Aug.	Cicero receives news about the events at Rome and decides to return immediately
late Aug./ early Sept.	M. Brutus and C. Cassius leave Italy, moving towards Macedonia and Syria respectively

1 Sept.	In the morning Cicero returns to Rome, but does not attend a meeting of the senate in the Temple of Concord; Antony threatens to punish Cicero for his absence
2 Sept.	*Philippic* 1: delivered at a meeting of the senate chaired by Dolabella in Antony's absence; Cicero criticizes Antony's policies
2–19 Sept.	Antony withdraws from Rome to prepare a response to the *First Philippic*, assisted by his rhetoric teacher Sex. Clodius
19 Sept.	Antony's invective against Cicero at a meeting of the senate in the Temple of Concord; Cicero is absent
9 Oct.	Antony leaves Rome for Brundisium to take command of legions transferred from Macedonia and to raise new legions of veterans in Campania
c. 10–12 Oct.	Cicero leaves Rome and withdraws to his rural estates
mid.-Oct./ late Nov.	Octavian attempts to make Antony's soldiers defect, recruits new troops, and levies an army mainly from Caesar's veterans in Campania
25 Oct.	*Philippic* 2: Cicero's response (never delivered) to Antony's invective of 19 Sept. sent to Atticus
c. 10 Nov.	Octavian marches on Rome with a band of veterans but withdraws before Antony returns

mid-Nov.   Antony returns to Rome with *legio* V *Alaudae*

24 Nov.   Antony cancels a meeting of the senate when he receives news of the defection of the *legio Martia* to Octavian; postpones meeting to 28 Nov.

28 Nov.   Last meeting of the senate presided over by Antony as consul: Antony drops intention to have Octavian declared a public enemy when he receives news of the defection of the *legio IV* to Octavian; he has senate decree a public thanksgiving (*supplicatio*) for M. Aemilius Lepidus and carries out distribution of praetorian provinces

28/29 Nov.   During the night, Antony leaves Rome for the rest of his consular year to take possession of Cisalpine Gaul from D. Brutus

9 Dec.   Cicero returns to Rome

10 Dec.   Tribunes of the plebs for 43 enter office

20 Dec.   Dispatch from D. Iunius Brutus arrives in Rome stating his intention not to hand over Cisalpine Gaul to Antony

Philippic 3: delivered at a meeting of the senate called by the tribunes of the plebs to discuss security measures for the senate to meet on 1 January under the new consuls; senate adopts Cicero's motion that D. Brutus and the present provincial governors continue to hold their provinces and that activities against Antony be honored in the near future

| same day | *Philippic* 4: Cicero informs the populace of the senate's decree |
| late Dec. | *Bellum Mutinense* breaks out: D. Iunius Brutus is besieged by Antony in Mutina |

43 B.C.

consuls: A. Hirtius (d. Apr.) and C. Vibius Pansa (d. Apr.)
Octavian and Q. Pedius (19 Aug.–*c.* 27 Nov.)
C. Carrinas and P. Ventidius Bassus (*c.* 28 Nov.–31 Dec.)

1 Jan.	*Philippic* 5: delivered at a meeting of the senate in the Temple of Jupiter on the Capitoline Hill: Cicero argues against proposal to send embassy to Antony and for immediate declaration of war and specific honors for Antony's opponents
2–4 Jan.	Continuation of debate in the senate, in Temple of Concord:
4 Jan.	Senate votes honors for Antony's opponents, embassy to Antony, and annulment of *Lex Antonia agraria*
same day	*Philippic* 6: Cicero informs the people of action taken by senate

5 Jan.	Three envoys (Ser. Sulpicius Rufus, L. Marcius Philippus, L. Calpurnius Piso Caesoninus) set off to Antony; one of them (Sulpicius) will die on the journey
slightly later	Senate authorizes military levies: one consul chosen by lot (Hirtius) to set forth to relieve D. Brutus; the other (Pansa) to oversee levies in Italy
mid-Jan.	*Philippic* 7: delivered at routine meeting of the senate: Cicero argues against peace with Antony and for a strict war policy
c. 1 Feb.	Piso and Philippus return from embassy and report that Antony has not complied with the instructions of the senate, but instead has made demands of his own; they are accompanied by an envoy of Antony, L. Varius Cotyla
2 Feb.	Senate declares a state of *tumultus* (but not of *bellum*); orders that *saga* ('military cloaks') be put on from 4 February onwards
3 Feb.	*Philippic* 8: delivered at a meeting of the senate called by Pansa because of a dispatch from Hirtius about the situation in northern Italy; Cicero criticizes *tumultus* decree of previous day, conduct of the consulars, and Antony's counter-demands; senate adopts Cicero's motion to set a date

	for deserters from Antony to be granted amnesty
4 Feb.	Populace dons *saga* ('military cloaks') in place of togas ('garbs of peace')
c. 4 Feb.	*Philippic* 9: Cicero moves that extensive posthumous honors be conferred on Sulpicius Rufus, which the senate adopts
mid-Feb.	Dispatch of M. Brutus arrives reporting that he had wrested Macedonia from C. Antonius and the Illyrian legions from P. Vatinius
	Philippic 10: Cicero moves that senate sanction Brutus' acts and give him *imperium* in Macedonia, Illyricum and all of Greece, which is passed
late Feb.	Senate declares Dolabella a public enemy for treacherously putting to death the governor of Asia, C. Trebonius, one of Caesar's assassins
1 day later	*Philippic* 11: Cicero urges senate to empower C. Cassius to make war on Dolabella, but senate commissions consuls instead
late Feb./ early Mar.	Senate decrees second embassy consisting of Q. Fufius Calenus, L. Calpurnius Piso Caesoninus, L. Iulius Caesar, P. Servilius Isauricus, and M. Tullius Cicero
a few days later	Isauricus states in the senate his reluctance to go on embassy;

	Philippic 12: Cicero points out uselessness of a second embassy and personal danger to himself
19/20 Mar.	Consul Pansa leaves Rome to join his colleague in the north of Italy after presiding at a meeting of the senate on 19 Mar.
20 Mar.	City praetor M. Caecilius Cornutus convenes senate to react to letters from the provincial governors M. Aemilius Lepidus and L. Munatius Plancus recommending peace with Antony;
	Philippic 13: Cicero disapproves of call for peace; reads and criticizes a letter from Antony to Hirtius and Octavian
14 Apr.	Battle at Forum Gallorum near Mutina fought
c. 18/19 Apr.	False report of Antony's victory on 14 Apr. arrives in Rome; rumor is spread that Cicero intends to have himself declared dictator on 21 Apr., the city's foundation day
20 Apr.	Tribune of the plebs P. Apuleius invites Cicero to address public meeting to respond to slanders; later in the day, news of Antony's defeat on 14 Apr. arrives in Rome; crowd celebrates by escorting Cicero to Capitoline
21 Apr.	Senate meets to react to report of victory at the battle of Forum Gallorum;

	Philippic 14: Cicero successfully moves that senate authorize a public thanksgiving (*supplicatio*) lasting fifty days, the renewal of the promises given to soldiers, and the erection of a monument for those killed in action
same day	Battle of Mutina fought: D. Brutus liberated from siege; Antony forced to flee after defeat; consul Hirtius killed in battle
23 Apr.	Consul Pansa dies in town of Bononia from wounds received in battle at Forum Gallorum on 14 Apr.
c. 26 Apr.	News of Antony's defeat on 21 Apr. reaches Rome; Antony declared public enemy; victors honored
27 Apr.	Senate empowers C. Cassius to hunt down Dolabella in Syria
30 June	M. Lepidus declared public enemy
19 Aug.	Octavian and Q. Pedius elected consuls
late Oct.	Triumvirate formed by Antony, Octavian and Lepidus, meeting in the north of Italy; Cicero and others marked for death in proscriptions
27 Nov.	Triumvirate is officially sanctioned by *Lex Titia*
7 Dec.	Cicero is hunted down and killed; his head and hand(s) are cut off and carried to Rome for presentation to Antony

BRITANNIA

GALLIA
TRANSALPINA
(NARBONENSIS)

CISALPINA

Novum
Comum
Avennio
Arelate
Narbo   Massilia   Forum   Luca
                    Julii

HISPANIA   Numantia
CITERIOR   Ilerda
           Tarraco

CORSICA

ULTERIOR   Sisapo(?)
                       Saguntum

SARDINIA

Urso
Munda   Carthago Nova   MEDITE

MAURETANIA
                    Cirta   Utica
                    NUMIDIA   AFRICA   Carthage
                                       Thapsu

0   100   200   300 miles

The Roman World in 44 B.C. (West)

NORICUM

ILLYRICUM

Mutina
Bononia
Ariminum

ITALY

Rome
Corfinium
Cumae
Naples
Brundisium

TYRRHENIAN
SEA

Dyrrachium
Apollonia

MACEDONIA

Pella
Pydna
Thessalonica
Philippi

PONTUS
EUXINUS

THRACE

Cyzicus
Ilium

SICILY
Leontini
Syracuse

IONIAN
SEA

Gomphi
Pharsalus

Delphi
Patrae
Corinth
Athens

ACHAEA

LESBOS
CHIOS

Ephesus

Pergamum

ASIA
Tralles
Aphrodisias
Mylasa

Apamea
CILICIA

MEDITERRANEAN SEA

Cnidus

DELOS

RHODES

CRETE
Gortyn

Cyrene
CYRENAICA

Alexandria

EGYPT

The Roman World in 44 B.C. (East)

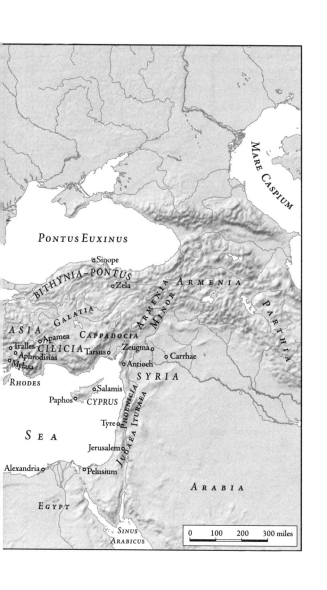

MARE CASPIUM

PONTUS EUXINUS

Sinope

BITHYNIA-PONTUS

Zela

ARMENIA MINOR   ARMENIA

PARTHIA

ASIA   GALATIA

CAPPADOCIA

Tralles   Apamea

Aphrodisias   CILICIA   Tarsus   Zeugma   Carrhae

Mylasa

Antioch

RHODES

SYRIA

Salamis

Paphos   CYPRUS

PHOENICIA

Tyre

SEA

JUDAEA ITURAEA

Jerusalem

Alexandria   Pelusium

ARABIA

EGYPT

SINUS
ARABICUS

0   100   200   300 miles

Italy & Sicily

Inset (upper region):

Ameria
Saxa Rubra
Fidenae
Rome ◎
Alba
Aricia
Antium
Astura
Tibur
Tusculum
Alba Fucens
Corfinium
SAMNIUM
Sora
Arpinum
Fregellae
Suessa
Fundi
Capua
Baiae
Misenum
Naples
LATIUM
Casilinum
Calatia
Pompeii

0   15 miles

Main map:

PROVINCE OF CISALPINE GAUL
Patavium
Po
Parma
Mutina
Bononia
Forum Gallorum
VIA AEMILIA
Claterna
Luca
Pistoria
Faesulae
Pisae
Ariminum
VIA FLAMINIA
Pisaurum
VIA AURELIA
Volaterrae
Arretium
Ancona
VIA CASSIA
Tiber
ETRURIA
PICENUM
Ameria
Saxa Rubra
Rome ◎
Alba Fucens
Corfinium
Sora
Arpinum
SAMNIUM
LATIUM
Antium
Astura
Fundi
Suessa
Capua
Baiae
Misenum
Naples
Casilinum
Calatia
CAMPANIA
Pompeii
Luceria
VIA
Venusia
APPIA
CALABRIA
Brundisium
Hydrus
LUCANIA
Velia
Tarentum

CORSICA

ADRIATIC
SEA

SARDINIA

TYRRHENIAN
SEA

IONIAN
SEA

Vibo
BRETTIUM
Locri
Messana
Rhegium

Mt. Eryx
Thermae
Lilybaeum
Entella
PROVINCE OF SICILY
Leucopetra
Promontory
Leontini
Syracuse

MEDITERRANEAN
SEA

Utica
Carthage
PROVINCE OF AFRICA

Thapsus

0   100 miles

PHILIPPIC 1

INTRODUCTION

The speech known today as the *First Philippic*[1] was delivered on 2 September 44 (5.19), at a meeting of the senate convened by the consul P. Dolabella (1.29) and held in the Temple of Concord (2.19). Mark Antony was not present (1.16), but on the previous day Antony had presided over a senatorial meeting in the same temple (5.18–19), at which he had proposed the addition of a day in honor of the late dictator Caesar to all future public thanksgivings (1.13; 2.110). Cicero, who had recently returned to Rome, most likely on that same day, 1 September (*Fam.* 12.25.3),[2] sent word to excuse his absence on the grounds of fatigue. The real reason why he avoided the meeting, as the *First Philippic* makes plain, was that Antony's proposal was ex-

[1] It was not until the spring of 43 that Cicero appears to have adopted the title *Philippics* to describe his speeches against Antony (see Introduction). Hence this speech, which appears to have been put into circulation soon after its delivery (*Fam.* 12.2.1 of *c.* 25 Sept. 44), was most likely known at first by the title *Oratio in M. Antonium*, or possibly as simply *Oratio in senatu de re publica*.

[2] Plutarch (*Cic.* 43.5–6) assigns Cicero's return to the day before the meeting called by Antony, doubtless an invention on the part of the biographer, designed to make room for the whole day of celebration that Plutarch alone claims greeted Cicero's return to Rome.

tremely distasteful to Cicero (§13). Antony reacted angrily to Cicero's failure to attend and lashed out with verbal abuse, even threatening to send public slaves to damage Cicero's house both as punishment and to humiliate him (1.12; 5.19).

The *First Philippic* offers Cicero's response to Antony's angry outburst (§§11–13), but first Cicero discusses his aborted plan to go abroad for the remainder of 44 and his reason for breaking off that journey (§§1–10). As we learn from a letter written on 7 August (*Att.* 16.7.1–5), Cicero had been informed by his friend Atticus that the public was reacting unfavorably to Cicero's departure in mid-July, viewing it as equivalent to flight at a time when Cicero's country desperately needed his wisdom and leadership. And so, Cicero seized the opportunity presented by this first speech after his return to justify his conduct. He insists that he hurried back to Rome just as soon as it appeared to him that he might be able to play a meaningful role. News brought to Cicero while on his journey led him to believe, he claims, that Antony was altering political course and showing signs of being willing to be guided by the senate (1.8–9).

A senator much praised in this section of the *First Philippic* (§10) is the consular L. Piso, the father of Caesar's widow Calpurnia. That same Piso is the object of an all-out attack in Cicero's *In Pisonem* of 55 B.C. because he had earned Cicero's enmity for failing to prevent Publius Clodius from driving Cicero into exile in 58 when Piso was consul. On 1 August 44, however, Piso had the boldness to criticize Antony's policies in a speech delivered in the senate, and this act elevated Piso to the status of a hero in the eyes of Brutus (1.10) and of Cicero himself (1.14–

3

15). Cicero laments that Piso did not receive the support he deserved from his consular colleagues on 1 August, and Cicero makes it plain that Piso will serve as his model (1.15). By adopting that stance, Cicero sent a clear and unmistakable signal to Antony and his backers that the orator intended to lead the opposition. Cicero had been warned in advance, it seems, not to adopt this course (1.28), and his act of doing so nonetheless, and doing it so blatantly, helps explain why Antony reacted so angrily to the *First Philippic* (see Introd. to *Phil.* 2). Although the *First Philippic* is outwardly cast as a speech of friendly, constructive criticism of Antony's policies, Cicero himself later characterized it as an invective (*Fam.* 12.25.4).

The bulk of the *First Philippic* (§§16–26) attempts first to demonstrate that Antony and his colleague Dolabella are not upholding the acts of Caesar and next to persuade them to come to their senses (§§27–38a). The basis of Cicero's argument is that Antony and Dolabella are betraying Caesar's legacy because they have caused laws to be passed, or are proposing laws, that will sweep away sound legislation put in place by Caesar. By leveling this criticism, Cicero blatantly launched an assault on the very foundation of Antony's power which rested on his claim to be a champion and guardian of Caesar's legacy. Cicero also insinuated that Antony was abusing Caesar's private papers, which had been entrusted to his care by Caesar's widow; by forging documents in Caesar's name Antony conferred all sorts of favors in exchange for bribes (§§16, 24, 29, 33). By innuendo, the speech also suggests that Antony and his colleague Dolabella were guilty of bribing leading senators to purchase their cooperation in their nefarious doings (§16), of employing armed supporters to intimidate their political opponents (§§16, 27), and of being so tyrannical as to threaten death to any opponent (§28). Cicero even goes so far as to suggest that the conduct of Antony and Dolabella will cause them soon to suffer the fate of Caesar, if they do not mend their misguided ways (§§38, cf. 35).

STRUCTURE

Narratio

(1–10) Events from 17 March to 1 September 44 B.C.

Digressio

(11–13) Reply to Antony's threats on the previous day

Propositio

(14–15) Cicero must speak out: (16–18) Caesar's actions must be upheld

Argumentatio

(19–26) Antony's new legislation overturns Caesar's acts

Refutatio

(27–38a) Rebuttal of possible objections

Peroratio

(38b) Pledge to stand by the Republic

M. TULLI CICERONIS
IN M. ANTONIUM
ORATIO PHILIPPICA PRIMA

1   [1] Ante quam de re publica, patres conscripti, dicam
ea quae dicenda hoc tempore arbitror, exponam vobis breviter consilium et profectionis et reversionis meae.

Ego cum sperarem aliquando ad vestrum consilium
auctoritatemque rem publicam esse revocatam, manen-
dum mihi statuebam quasi in vigilia quadam consulari ac
senatoria. Nec vero usquam discedebam nec a re publica
deiciebam oculos ex eo die quo in aedem Telluris convocati sumus, in quo templo, quantum in me fuit, ieci fundamenta pacis Atheniensiumque renovavi vetus exemplum;
Graecum etiam verbum usurpavi quo tum in sedandis dis-
cordiis usa erat civitas illa, atque omnem memoriam dis-
cordiarum oblivione sempiterna delendam censui.

2   Praeclara tum oratio M. Antoni, egregia etiam voluntas;
pax denique per eum et per liberos eius cum praestantissimis civibus confirmata est. Atque his principiis reliqua

---

¹ See §§6–9.   ² On 17 March 44, the first meeting after
Caesar's assassination.   ³ Cicero, in fact, left Rome on 7
April 44 and did not return until 1 Sept.

⁴ Doubtless *amnestia*.   ⁵ An infant employed as a hostage to guarantee good faith (cf. §31).

MARCUS TULLIUS CICERO'S
FIRST PHILIPPIC ORATION
AGAINST MARCUS ANTONIUS

[1] Before I say, Members of the Senate, what I think
ought to be said at this time concerning public affairs, I
shall briefly explain to you my rationale both for setting out
on my journey and for turning back.[1]

Hoping, as I did, that the Republic had at last been restored to your guidance and authority, I took the view that
I ought to stay on a vigil, so to speak, of the sort that befits a
consular and a senator. In fact, from that day on which we
were summoned to the Temple of Tellus,[2] neither did I
withdraw anywhere from, nor did I take my eyes off public
affairs.[3] In that temple, so far as was in my power, I laid the
foundations of peace and revived the ancient Athenian
precedent, even adopting the Greek term[4] that was used
by that community in laying their quarrels to rest at that
time; that is, I proposed that all recollection of disputes
should be obliterated and forgotten for all time.

Marcus Antonius made a fine speech on that occasion
and also showed outstanding goodwill. Finally, through
him and his son,[5] peace with our most distinguished fellow
countrymen was established. And the sequel was in har-

consentiebant. Ad deliberationes eas quas habebat domi
de re publica principes civitatis adhibebat; ad hunc ordinem res optimas deferebat; nihil tum nisi quod erat notum
omnibus in C. Caesaris commentariis reperiebatur; summa constantia ad ea quae quaesita erant respondebat.
3 Num qui exsules restituti? Unum aiebat, praeterea neminem. Num immunitates datae? "Nullae," respondebat.
Adsentiri etiam nos Ser. Sulpicio, clarissimo viro, voluit, ne
qua tabula post Idus Martias ullius decreti Caesaris aut
benefici figeretur.

Multa praetereo eaque praeclara; ad singulare enim M.
Antoni factum festinat oratio, dictaturam, quae iam vim
regiae potestatis obsederat, funditus ex re publica sustulit;
de qua ne sententias quidem diximus. Scriptum senatus
consultum quod fieri vellet attulit, quo recitato auctoritatem eius summo studio secuti sumus eique amplissimis
verbis per senatus consultum gratias egimus.

4 [2] Lux quaedam videbatur oblata non modo regno,
quod pertuleramus, sed etiam regni timore sublato,
magnumque pignus ab eo rei publicae datum, se liberam
civitatem esse velle, cum dictatoris nomen, quod saepe
iustum fuisset, propter perpetuae dictaturae recentem
5 memoriam funditus ex re publica sustulisset. Liberatus

---

6 Sc. under the terms of any entries in Caesar's private memoranda.   7 Sex. Cloelius (not "Clodius," as his name used to
be incorrectly spelled), a former henchman of Cicero's bitter enemy P. Clodius Pulcher; cf. 2.7–10.

8 Such bronze tablets were posted in public places, especially
on the Capitol.   9 Cicero deliberately oversimplifies the
nature of this restriction. It did not ban the implementation of all
of Caesar's planned acts but rather called for a review by the two
consuls and an advisory board to decide which acts were to be implemented (cf. §23; 2.100, n. 127).

mony with these beginnings. Antonius regularly brought
the leaders of our community into the deliberations on
state affairs that he was in the habit of holding at his home.
He laid admirable proposals before this body. Nothing at
that time was discovered in Gaius Caesar's memoranda except what was common knowledge. His replies to questions were perfectly consistent. Had any exiles been re-   3
stored?[6] He mentioned just one,[7] nobody else. Had any
exemptions from taxes been granted? "None," was his reply. He even wanted us to vote for a motion by the distinguished gentleman Servius Sulpicius, the terms of which
were that no tablet[8] inscribed with any order or grant of
Caesar's should be posted after the fifteenth of March.[9]

I pass over many items, notable ones too, as my tongue
hastens on to Marcus Antonius' most remarkable gesture,
the total removal of the office of dictator from our constitution, an office that had usurped the power of absolute
monarchy.[10] We did not so much as debate the subject.
Antonius brought the draft of a decree that he said he
wished the senate to pass. As soon as it had been read
aloud, we followed his lead with the utmost enthusiasm
and by a decree voted him our unstinted thanks.

[2] It seemed as though a light of sorts had dawned,   4
with the removal not only of the monarchy which we had
endured, but even of the fear of its recurrence; it seemed
as though Antonius had given the Republic a mighty pledge
of his desire for a free community when, because of the
recollection of the recent "Dictatorship for Life," he totally removed from our constitution the office of dictator,
legitimate though it had often been. A few days later the   5

[10] Antony wished to forestall potential rivals from aspiring to
this office, which would trump his consulship.

periculo caedis paucis post diebus senatus; uncus impac-
tus est fugitivo illi qui in Mari nomen invaserat, atque haec
omnia communiter cum collega; alia porro propria Dolabellae quae, nisi collega afuisset, credo eis futura fuisse
communia. Nam cum serperet in urbe infinitum malum
idque manaret in dies latius, idemque bustum in foro facerent qui illam insepultam sepulturam effecerant, et cotidie
magis magisque perditi homines cum sui[s][1] similibus servis tectis ac templis urbis minarentur, talis animadversio
fuit Dolabellae cum in audacis sceleratosque servos, tum
in impuros et nefarios liberos, talisque eversio illius ex-
secratae columnae ut mihi mirum videatur tam valde reliquum tempus ab illo uno die dissensisse.

6   Ecce enim Kalendis Iuniis, quibus ut adessemus edixe-
rant, mutata omnia: nihil per senatum, multa et magna per
populum et absente populo et invito. Consules designati
negabant se audere in senatum venire; patriae liberatores
urbe carebant ea cuius a cervicibus iugum servile deiece-
rant, quos tamen ipsi consules in contionibus et in omni

---

[1] *corr. Angelius*

---

[11] The body of an executed criminal was dragged by a hook
and thrown into the Tiber.   [12] A man who claimed to be
the grandson of Gaius Marius and his wife Julia (Caesar's aunt).
He led a movement to institute divine rites for the murdered dictator. Antony had him summarily executed *c.* 13 April, not wanting
a rival to champion the cause of Caesar.

[13] Lit. "unburied"; a reference to the makeshift funeral pyre
that was heaped up in the Forum and used to burn Caesar's body
after the mob had been whipped into a frenzy of grief by Antony's
funeral speech.

senate was relieved from the threat of a massacre. The hook[11] was planted in the body of that runaway slave who had usurped the name of Marius.[12] In all of this Antonius acted jointly with his colleague; there were other acts besides for which Dolabella was solely responsible, acts which, I imagine, would have been their joint responsibility but for the absence of his colleague. For when a boundless infection was gaining ground in Rome and spreading wider and wider day by day, and when the authors of Caesar's abortive[13] burial were raising a tomb in the Forum, and when more and more desperados with slaves like themselves were daily threatening the houses and temples of our city, such was action taken by Dolabella in punishing not only the bold and criminal slaves but also the foul ruffians consisting of free men, such was his demolition of that accursed pillar[14] that I find it strange that his subsequent record stands in such sharp contrast to that one day's work.

Well, on the first of June, the day of the meeting to 6 which we had been summoned, everything was changed.[15] Nothing was enacted through the senate, but many important measures were put through the popular assembly— in the absence of the people and against their will. The consuls-elect said they did not dare attend the senate. The liberators of their native land were parted from the very city from whose neck they had cast off the yoke of slavery; and yet the consuls themselves praised them in public

[14] Raised to Caesar in the Forum in Apr. 44, on the spot where he had been cremated.   [15] Cicero distorts the chronology for rhetorical effect. As early as 22 April, Cicero began criticizing Antony's highhanded, unscrupulous conduct (*Att.* 14.12.1).

sermone laudabant. Veterani qui appellabantur, quibus hic
ordo diligentissime caverat, non ad conservationem earum
rerum quas habebant, sed ad spem novarum praedarum
incitabantur. Quae cum audire mallem quam videre habe-
remque ius legationis liberum, ea mente discessi ut ades-
sem Kalendis Ianuariis, quod initium senatus cogendi fore
videbatur.

7   [3] Exposui, patres conscripti, profectionis consilium:
nunc reversionis, quae plus admirationis habet, breviter
exponam. Cum Brundisium iterque illud quod tritum in
Graeciam est non sine causa vitavissem, Kalendis Sextilibus veni Syracusas, quod ab ea urbe transmissio in Graeciam laudabatur: quae tamen urbs mihi coniunctissima
plus una me nocte cupiens retinere non potuit, veritus sum
ne meus repentinus ad meos necessarios adventus suspi-
cionis aliquid adferret, si essem commoratus. Cum autem
me ex Sicilia ad Leucopetram, quod est promunturium
agri Regini, venti detulissent, ab eo loco conscendi ut trans-
mitterem; nec ita multum provectus reiectus Austro sum

8 in eum ipsum locum unde conscenderam. Cumque intem-
pesta nox esset mansissemque in villa P. Valeri, comitis et
familiaris mei, postridieque apud eundem ventum exspectans manerem, municipes Regini complures ad me vene-

---

16 In June 44, Dolabella, the incoming governor of Syria, had
made Cicero a *legatus* ("staff officer"), thus enabling him to leave
Italy (for which senators needed official authorization).

17 I.e., when the senate might be free of domination because
Antony would no longer be consul.

18 For fear of encountering the legions being transferred by
Antony from Macedonia via Brundisium (*Att.* 16.5.3).

19 Antony had recently courted the Sicilians by granting them

speeches and in all their conversation. The veterans, who were being called upon as supporters, of whose interests this body had taken the greatest care, were stirred up, not to preserve what they already had but to hope for fresh plunder. Since I preferred to hear of than to see all this, and since I had an unrestricted right to exercise a commission,[16] I set out with the intention of returning by the first of January, the earliest date, as appeared likely, for a convocation of the senate.[17]

[3] So much, Members of the Senate, for my reason   7
for leaving. As for my turning back, which entails more astonishment, I shall now briefly explain the reason. Avoiding for good cause[18] the beaten track to Greece via Brundisium, I arrived at Syracuse on the first of August, since the crossing to Greece from that city had a good reputation. I have very close ties with that city, but they could not keep me more than a single night, much as they wished it. I was fearful that if I made a stay, my sudden arrival among my old connections might give rise to some suspicion.[19] So when the wind carried me from Sicily to Leucopetra, a promontory in the district of Rhegium, I embarked from there for the crossing; but I had not proceeded so very far when the south wind carried me back right to my point of embarkation. Since it was the dead of night, and after I had   8
put up in a country house belonging to my friend and traveling companion Publius Valerius, on the following day, while I continued to stay there and wait for a favorable wind, a number of residents of Rhegium came over to see

Roman citizenship (*Att.* 14.12.1), whereas Cicero's ties to the island dated back to his quaestorship in 75 and his prosecution of Verres in 70.

runt, ex eis quidam Roma recentes: a quibus primum accipio Antoni contionem, quae mihi ita placuit ut ea lecta de
reversione primum coeperim cogitare, nec ita multo post
edictum Bruti adfertur et Cassi, quod quidem mihi, fortasse quod eos plus etiam rei publicae quam familiaritatis
gratia diligo, plenum aequitatis videbatur, addebant praeterea—fit enim plerumque ut ei qui boni quid volunt ad-
ferre adfingant aliquid quo faciant id quod nuntiant lae-
tius—rem conventuram: Kalendis Sextilibus senatum
frequentem fore; Antonium, repudiatis malis suasoribus,
remissis provinciis Galliis, ad auctoritatem senatus esse
rediturum.

9   [4] Tum vero tanta sum cupiditate incensus ad reditum
ut mihi nulli neque remi neque venti satis facerent, non
quo me ad tempus occursurum non putarem, sed ne tar-
dius quam cuperem rei publicae gratularer. Atque ego celeriter Veliam devectus Brutum vidi, quanto meo dolore
non dico. Turpe mihi ipsi videbatur in eam urbem me audere reverti ex qua Brutus cederet, et ibi velle tuto esse ubi
ille non posset. Neque vero illum similiter atque ipse eram
commotum esse vidi. Erectus enim maximi et pulcherrimi
facti sui conscientia nihil de suo casu, multa de vestro que-

10   rebatur. Exque eo primum cognovi quae Kalendis Sextilibus in senatu fuisset L. Pisonis oratio: qui quamquam parum erat—id enim ipsum a Bruto audieram—a quibus
debuerat adiutus, tamen et Bruti testimonio—quo quid

20 Delivered most likely *c.* mid-July when Antony thwarted
Octavian's plans to confer lavish honors on Caesar at funeral
games: thus signaling a rift among the Caesarians.
21 Addressed to the senate as a whole.

14

me, among them some recently returned from Rome. It was from them I first received a copy of Marcus Antonius' address to the people,[20] which pleased me so much that after reading it I first began to think of turning back; and not very long afterwards, I was brought a copy of Brutus' and Cassius' manifesto, which struck me—perhaps because I regard them even more highly on public grounds than I do for friendship's sake—as eminently fair. My callers added that there would be a settlement—for it generally happens that would-be bearers of good news add a little of their own invention to make their report the more agreeable—that there was to be a full meeting of the senate on the first of August, and that Antonius would divorce himself from his bad advisors, give up the Gallic provinces, and return to the guidance of the senate.

[4] That news fired me with such eagerness to get home that no oars, no winds satisfied my desire for speed, not because I thought I would not arrive in time, but so that I might congratulate the Republic no later than I was anxious to do so. So I made good time to Velia, where I saw Brutus, I do not say with what distress. I felt ashamed to be daring to return to the city from which Brutus was withdrawing, and to be wishing to live in safety in a place where he could not. However, I perceived no such agitation on his part as I felt myself. Exalted by the consciousness of his tremendously great and noble deed, he said no word of complaint about his own predicament, but many about yours.[21] It was from him that I first learned of Lucius Piso's speech in the senate on the first of August, and although Piso received too little support from those who ought to have backed him—that too I heard from Brutus—nevertheless, on Brutus' testimony, the weightiest in the world,

potest esse gravius?—et omnium praedicatione quos postea vidi, magnam mihi videbatur gloriam consecutus. Hunc igitur ut sequerer properavi quem praesentes non sunt secuti, non ut proficerem aliquid—nec enim sperabam id nec praestare poteram—sed ut, si quid mihi humanitus accidisset—multa autem impendere videntur praeter naturam etiam praeterque fatum—huius tamen diei vocem testem rei publicae relinquerem meae perpetuae erga se voluntatis.

11   Quoniam utriusque consili causam, patres conscripti, probatam vobis esse confido, prius quam de re publica dicere incipio, pauca querar de hesterna M. Antoni iniuria: cui sum amicus, idque me non nullo eius officio debere esse prae me semper tuli.

[5] Quid tandem erat causae cur die hesterno in senatum tam acerbe cogerer? Solusne aberam, an non saepe minus frequentes fuistis, an ea res agebatur ut etiam aegrotos deferri oporteret? Hannibal, credo, erat ad portas aut de Pyrrhi pace agebatur, ad quam causam etiam Appium illum et caecum et senem delatum esse memoriae

12   proditum est. De supplicationibus referebatur, quo in genere senatores deesse non solent. Coguntur enim non pignoribus, sed eorum de quorum honore agitur gratia; quod idem fit, cum de triumpho refertur. Ita sine cura consules sunt, ut paene liberum sit senatori non adesse. Qui cum

---

22 See 2.5–6.

23 Appius Claudius Caecus, in 279 (*Sen.* 16).

24 Liable to forfeiture, if a senator was absent without good cause.

and on the laudatory report of all whom I saw later, it seemed to me that Piso had covered himself with glory. Consequently, I hastened in order to follow the lead of a man whom those present failed to follow, not in order to achieve anything—that was not in my hopes or power to guarantee—but so that I might leave the words I speak today as witnesses to the Republic of my abiding loyalty, in case anything befall me such as may happen to any of us—many dangers, moreover, appear to loom even beyond the course of nature and destiny.

Members of the Senate, inasmuch as I am confident   11 that my reasons for both decisions have met with your approval, I shall, before I begin to speak on public affairs, say a few words in protest against Marcus Antonius' offensive behavior yesterday—I am his friend, and I have always acknowledged that I ought to be such on account of some service he once rendered me.[22]

[5] Now what cause was there yesterday for me to be summoned to attend the senate in such harsh terms? Was I the only absentee? Has this body not often been less well attended? Was the business in hand such as to demand the attendance even of invalids? Hannibal was at the gates, I suppose; or peace with Pyrrhus was at issue—the business for which tradition has it that the great Appius[23] was brought in, blind and aged as he was. In fact, the business   12 under discussion concerned public thanksgivings, and senators are usually in good attendance on such occasions. They are brought to the meeting not by pledges[24] but by their willingness to oblige the persons whose honors are under consideration. The same applies when the debate concerns a triumph. The consuls are so free of worry about a quorum that a senator is pretty much at liberty to stay

17

mihi mos notus esset cumque e via languerem et mihimet
displicerem, misi pro amicitia qui hoc ei diceret. At ille vobis audientibus cum fabris se domum meam venturum
esse dixit. Nimis iracunde hoc quidem et valde intemperanter. Cuius enim malefici tanta ista poena est ut dicere in
hoc ordine auderet se publicis operis disturbaturum publice ex senatus sententia aedificatam domum? Quis autem umquam tanto damno senatorem coegit? Aut quid est
ultra pignus aut multam?

13   Quod si scisset quam sententiam dicturus essem, remi-
sisset aliquid profecto de severitate cogendi. [6] An me
censetis, patres conscripti, quod vos inviti secuti estis, decreturum fuisse, ut parentalia cum supplicationibus mis-
cerentur, ut inexpiabiles religiones in rem publicam indu-
cerentur, ut decernerentur supplicationes mortuo? Nihil
dico cui. Fuerit ille L. Brutus qui et ipse dominatu regio
rem publicam liberavit et ad similem virtutem et simile
factum stirpem iam prope in quingentesimum annum pro-
pagavit: adduci tamen non possem ut quemquam mortuum coniungerem cum deorum immortalium religione;
ut, cuius sepulcrum usquam[2] exstet ubi parentetur, ei publice supplicetur. Ego vero eam sententiam dixissem ut me

---

[2] *b*: nusquam *Vcnstv*

---

[25] After Cicero's return from exile in 57, his house on the Pala-
tine, which had been demolished (and the land confiscated), was
rebuilt with a grant from the senate.   [26] Lit. the "Parentalia," a festival (13–21 February) at which offerings were made to
the dead, likened here to Antony's proposal to honor a dead man
(Caesar) at festivals (*supplicationes*) reserved for the living.

[27] The liberators Decimus and Marcus Brutus.

[28] The bulk of the MSS read "nowhere" (*nusquam*), which can

away. Knowing the custom and feeling weak and out of sorts from my journey, I sent a message to that effect to Antonius in keeping with our friendship. But Antonius declared in your presence that he would come to my house with a squad of workmen! That was really letting his temper run away with him! Of what misdeed is the penalty so grave that Antonius dared to say in this body that he would use public employees to demolish a house built at public expense by order of the senate?[25] Who ever compelled a senator's attendance by so heavy a forfeit? What is there beyond a pledge or a fine?

But if Antonius had known what I would have said in that debate, he would undoubtedly have somewhat toned down the sternness of his summons. [6] Or do you suppose, Members of the Senate, that I would have voted for the proposal to which you agreed against your will, namely that offerings to the dead[26] be mixed up with public thanksgivings, that inexpiable sacrilege be introduced into the Republic, that public thanksgivings be decreed to a *dead man*? Never mind to *which* dead man. Let us say it was Lucius Brutus, who freed the Republic from regal despotism and now, almost five hundred years later, has inspired his stock[27] to a courageousness and a deed like to his own: even so, I would not be able to be led to link any dead man with the worship of the immortal gods, so that prayers of public thanksgiving are addressed to one whose tomb, where offerings can be made to the departed spirit, exists somewhere.[28] No, I would have spoken in such a vein that

13

be defended only by supposing that Cicero is alluding to the removal of the grave monument to Caesar in the Forum (2.107). There was, however, a place elsewhere in which his bones were interred (Cass. Dio 44.51.1).

adversus populum Romanum, si qui accidisset gravior rei
publicae casus, si bellum, si morbus, si fames, facile possem defendere; quae partim iam sunt, partim timeo ne im-
pendeant. Sed hoc ignoscant di immortales velim et populo Romano, qui id non probat, et huic ordini, qui decrevit
invitus.

14   Quid? De reliquis rei publicae malis licetne dicere?
Mihi vero licet et semper licebit dignitatem tueri, mortem
contemnere. Potestas modo veniendi in hunc locum sit: dicendi periculum non recuso. Atque utinam, patres conscripti, Kalendis Sextilibus adesse potuissem! Non quo
profici potuerit aliquid, sed ne unus modo consularis,
quod tum accidit, dignus illo honore, dignus re publica in-
veniretur. Qua quidem ex re magnum accipio dolorem, homines amplissimis populi Romani beneficiis usos L. Pisonem ducem optimae sententiae non secutos. Idcircone nos
populus Romanus consules fecit ut in altissimo gradu dignitatis locati rem publicam pro nihilo haberemus? Non
modo voce nemo L. Pisoni consularis sed ne voltu quidem
15 adsensus est. Quae, malum, est ista voluntaria servitus?
Fuerit quaedam necessaria; ‹nunc non est ita›.[3] Neque
ego hoc ab omnibus eis desidero qui sententiam consulari
loco dicunt. Alia causa est eorum quorum silentio ignosco,
alia eorum quorum vocem requiro. Quos quidem doleo in

[3] *suppl. SB*

[29] Under Caesar's dictatorship.
[30] Lit. "in the consular position." The ex-consuls spoke first
(after the consuls-elect, if any), their order being determined each
year by whichever consul presided during January.

in the event of some serious national disaster—war, pestilence, famine—I could easily defend myself before the Roman people. Some of these disasters are already upon us; others, I fear, hang over our heads. But I could wish that the immortal gods may pardon the Roman people, who do not approve of what was done, and pardon this body, which passed the decree against its will.

What of other public ills? Is it permitted to speak of   14
them? Permitted it is to me, and ever shall be, to maintain honor and despise death. Just let me have the power to enter this place, and I do not decline the risk of speaking. And I only wish, Members of the Senate, that I could have been present on the first of August; not because anything could have been accomplished, but to prevent what actually occurred, namely that only one consular was found worthy of that rank, worthy of the Republic. Indeed, it grieves me to the heart that persons who have enjoyed the highest gifts the Roman people can bestow did not follow the lead given by Lucius Piso in his most admirable motion. Was it for this reason that the Roman people made us consuls, in order that we in so exalted a station, the highest in the land, might set the Republic at naught? Not only did no consular support Lucius Piso by word but not even by look. For   15
pity's sake, what is this voluntary slavery? Granted that slavery of a sort was unavoidable in time past:[29] it is not so now. At the same time, I do not expect this from all senators who express their views with the status of an ex-consul.[30] It is not the same with those whose silence I pardon,[31] as with those whose voice I demand. I am sorry

[31] I.e., persons who have a close connection with Antony such as his maternal uncle, L. Caesar, and paternal uncle, C. Antonius.

suspicionem populo Romano venire non metu, quod ipsum esset turpe, sed alium alia de causa deesse dignitati
suae. [7] Qua re primum maximas gratias et ago et habeo
Pisoni, qui non quid efficere posset in re publica cogitavit,
sed quid facere ipse deberet. Deinde a vobis, patres conscripti, peto ut, etiam si sequi minus audebitis orationem
atque auctoritatem meam, benigne me tamen, ut fecistis
adhuc, audiatis.

16   Primum igitur acta Caesaris servanda censeo, non quo
probem—quis enim id quidem potest?—sed quia rationem habendam maxime arbitror pacis atque oti. Vellem
adesset M. Antonius, modo sine advocatis—sed, ut opinor,
licet ei minus valere, quod mihi heri per illum non licebat;
doceret me vel potius vos, patres conscripti, quem ad modum ipse Caesaris acta defenderet. An in commentariolis
et chirographis et libellis se uno auctore prolatis, ne prolatis quidem sed tantum modo dictis, acta Caesaris firma
erunt: quae ille in aes incidit, in quo populi iussa perpe-
17 tuasque leges esse voluit, pro nihilo habebuntur? Equidem existimo nihil tam esse in actis Caesaris quam leges
Caesaris. An, si cui quid ille promisit, id erit fixum, quod
idem non facere potuit? Ut multis multa promissa non fecit: quae tamen multo plura illo mortuo reperta sunt quam
a vivo beneficia per omnis annos tributa et data. Sed ea non

---

32 Cicero alludes to bribes and pressure of various sorts
brought to bear by Antony (see *Fam.* 12.2.2).

33 Antony's armed guards, sarcastically styled *advocati* ("consultants").

indeed that in the eyes of the Roman people the latter fall under suspicion of not living up to their high rank, not out of fear, which would be dishonorable enough, but for their several particular reasons.[32] [7] And so in the first place I both express and feel sincere gratitude to Piso, who did not think about how much he could achieve politically but about his own duty. In the second place, Members of the Senate, let me request of you to give me a courteous hearing, as you have thus far, even if you will be somewhat hesitant to fall in with what I say and advise.

First, then, I declare myself in favor of maintaining Caesar's acts; not that I approve of them—who can do that?—but because I think peace and quiet should be our first consideration. I could have wished that Marcus Antonius were here present, only without his consultants;[33] but I suppose he has a right to be indisposed, a right he did not allow *me* yesterday. If he were here, he would show me, or rather you, Members of the Senate, how *he* goes about defending Caesar's acts. Will it be in scraps of memoranda and holographs and papers produced on Antonius' sole authority, or not so much as produced but merely alleged, that the acts of Caesar will be unshakable; whereas measures that Caesar inscribed on bronze, as legislative acts of the people and permanently valid statutes, will be treated as of no account? I indeed consider that nothing is so decidedly a part of Caesar's acts as Caesar's laws. Or, if he made some promise to somebody, is it to be hard and fast, a promise that Caesar could have failed to carry out? Just as he did not carry out many promises made to many people. And yet the promises brought to light after his death far outnumber the favors granted and given by him throughout all the years of

16

17

23

muto, non moveo: summo etiam studio illius praeclara acta
defendo. Pecunia utinam ad Opis maneret! Cruenta illa
quidem, sed his temporibus, quoniam eis quorum est non
redditur, necessaria. Quamquam ea quoque sit effusa, si
18   ita in actis fuit. Ecquid est quod tam proprie dici possit actum eius qui togatus in re publica cum potestate impe-
rioque versatus sit quam lex? Quaere acta Gracchi: leges
Semproniae proferentur. Quaere Sullae: Corneliae. Quid?
Pompei tertius consulatus in quibus actis constitit? Nempe
in legibus. De Caesare ipso si quaereres quidnam egisset
in urbe et in toga, leges multas responderet se et praeclaras
tulisse, chirographa vero aut mutaret aut non daret aut, si
dedisset, non istas res in actis suis duceret, sed haec ipsa
concedo; quibusdam etiam in rebus coniveo; in maximis
vero rebus, id est in legibus, acta Caesaris dissolvi feren-
dum non puto.

19   [8] Quae lex melior, utilior, optima etiam re publica saepius flagitata quam ne praetoriae provinciae plus quam annum neve plus quam biennium consulares obtinerentur?
Hac lege sublata videturne vobis posse Caesaris acta servari? Quid? Lege quae promulgata est de tertia decuria

---

34 Because derived largely from the sales of confiscated property; its embezzlement by Antony and Dolabella started in March
(2.93a; *Att.* 14.14.5).

35 For rhetorical effect, Cicero characterizes the legislation
granting extended terms to Antony and his colleague as the abolition of Caesar's law.

36 In 46, Caesar restricted jury service from three panels to
two (composed of senators and of knights); in 44 Antony restored

his life. However, I am not tampering with them, not at all; I am a most enthusiastic defender of Caesar's splendid acts. One *could* wish the money in the Temple of Ops were still there. To be sure, it is stained with blood,[34] but it is really needed in these circumstances, since it is not being returned to its rightful owners. And yet, let it also be dissipated, if it was so ordered in Caesar's acts. Is there anything at all so much as a law that can properly be called an act of one who in a civilian capacity has wielded power and authority in public life? Ask to be shown the acts of Gracchus: the Sempronian laws will be held up. Ask to be shown Sulla's: voilà, the Cornelian laws. Come, what were the acts that made up Pompey's third consulship? Why, his legislation. If you could ask Caesar himself what he had done in Rome, in a civilian capacity, he would answer that he had passed many fine laws, but as for his handwritten notes, he would either change them or not produce them or, if he did produce them, he would not consider such jottings among his acts. However, this also I concede; in certain matters I am even ready to turn a blind eye; but in the most important matters of all, that is to say laws, I do not think it tolerable that Caesar's acts should be set aside.

[8] What better, more useful law, more often demanded even in the best days of the Republic is there than the law providing that praetorian provinces be held for not more than one year and consular for not more than two? When this law is abolished, do you think it possible for Caesar's acts to be maintained?[35] What about the law that has been promulgated concerning a third panel of jurors;[36]

a third panel henceforth comprising citizens drawn from lower census classes.

nonne omnes iudiciariae leges Caesaris dissolvuntur? Et
vos acta Caesaris defenditis qui leges eius evertitis? Nisi
forte, si quid memoriae causa rettulit in libellum, id nume-
rabitur in actis et, quamvis iniquum et inutile sit, defende-
tur: quod ad populum centuriatis comitiis tulit, id in actis
20 Caesaris non habebitur. At quae est ista tertia decuria?
"Centurionum," inquit. Quid? Isti ordini iudicatus lege Iulia, etiam ante Pompeia, Aurelia non patebat? "Census
praefiniebatur," inquit. Non centurioni quidem solum sed
equiti etiam Romano; itaque viri fortissimi atque honestissimi qui ordines duxerunt res et iudicant et iudicaverunt.
"Non quaero," inquit "istos: quicumque ordinem duxit, iu-
dicet." At si ferretis quicumque equo meruisset, quod est
lautius, nemini probaretis; in iudice enim spectari et fortuna debet et dignitas. "Non quaero," inquit, "ista: addo
etiam iudices manipularis ex legione Alaudarum. Aliter
enim nostri negant posse se salvos esse." O contumeliosum
honorem eis quos ad iudicandum nec opinantis vocatis!
Hic enim est ⟨prope dicam⟩[4] legis index ut ei res in tertia

4 *suppl. SB*

---

37 The voting units in the *comitia centuriata* were formed according to census class, and voting was weighted in favor of the
wealthy.

38 The Aurelian law of 70 provided for juries to be drawn
equally from three panels (of senators, of knights, and of *tribuni
aerarii*, citizens on a par with knights). Pompey's law of 55 called
for the richest citizens from the three classes to be placed on the
panels (*Pis.* 94; Ascon. p. 17C).

39 The officers (legates, military tribunes and prefects),
chiefly drawn from the equestrian class but not always persons in
the best of financial circumstances (and hence ineligible for jury
service under previous laws).

does it not set aside the whole of Caesar's judiciary legislation? And do you defend Caesar's acts while you subvert his laws? Or perhaps we should say that if Caesar jotted something in a notebook as an aid to memory, we must count that among his acts and defend it, no matter how unjust and inadvisable it may be, whereas a law that he submitted to the people at the centuriate assembly is not to be regarded as an act of Caesar's?[37] However, what is this 20 third jury panel? "It is composed of centurions," he says. Indeed? Service as a juror was not open to that class under the Julian law, and even earlier under the Pompeian and Aurelian?[38] "That was with a property qualification," he says. Well, but this applied not merely to a centurion but to a Roman knight as well. And so, brave and respectable persons who have served as centurions are sitting on juries and have done so in the past. "I am not interested in those individuals," he says. "Let every man who has served as centurion sit on juries." But if you and your colleague were making the same proposal with respect to every man who has served in the army on horseback,[39] which carries more distinction, you would win support from no one. In a juror both financial means and status ought to be considered. "I am not interested in all that," he says. "In addition, I am giving the right to private soldiers of the Larks Legion.[40] Our people[41] say that otherwise they cannot be safe from prosecution." Oh what an insulting honor for those whom you and your colleague are summoning out of the blue to sit as jurors. The rubric to the law states, I might almost say, that the third panel shall consist of jurors who dare

[40] Raised by Caesar from Transalpine Gaul and later granted Roman citizenship.

[41] Antony and his followers (cf. 5.15; 8.27).

decuria iudicent qui libere iudicare non audeant. In quo
quantus error est, di immortales, eorum qui istam legem
excogitaverunt! Ut enim quisque sordidissimus videbitur,
ita libentissime severitate iudicandi sordis suas eluet labo-
rabitque ut honestis decuriis potius dignus videatur quam
in turpem iure coniectus.

21   [9] Altera promulgata lex est ut de vi et maiestatis dam-
nati ad populum provocent, si velint. Haec utrum tandem
lex est an legum omnium dissolutio? Quis est autem[5] hodie
cuius intersit istam legem rogari?[6] Nemo reus est legibus
illis, nemo quem futurum putemus. Armis enim gesta numquam profecto in iudicium vocabuntur. "At res popularis."
Utinam quidem aliquid velletis esse populare! Omnes
enim iam cives de rei publicae salute una et mente et voce
consentiunt. Quae est igitur ista cupiditas legis eius fe-
rendae quae turpitudinem summam habeat, gratiam nullam? Quid enim turpius quam qui maiestatem populi Romani minuerit per vim, eum damnatum iudicio ad eam
22 ipsam vim reverti propter quam sit iure damnatus? Sed
quid plura de lege disputo? Quasi vero id agatur ut quisquam provocet: id agitur, id fertur ne quis omnino umquam istis legibus reus fiat. Quis enim aut accusator tam
amens reperietur qui reo condemnato obici se multitudini
conductae velit, aut iudex qui reum damnare audeat, ut
ipse ad operas mercennarias statim protrahatur? Non igitur provocatio ista lege datur, sed duae maxime salutares

---

5 *SB*: enim *codd.*
6 *SB in app.*: manere *V*: venire *D*

---

42 Cicero likes to make play with *popularis* in its general
meaning, "pleasing to the people," and its use as a political term
for "democratic"—i.e. antisenatorial—politicians and measures.

not render an independent verdict. Ah, but by the immortal gods, what a monumental error the contrivers of this law are making! Why, the spottier a man's credentials, the more eager he will be to wash away his spots by strictness in the jury box, the harder he will try to look as though he ought to be on a respectable panel, instead of being rightly thrust into a disreputable one.

[9] Another law has been promulgated permitting persons convicted of violence and treason to appeal to the people, if they wish. Is this a law or the cancellation of all laws? Besides, who is there today who has any stake in having such a law put to a vote? Nobody stands accused under those laws, nobody is expected to be accused, for obviously acts of warfare will never be brought before a court of law. "But it's a popular measure." I only wish you gentlemen wanted anything you do to be truly pleasing to the people,[42] for all citizens are now of one mind and voice concerning the welfare of the Republic. So why are you so anxious to pass this law which entails the utmost disgrace and no goodwill? For what is more disgraceful than a return to violence on the part of a man justly convicted for such conduct, one who has committed treason by resorting to violence and hence been condemned in a court? But I need not go on talking about the law, as though its purpose were to allow appeals; its purpose, its intent, is that nobody should ever be charged under the laws punishing violence and treason. For what prosecutor will be found crazy enough to be willing to allow himself to be exposed to a hired crowd after the accused is found guilty, or what juror crazy enough to dare convict a defendant when the juror himself faces the prospect of being dragged up immediately before a mercenary gang? Therefore, this law does not grant a right of appeal, but it does away with two very

21

22

CICERO

leges quaestionesque tolluntur. Quid est aliud hortari adulescentis ut turbulenti, ut seditiosi, ut perniciosi cives velint esse? Quam autem ad pestem furor tribunicius impelli
non poterit his duabus quaestionibus de vi et maiestate
23 sublatis? Quid quod obrogatur legibus Caesaris, quae iu-
bent ei qui de vi itemque ei qui maiestatis damnatus sit
aqua et igni interdici? Quibus cum provocatio datur, nonne acta Caesaris rescinduntur? Quae quidem ego, patres
conscripti, qui illa numquam probavi, tamen ita conser-
vanda concordiae causa arbitratus sum ut non modo, quas
vivus leges Caesar tulisset, infirmandas hoc tempore non
putarem, sed ne illas quidem quas post mortem Caesaris
prolatas esse et fixas videtis.
24 [10] De exsilio reducti a mortuo; civitas data non solum
singulis sed nationibus et provinciis universis a mortuo;
immunitatibus infinitis sublata vectigalia a mortuo. Ergo
haec uno verum optimo auctore domo prolata defendimus: eas leges quas ipse nobis inspectantibus recitavit,
pronuntiavit, tulit, quibus latis gloriabatur eisque legibus
rem publicam contineri putabat, de provinciis, de iudiciis,
eas, inquam, Caesaris leges nos qui defendimus acta Cae-
25 saris evertendas putamus? Ac de his tamen legibus quae
promulgatae sunt saltem queri possumus: de eis quae iam
latae dicuntur ne illud quidem licuit. Illae enim sine ulla
promulgatione latae sunt ante quam scriptae.

---

43 An exaggeration. The only province granted Roman citizenship was Sicily, which already possessed it in large measure.
Crete was given "free" status (see 2.97).

44 Sc. the law adding the third jury panel and the law allowing
appeal.   45 Cicero uses similar language in 5.7 to describe
the tribunician legislation in June that granted provinces to Antony and Dolabella for an extended term.

salutary laws and courts. Does not this constitute an invitation to our young men to become turbulent agitators and harmful citizens? To what ruinous act will the subversive tendencies of tribunes not be able to be incited, once these two courts, of violence and of treason, have been abolished? Again, is not this to alter the laws of Caesar, which 23
declare that any man found guilty of violence, and likewise any man found guilty of treason, is to be outlawed? When the right of appeal is granted to such, are not Caesar's acts rescinded? I, who never approved those acts, Members of the Senate, nevertheless judged that they should be retained for concord's sake, and consequently I arrived at the opinion that we should not abolish at this time not only the laws passed by Caesar while yet alive but even those that you see produced and posted after Caesar's death.

[10] Exiles have been restored by a dead man; citizen- 24
ship has been conferred by a dead man, not only upon individuals but on peoples and whole provinces;[43] through the granting of countless exemptions, revenues have been abolished by a dead man. Well, we defend these ordinances, produced from a private house on the authority (admittedly excellent) of one individual. What of the laws that Caesar in person read out and published and carried before our eyes, the laws in which he gloried as their sponsor, on which he believed the existence of the Republic to depend, the laws on the provinces and the courts? Yes, those laws of Caesar: do we, who defend Caesar's acts, think they ought to be overturned? And these laws,[44] 25
which have been promulgated, are at least open to protest on our part; but not even that was permitted in the case of laws alleged to have been already passed. They were passed without any promulgation before they were committed to writing.[45]

Quaero autem quid sit cur aut ego aut quisquam vestrum, patres conscripti, bonis tribunis plebi leges malas
metuat. Paratos habemus qui intercedant, paratos qui rem
publicam religione defendant: vacui metu esse debemus.
"Quas tu mihi," inquit "intercessiones, quas religiones?"
Eas scilicet quibus rei publicae salus continetur. "Neglegi-
mus ista et nimis antiqua ac stulta ducimus: forum saepie-
tur; omnes claudentur aditus; armati in praesidiis multis
26   locis collocabuntur." Quid tum? Quod ita erit gestum, id
lex erit? Et in aes incidi iubebitis, credo, illa legitima:
CONSULES POPULUM IURE ROGAVERUNT—hocine a maioribus accepimus ius rogandi?—POPULUSQUE IURE SCI-
VIT. Qui populus? Isne qui exclusus est? Quo iure? An eo
quod vi et armis omne sublatum est? Atque haec dico de
futuris, quod est amicorum ante dicere ea quae vitari possint: quae si facta non erunt, refelletur oratio mea. Loquor
de legibus promulgatis, de quibus est integrum vobis, de-
monstro vitia. Tollite! Denuntio vim, arma. Removete!
27   [11] Irasci quidem vos mihi, Dolabella, pro re publica
dicenti non oportebit. Quamquam te quidem id facturum
non arbitror—novi facilitatem tuam; collegam tuum aiunt
in hac sua fortuna, quae bona ipsi videtur—mihi, ne gravius quippiam dicam, avorum et avunculi sui consulatum si
imitaretur, fortunatior videretur—sed eum iracundum au-

---

46 M. Antonius (cos. 99), L. Julius Caesar (cos. 90), and L. Julius Caesar (cos. 64), repectively.

And now I put a question: why should I or any of you, Members of the Senate, fear bad laws when we have good tribunes of the plebs? There they are, ready to use their veto, ready to defend the Republic by the sanctity of their office. Our minds should be at ease. "Vetoes?" says he. "Religious sanctions? What are you talking about?" Why, naturally, those which are bound up with the welfare of the Republic. "Oh, we take no notice of that sort of thing. Antiquated nonsense, that's what we think of it. The Forum will be fenced off, all entries barred. Armed men will be posted on guard at many points." And then what? Will something 26 transacted in this fashion be a law? I suppose you will have the stock formula in legislation engraved on bronze: "The Consuls lawfully proposed to the people"– is *this* the traditional right of proposal?—"and the people lawfully enacted." What people? The people who were shut out? Lawfully? Are you referring to a legality that has been entirely abolished by armed violence? Now understand, I am speaking of the future—it is the part of friends to speak beforehand of such things as can be avoided. If they do not come to pass, my words will be refuted. I am talking about promulgated laws, as to which your hands are still free, and I am pointing out flaws. Remove them! I warn of violence, of armed force. Take it away!

[11] It will not be proper for you and your colleague, 27 Dolabella, to be angry with me for speaking out on behalf of the Republic. To be sure, I do not suppose that *you* will react that way—I know your easy temper; as to your colleague, they say that he in this fortune of his, which in his eyes is good—to me, to put it thus mildly, he would appear more fortunate, if he took as his models the consulships of his grandfathers and his maternal uncle[46]—anyhow, I hear

dio factum. Video autem quam sit odiosum habere eundem iratum et armatum, cum tanta praesertim gladiorum sit impunitas: sed proponam ius, ut opinor, aequum, quod M. Antonium non arbitror repudiaturum. Ego, si quid in vitam eius aut in mores cum contumelia dixero, quo minus mihi inimicissimus sit non recusabo; sin consuetudinem meam quam in re publica semper habui tenuero, id est si libere quae sentiam de re publica dixero, primum deprecor ne irascatur; deinde, si hoc non impetro, peto ut sic irascatur ut civi. Armis utatur, si ita necesse est, ut dicit, sui defendendi causa: eis qui pro re publica quae ipsis visa erunt dixerint ista arma ne noceant. Quid hac postulatione

28   dici potest aequius? Quod si, ut mihi a quibusdam eius familiaribus dictum est, omnis eum quae habetur contra voluntatem eius oratio graviter offendit, etiam si nulla inest contumelia, feremus amici naturam. Sed idem illi ita mecum loquuntur: "non idem tibi adversario Caesaris licebit quod Pisoni socero," et simul admonent quiddam quod cavebimus; nec erit iustior in senatum non veniendi morbi causa quam mortis.

29   [12] Sed per deos immortalis!—te enim intuens, Dolabella, qui es mihi carissimus, non possum de utriusque vestrum errore reticere. Credo enim vos nobilis homines magna quaedam spectantis non pecuniam, ut quidam nimis creduli suspicantur, quae semper ab amplissimo quoque clarissimoque contempta est, non opes violentas

that he has become irascible. And I am well aware how disagreeable it is to have a man angry when he carries a weapon, especially in times when swords are used with so much impunity. But I shall make what seems to me a fair proposition, one which I do not think Marcus Antonius will reject. If I say anything offensive concerning his career or character, I shall not object to his becoming my mortal enemy. On the other hand, if I hold to my invariable practice in public life, that is, if I speak my mind freely on public affairs, in the first place I beg him not to be angry; and if that plea fails, then I ask him to be angry with me as a fellow citizen. Let him use arms, if that is necessary (as he says it is), for his own defense, but let those arms do no injury to people who speak their own minds on behalf of the Republic. Well, what can be fairer than what I am asking? Certain of 28 his closest friends, however, tell me that all speech that is held to be contrary to his wishes gravely offends him, even if no insult is involved. If that be so, I shall put up with a friend's humor. But I am told by these same persons: "You were an adversary of Caesar; you cannot expect to be allowed the same license as Piso, Caesar's father-in-law." And they go on to give me a hint that I shall bear in mind: as a reason for not attending the senate, death will be as good an excuse as illness.

[12] But in the name of the immortal gods!—when I 29 look at you, Dolabella, very dear to me as you are, I cannot keep silent about the mistake which both of you gentlemen are making. I do not suppose that you, being men of noble birth with lofty aims, have set your sights on money, as certain over-credulous folk suspect—for money has ever been despised by all the greatest and most renowned men—nor yet on might backed by violence and on power such as the

et populo Romano minime ferendam potentiam, sed cari-
tatem civium et gloriam concupivisse. Est autem gloria
laus recte factorum magnorumque in rem publicam fama
meritorum, quae cum optimi cuiusque, tum etiam multi-
30 tudinis testimonio comprobatur. Dicerem, Dolabella, qui
recte factorum fructus esset, nisi te praeter ceteros paulis-
per esse expertum viderem. Quem potes recordari in vita
illuxisse tibi diem laetiorem quam cum expiato foro, dissi-
pato concursu impiorum, principibus sceleris poena ad-
fectis, ⟨urbe incendio et caedis metu liberata⟩,[7] te domum
recepisti? Cuius ordinis, cuius generis, cuius denique fortunae studia tum laudi et gratulationi tuae se non obtule-
runt? Quin mihi etiam, quo auctore te in his rebus uti
arbitrabantur, et gratias boni viri agebant et tuo nomine
gratulabantur. Recordare, quaeso, Dolabella, consensum
illum theatri, cum omnes earum rerum obliti propter quas
fuerant tibi offensi significarent se beneficio novo memo-
31 riam veteris doloris abiecisse. Hanc tu, P. Dolabella—
magno loquor cum dolore—hanc tu, inquam, potuisti aequo animo tantam dignitatem deponere?

[13] Tu autem, M. Antoni—absentem enim appello—
unum illum diem quo in aede Telluris senatus fuit non omnibus his mensibus quibus te quidam multum a me dissen-
tientes beatum putant anteponis? Quae fuit oratio de concordia! Quanto metu senatus, quanta sollicitudine civitas

7 *add.* V[2]

47 *Boni viri* (lit. "good men") are solid, substantial citizens and
supporters of the existing order.   48 An allusion to Dolabella's tribunate in 47, when by agitating unsuccessfully for the
cancellation of debts he sparked violent riots.

Roman people can in no way tolerate; not on these then, but on glory and a place in the hearts of your countrymen. Glory, moreover, consists in the credit for honorable deeds and the reputation for great services benefiting the Republic, approved by the testimony of the best among us and also by that of the multitude. I would be telling you, 30 Dolabella, what the reward of good deeds is, if I were not aware of the fact that for a short while you had more experience of it than any other man. What happier or brighter day in your life can you remember than the day you returned home after purging the Forum, dispersing the concourse of traitors, punishing the ringleaders, and freeing Rome from the threat of arson and the fear of massacre? People of all classes, sorts, and conditions came up to you on your way with enthusiastic praise and congratulation. Indeed, decent men[47] were actually thanking *me* and congratulating me on your account under the impression that I had been your mentor in these proceedings. Please recall, Dolabella, the unanimous applause in the theater, when all present, forgetting their past grievances against you,[48] made it plain that after this recent benefaction they had cast aside the recollection of old bitterness. Could you, 31 Publius Dolabella—I speak with much pain—could you, I say, calmly lay down such high standing as this?

[13] And you, Marcus Antonius—I address you though you are not here—surely you prize that one day when the senate met in the Temple of Tellus beyond all these recent months in which some folk with whom I profoundly disagree regard you as felicitous? What a speech you made about concord! From what fear did you deliver the senate, from what anxiety did you deliver the community, when

tum a te liberata est cum collegam tuum, depositis inimici-
tiis, oblitus auspiciorum a te ipso augure populi Romani
nuntiato‹rum›,[8] illo primum die collegam tibi esse voluisti; cum tuus parvus filius in Capitolio a te missus pacis
32 obses fuit! Quo senatus die laetior, quo populus Romanus?
Qui quidem nulla in contione umquam frequentior fuit.
Tum denique liberati per viros fortissimos videbamur,
quia, ut illi voluerant, libertatem pax consequebatur.

Proximo, altero, tertio, denique reliquis consecutis diebus non intermittebas quasi donum aliquod cotidie ad-
ferre rei publicae; maximum autem illud quod dictaturae
nomen sustulisti. Haec inusta est a te, a te, inquam, mortuo
Caesari nota ad ignominiam sempiternam. Ut enim propter unius M. Manli scelus decreto gentis Manliae neminem patricium Manlium ‹Marcum›[9] vocari licet, sic tu
propter unius dictatoris odium nomen dictatoris funditus
33 sustulisti. Num te, cum haec pro salute rei publicae tanta
gessisses, fortunae tuae, num amplitudinis, num claritatis,
num gloriae paenitebat? Unde igitur subito tanta ista mu-
tatio? Non possum adduci ut suspicer te pecunia captum.
Licet quod cuique libet loquatur, credere non est necesse.
Nihil enim umquam in te sordidum, nihil humile cognovi.
Quamquam solent domestici depravare non numquam;

---

8 *corr. Faërnus*
9 *add. Gulielmius*

---

49 Cf. 2.79–84.   50 Cf. §2.   51 Caesar's assassins.

52 Suspected of aiming at despotic power, he was killed in 384.
On the action taken by the *gens* Manlia to blackball henceforth
the name Marcus, see Liv. 6.20.14.

53 An allusion to Antony's wife Fulvia, whose greed and corrupt dealings are criticized elsewhere (2.93; 3.10; 6.4), and possibly also to Antony's brother Lucius, who wielded great power

you dropped your quarrel with your colleague and, forgetting the auspices previously announced by yourself as augur of the Roman people,[49] you desired him on that day, for the first time, to *be* your colleague; and you sent your little son up to the Capitol as a hostage for peace.[50] What 32 day was happier for the senate, what day for the Roman people, who never attended any public assembly in greater numbers? Only then did we feel liberated by that brave company,[51] because peace was following in the wake of freedom, as they had wanted.

The next day and the next and the next and onwards, one day after another, you did not cease to bring the Republic a daily gift, so to speak; the greatest of all was your act of abolishing the title dictator. Thereby you   yes, *you*, I say—branded Caesar in his grave with everlasting infamy. For, just as because of a crime committed by one of its members, Marcus Manlius,[52] no patrician belonging to the Manlian clan is permitted to be called Marcus Manlius by decree of the clan, so because of the hatred felt for one particular dictator you totally abolished the name of dictator. After these magnificent contributions to the welfare of 33 the Republic, surely you felt no regret for your success, did you, no regret for your greatness, none for your fame, none for your glory? What, then, is the cause of this sudden and significant change in your course? I cannot bring myself to suspect that you yielded to a pecuniary temptation. People may say what they please; one does not have to believe them. I have never known anything mean, anything sordid in your character. True, men are sometimes corrupted by those close to them.[53] But I know what stout stuff you are

thanks to his appointment as chairman of the Agrarian Board of Seven, of which Antony was also a member (5.7; 6.12–15).

sed novi firmitatem tuam. Atque utinam ut culpam, sic etiam suspicionem vitare potuisses! [14] Illud magis vereor ne ignorans verum iter gloriae gloriosum putes plus te unum posse quam omnis et metui a civibus tuis quam diligi malis. Quod si ita putas, totam ignoras viam gloriae. Carum esse civem, bene de re publica mereri, laudari, coli, diligi gloriosum est; metui vero et in odio esse invidiosum,

34 detestabile, imbecillum, caducum. Quod videmus etiam in fabula illi ipsi qui "oderint, dum metuant" dixerit perniciosum fuisse. Utinam, M. Antoni, avum tuum meminisses! De quo tamen audisti multa ex me eaque saepissime. Putasne illum immortalitatem mereri voluisse, ut propter armorum habendorum licentiam metueretur? Illa erat vita, illa secunda fortuna, libertate esse parem ceteris, principem dignitate. Itaque, ut omittam res avi tui prosperas, acerbissimum eius supremum diem malim quam L. Cinnae dominatum, a quo ille crudelissime est interfectus.

35 Sed quid oratione te flectam? Si enim exitus C. Caesaris efficere non potest ut malis carus esse quam metui, nihil cuiusquam proficiet nec valebit oratio. Quem qui beatum fuisse putant, miseri ipsi sunt. Beatus est nemo qui ea lege vivit ut non modo impune sed etiam cum summa interfectoris gloria interfici possit.

Qua re flecte te, quaeso, et maiores tuos respice atque

---

54 Atreus, Greek king of Mycene and father of Agamemnon and Menelaus. The words quoted are from Accius' play *Atreus*.

55 M. Antonius (cos. 99), a famous orator, who is made one of the interlocutors in *De oratore*. He lost his life in the proscriptions of 87.

made of. It is a pity you could not avoid the suspicion, as you avoided the guilt. [14] What I am more afraid of is that in ignorance of the true path of glory, you think it glorious to have more power than the rest of us put together and prefer the fear of your countrymen to their esteem. If you think along those lines, you are utterly ignorant of the road to glory. It is glorious to be a citizen dear to the community, to deserve well of the Republic, to be praised and courted and esteemed. But to be feared and hated carries ill-will, execration, weakness, insecurity. Even in the play we see 34 that it was ruinous to the very character[54] who said "Let them hate me, so long as they fear me." Ah, Marcus Antonius, would that you remembered your grandfather![55] But you have heard me talk of him much and very often! Do you think *he* would have wished to earn immortality, if that involved being feared on account of a license to keep an armed following? No, the life and success he wanted meant parity in freedom, primacy in prestige. And so, to say nothing of your grandfather's time of prosperity, I would prefer that bitterest last day of his life to the autocracy of Lucius Cinna, who cruelly murdered him. But why 35 do I try to turn you from your course with words? If Gaius Caesar's end cannot cause you to prefer to be loved than to be feared, nobody's words will do any good or make any impression. Those who think Caesar was happy are themselves miserable. No man is happy who lives on such terms that he can be killed not only with impunity but even to the supreme glory of his killer.

Therefore, alter your course, I beg you, and look back

ita guberna rem publicam ut natum esse te cives tui gau-
deant: sine quo nec beatus nec clarus nec tutus[10] quisquam
36   esse omni‹no›[11] potest. [15] ‹At›[12] populi quidem Romani iudicia multa ambo habetis, quibus vos non satis moveri
permoleste fero. Quid enim gladiatoribus clamores innu-
merabilium civium? Quid populi versus? Quid Pompei
statuae plausus infiniti? Quid duobus[13] tribunis plebis qui
vobis adversantur? Parumne haec significant incredibili-
ter consentientem populi Romani universi voluntatem?
Quid? Apollinarium ludorum plausus vel testimonia potius
et iudicia populi Romani parum magna vobis videbantur?
O beatos illos qui, cum adesse ipsis propter vim armorum
non licebat, aderant tamen et in medullis populi Romani
ac visceribus haerebant! Nisi forte Accio tum plaudi et
sexagesimo post anno palmam dari, non Bruto putabatis;
qui ludis suis ita caruit ut in illo apparatissimo spectaculo
studium populus Romanus tribueret absenti, desiderium
37   liberatoris sui perpetuo plausu et clamore leniret. Equidem is sum qui istos plausus, cum popularibus civibus tri-
buerentur, semper contempserim; idemque cum a sum-

---

10 *coni. Muretus*: nec unctus V: *om. D*
11 *corr. Muretus*   12 *suppl. Deycks*
13 *forte* tribus: ii *Vc*: u *t*: hi *vn²*: his *n¹s*

---

56 Most likely the one restored to the Rostra by Caesar in 44,
shortly before his assassination (Cass. Dio 43.49.1). It would stand
in close proximity to the gladiatorial shows just mentioned.

57 There were, in fact, three, not two, hostile tribunes: Ti.
Cannutius, L. Cassius Longinus, brother of the tyrannicide, and
D. Carfulenus (3.23). Possibly *"ii"* of the codd. should be
emended to *"ii‹i›."*

58 As city praetor, M. Brutus was responsible for producing

on your ancestors, and so guide the Republic that your
fellow countrymen will be glad that you were born. Without that, it is completely impossible for anyone to be happy
or famous or safe. [15] But the Roman people have expressed their sentiments to both of you by many signs, and
I am very sorry that these have not had as much effect
upon you as they should. What of the shouts of countless
voices at the show of gladiators, what of the verses chanted
by the people, what of the endless applause for Pompeius'
statue[56] and for two tribunes of the plebs[57] who oppose you
and your colleague—is not all this enough to signify a truly
extraordinary consensus of the entire Roman people? And
then there was the applause at the Apollinarian games,[58] or
rather the people's testimony and expression of their feelings. Did you find that insufficient? Happy were they who
were kept away by force of arms but were present none the
less, deep down in the hearts of the Roman people. Or did
you think it was Accius who won the applause and the prize
sixty years later,[59] and not Brutus? Brutus could not be
present at his own games, but at that magnificent spectacle
the Roman people paid him in his absence the tribute of
their affection, assuaging their longing for their deliverer
with sustained clapping and shouting. For my part, I am
one who has always scorned such applause when bestowed
on demagogues; but when it comes from all ranks, from

these games, which began on 6 July. Since a hostile climate in
Rome made it unsafe for Brutus to preside in person, his duties
were entrusted to Antony's brother Gaius, also a praetor in 44. For
the popular demonstration in favor of Brutus, cf. 10.8.

[59] Sc. after the premiere performance of Accius' play *Tereus*
(*Att.* 16.5.1).

36

37

mis, mediis, infimis, cum denique ab universis hoc idem fit, cumque ei qui ante sequi populi consensum solebant fugiunt, non plausum illum, sed iudicium puto. Sin haec leviora vobis videntur, quae sunt gravissima, num etiam hoc contemnitis quod sensistis tam caram populo Romano vitam A. Hirti fuisse? Satis erat enim probatum illum esse populo Romano, ut est; iucundum amicis, in quo vincit omnis; carum suis, quibus est ille[14] carissimus: tantam tamen sollicitudinem bonorum, tantum timorem in quo meminimus? Certe in nullo. Quid igitur? Hoc vos, per deos immortalis! Quale sit non interpretamini? Quid? Eos de vestra vita cogitare non censetis quibus eorum quos sperant rei publicae consulturos vita tam cara sit?

Cepi fructum, patres conscripti, reversionis meae, quoniam et ea dixi ut, quicumque casus consecutus esset, exstaret constantiae meae testimonium, et sum a vobis benigne ac diligenter auditus. Quae potestas si mihi saepius sine meo vestroque periculo fiet, utar: si minus, quantum potero, non tam mihi me quam rei publicae reservabo. Mihi fere satis est quod vixi vel ad aetatem vel ad gloriam: huc si quid accesserit, non tam mihi quam vobis reique publicae accesserit.

38 (margin)

---

14 *SB*: ipse V: *om. D*

---

60 Hirtius had recently been seriously ill and was still in poor health.

61 A not so veiled threat holding out for Antony (and his colleague) the same fate that befell Caesar for his tyranny.

62 In *Marc.* 25, Cicero attributes almost the same words to Caesar.

the highest to the lowest, from everybody present in fact, and when those who previously made it a habit to follow the popular consensus take to their heels, in that case, I do not regard it as applause but as a verdict. However, if these demonstrations, which are highly impressive, seem rather trivial in your eyes, surely you cannot dismiss, can you, your perception of the deep concern felt by the Roman people for Aulus Hirtius' life?[60] It was enough to be well thought of by the Roman people, as he is, a delight to his friends—no man is more so—loved by his family, who love him very dearly, but the anxiety expressed by decent folk, the alarm—do we remember the like of it in any other such case? Assuredly not. Well then, by the immortal gods, do 38 you gentlemen not understand what it means? What do you say? Do you suppose that people who set so high a value on the lives of those whom they expect to act for the good of the Republic entertain no thoughts about *your* lives?[61]

Members of the Senate, I am well rewarded for my return inasmuch as whatever chance may now befall, my words will stand as a witness to my steadfast purpose; and you have given me a courteous and attentive hearing. If I have the opportunity to address you more frequently without danger to you and myself, I shall take advantage of it. If not, I shall, to the best of my ability, preserve my life, not so much for myself as for the Republic. For myself, I have lived pretty well long enough, whether in years or in glory.[62] If more is to come, it will come not so much for me as for you and for the Republic.

PHILIPPIC 2

INTRODUCTION

Antony reacted to Cicero's *First Philippic* of 2 September 44 by declaring himself henceforth Cicero's enemy, and he called a meeting of the senate for 19 September to deliver his response (5.19). Antony then retired to his villa at Tibur (formerly the property of Pompey's father-in-law, Metellus Scipio) to prepare his speech over the next several weeks (ibid.; *Fam.* 12.2.1). On the 19ᵗʰ, the senate convened in the Temple of Concord, which was ringed with soldiers (5.18), and Antony delivered a scathing invective attacking Cicero's whole career (*ORF*, pp. 472–475). That speech went without an answer in the senate because Cicero did not attend out of fear for his safety (5.20). On 9 October, Antony left for Brundisium to take command of several Caesarian legions that were being transferred from Macedonia to his proconsular province of Cisalpine Gaul (*Fam.* 12.23.2). Cicero had remained in or near Rome but left for Campania not long after Antony's departure. On 25 October, Cicero sent to Atticus a draft of the *Second Philippic*, a work written in the form of a speech as though actually delivered on 19 September in response to Antony's invective: "to be kept back and put out at your discretion. But when shall we see the day when you will think it proper to publish it?" (*Att.* 15.13.1, trans. SB). On 5 November, Cicero replied to certain amendments suggested by Atticus and expressed the hope that the day would come when the work might circulate freely. For the time being, however, he cautioned Atticus to share the draft with only a few trusted friends and friendly critics (*Att.* 16.11.1).

That is the last we hear of Cicero's plans to revise and perhaps publish some day the *Second Philippic*, but after Antony's departure for Cisalpine Gaul at the end of November, there was no longer any compelling reason for Cicero to keep the *Second Philippic* under wraps. On the other hand, Cicero did not irrevocably commit himself to an open struggle with Antony until a few weeks later when he delivered his *Third Philippic* in the senate and his *Fourth Philippic* to a public meeting, both on 20 December. It was then that Cicero finally burned his bridges and embarked upon an all-out contest with Antony (*Fam.* 10.28.2; 12.25.2). Hence, it was most likely in late December, if at all in his lifetime,[1] that the *Second Philippic* was allowed by its author to be reproduced in multiple copies and given wider circulation.

Although the work is a pamphlet in oratorical form, it strives throughout to maintain the fiction that it was an actual speech delivered in Antony's presence on 19 September. Cicero conveys this impression by means of such devices as frequent allusions to the physical setting, both the day itself (§§110, 112) and the threatening conditions surrounding the place of delivery, especially Antony's armed followers (§§8, 46, 112); by repeatedly addressing his fel-

---

[1] Some scholars believe that the *Second Philippic* never circulated outside Cicero's immediate circle of friends until after his death: e.g., T. Rice Holmes, *The Architect of the Roman Empire* (Oxford, 1928), 1.198–199; M. Gelzer, *RE* VII A 1047 and *Cicero. Ein biographischer Versuch* (Wiesbaden, 1969), 352 n. 51.

low senators (§§1, 5, 10, 25, etc.) and requesting a friendly hearing (§47); and by imagining that Antony has suddenly shown signs of dismay or anger or alarm, as for instance, when Cicero assigns to him a powerful motive for wishing to murder Caesar (§36), or alludes to his foppish attire (§76), or raises the controversial subject of Antony's conduct at the Lupercalia (§84). Cicero is also very careful not to refer to a single event that occurred after the fictional date of the speech (19 Sept.), although he did not finish writing it until late October.

In his *Tenth Satire*, Juvenal singles out the *Second Philippic* as Cicero's masterpiece *(dīvina Philippica*, vs. 125), and it is easy to see why. Juvenal wanted to make the point that eloquence had cost Cicero his life, and certainly the *Philippics* provided Antony with a powerful motive for ordering Cicero's death at the time of the proscriptions in November 43 (Plut. *Cic.* 48.6). In fact, it became a stock exercise in the rhetorical schools under Augustus to debate the question whether Cicero should try to win a pardon from Antony by agreeing to burn his writings (Sen. *Suas.* 7; Quint. *Inst.* 3.8.46).[2] Hence the *Second Philippic*, which is not only by far the longest of the series but also the most sustained and bitter in attacking Antony personally, was clearly the one best suited to Juvenal's purposes.

The attractiveness of the speech for the modern reader, on the other hand, is its sweep of subject matter. No other extant speech of Cicero reviews the orator's career in such minute detail, from the year of his consulship in 63 to the autumn of 44, and no other speech provides such a rich narrative of political events in and outside Rome during the period of the Civil War (49–44) and slightly before.

---

[2] A *suasoria* originating with Asinius Pollio, Sen. *Suas.* 6.14.

In this regard, when compared with the speeches of the great, fourth-century Athenian orator Demosthenes, whose *Philippics* inspired Cicero to give his collection the same name, Cicero's *Second Philippic* bears a greater resemblance to Demosthenes' autobiographical *Speech on the Crown* (*De Corona*) than it does to Demosthenes' *Philippics* proper.

INTRODUCTION TO PHILIPPIC 2

STRUCTURE

Exordium

(1–2) Cicero's fate to wage war with the enemies of the state

Refutatio

(3–10a) Accusations concerning violated friendship
Partitio (10b): Cicero will defend himself and attack Antony
(11–36a) Accusations concerning Cicero's public career
(36b–42a) Minor accusations
Transitio (42b–43): Antony's lack of skill as an orator

Confirmatio

(44–50a) Attack on Antony's early years
(50b–78a) Attack on Antony's public career during the Civil War
(78b–111) Attack on Antony's consulship
(112–114) Warning concerning the path of true glory

Peroratio

(115–119) Appeal to Antony to be guided by Caesar's fate and to renounce tyranny

M. TULLI CICERONIS
IN M. ANTONIUM
ORATIO PHILIPPICA SECUNDA

1   [1] Quonam meo fato, patres conscripti, fieri dicam ut
nemo his annis viginti rei publicae fuerit hostis qui non
bellum eodem tempore mihi quoque indixerit? Nec vero
necesse est quemquam a me nominari: vobiscum ipsi recordamini. Mihi poenarum illi plus quam optarem dederunt: te miror, Antoni, quorum facta imitere, eorum exitus non perhorrescere. Atque hoc in aliis minus mirabar.
Nemo enim illorum inimicus mihi fuit voluntarius, omnes
a me rei publicae causa lacessiti. Tu ne verbo quidem viola-
tus, ut audacior quam Catilina, furiosior quam Clodius
viderere, ultro me maledictis lacessisti, tuamque a me alie-
nationem commendationem tibi ad impios civis fore pu-
2   tavisti. Quid ‹enim›[1] putem? Contemptumne me? Non
video nec in vita nec in gratia nec in rebus gestis nec in hac
mea mediocritate ingeni quid despicere possit Antonius.
An in senatu facillime de me detrahi posse credidit? Qui
ordo clarissimis civibus bene gestae rei publicae testi-

[1] *suppl. SB*

MARCUS TULLIUS CICERO'S
SECOND PHILIPPIC ORATION
AGAINST MARCUS ANTONIUS

[1] To what destiny of mine, Members of the Senate, should I ascribe the fact that in these twenty years there was never an enemy of the Republic who did not at the same time declare war on me too? There is no need for me to mention any names. Consult your own memories. Those persons have paid me penalties greater than I should have desired. It surprises me, Antonius, that you do not dread the fate of those whose actions you imitate. In other cases I was less surprised by this phenomenon, for none of those people became my enemy by choice; they were all challenged by me for the sake of the Republic. Whereas you, against whom I did not even say a word, have assailed me with unprovoked abuse, as though you wished to look more reckless than Catiline and madder than Clodius, reckoning that your alienation from me would recommend you to disloyal citizens. What else am I to think? That I am held in contempt? I really fail to see anything in my life, my connections, my public record, or such modest talent as I possess, for Antonius to despise. Perhaps he thought that the senate was the place where I could most easily be disparaged? Well, this body has given many famous Romans its testimonials of good service to the Republic rendered in

monium multis, mihi uni conservatae dedit. An decertare mecum voluit contentione dicendi? Hoc quidem est beneficium. Quid enim plenius, quid uberius mihi quam et pro me et contra Antonium dicere? Illud profecto est: non existimavit sui similibus probari posse se esse hostem patriae, nisi mihi esset inimicus.

3   Cui prius quam de ceteris rebus respondeo, de amicitia quam a me violatam esse criminatus est, quod ego gravissimum crimen iudico, pauca dicam. [2] Contra rem suam me nescio quando venisse questus est. An ego non venirem contra alienum pro familiari et necessario, non venirem contra gratiam non virtutis spe, sed aetatis flore collectam, non venirem contra iniuriam quam iste intercessoris iniquissimi beneficio obtinuit, non iure praetorio? Sed hoc idcirco commemoratum a te puto ut te infimo ordini commendares, ⟨cum omnes te⟩[2] recordarentur libertini generum et liberos tuos nepotes Q. Fadi, libertini hominis, fuisse.

At enim te in disciplinam meam tradideras—nam ita dixisti—domum meam ventitaras. Ne tu, si id fecisses, melius famae, melius pudicitiae tuae consuluisses. Sed neque fecisti nec, si cuperes, tibi id per C. Curionem facere licuisset.

[2] *om. V¹, D*: cum omnes V²: cum te omnes *ed. Aldina, corr. Halm*

---

[1] The friend's name was Sicca (*Att.* 16.11.1), but nothing is known of the case.

[2] The lowest tier of citizens comprised freedmen. The wording here and at 13.23 indicates that Antony was not actually married to Fadia, though he acknowledged paternity of her children.

positions of responsibility: only to me has it given one for saving it. Can it be that he wished to meet me in an oratorical duel? That is kind of him. Could I find any richer or more rewarding theme than in defending myself and attacking Antonius? No, it must be as I said: he did not think people like himself would accept him as an enemy of his native land unless he was an enemy of mine.

Before I reply to him concerning other matters, I shall say a few words about the friendship he charges me with violating, a charge that I take extremely seriously. [2] He has complained that at some time or other I appeared against his interests in a civil case. Can it be that I was not to appear against a stranger on behalf of a friend and connection,[1] in opposition to influence gathered not by the promise of manly excellence but by youthful good looks; was I not to appear in opposition to an unfair advantage which that opponent had gained thanks to a grossly biased veto, not by due process of law in the praetor's court. But I imagine you brought up this incident to recommend yourself to the lowest tier of citizens, since they will all bear in mind that you were a freedman's son-in-law and that your children were the grandchildren of a freedman, Quintus Fadius.[2]

Moreover, you say that you had put yourself under my direction—for so you claimed—had been a frequent visitor in my house. If indeed you had done so, you would have better looked after your reputation and your morals. But you did not; and even if you had so wished, Gaius Curio would not have let you.[3]

---

[3] Supposedly because he was a possessive lover (§§44–45).

4   Auguratus petitionem mihi te concessisse dixisti. O incredibilem audaciam, o impudentiam praedicandam! Quo
enim tempore me augurem a toto collegio expetitum Cn.
Pompeius et Q. Hortensius nominaverunt—nec enim licebat a pluribus nominari—tu nec solvendo eras nec te ullo
modo nisi eversa re publica fore incolumem putabas. Pote-
ras autem eo tempore auguratum petere cum in Italia Curio non esset, aut tum cum es factus unam tribum sine
Curione ferre potuisses? Cuius etiam familiares de vi
condemnati sunt quod tui nimis studiosi fuissent.

5   [3] At beneficio sum tuo usus. Quo? Quamquam illud
ipsum quod commemoras semper prae me tuli: malui me
tibi debere confiteri quam cuiquam minus prudenti non
satis gratus videri. Sed quo beneficio? Quod me Brundisi
non occideris? Quem ipse victor, qui tibi, ut tute gloriari
solebas, detulerat ex latronibus suis principatum, salvum
esse voluisset, in Italiam ire iussisset, eum tu occideres?
Fac potuisse. Quod est aliud, patres conscripti, beneficium
latronum nisi ut commemorare possint eis se dedisse vitam quibus non ademerint? Quod si esset beneficium,
numquam ei qui illum interfecerunt a quo erant conserva-
ti, quos tu ipse clarissimos viros soles appellare, tantam essent gloriam consecuti. Quale autem beneficium est quod

---

4 Cicero was elected in the summer of 53, or possibly in the
spring of 52, while Antony was elected in 50, through Caesar's
influence.   5 In the autumn of 48, Cicero was allowed to return to Italy but to go no farther than Brundisium until Caesar
returned in Sept. 47 and granted him a full pardon. Antony governed Italy in Caesar's absence as his Master of the Horse, and
Cicero's letters confirm that Antony treated him according to
Caesar's instructions.   6 Many of the conspirators, includ-

You have asserted that you left me a free field as candi- 4
date for the augurate.[4] Scandalous impudence! How dare
you make such a preposterous assertion? And at the time
when Gnaeus Pompeius and Quintus Hortensius put my
name forward at the instance of the entire College—no
more than two nominators being permitted—you were a
bankrupt who saw your only salvation in the overthrow of
the Republic. Besides, could you stand for the augurate at
that time seeing that Curio was out of Italy, or on that occasion when you were elected, would you have been able to
carry a single tribe without Curio? Friends of his were actually convicted of violence because of their excessive zeal
on your behalf.

[3] You say I availed myself of a kindness from you. 5
What kindness? To be sure, what you are talking about
is indeed something I have always been the first to acknowledge. I have preferred to confess myself in your debt
rather than let some foolish person think me wanting in
gratitude. But what was the kindness? That you did not kill
me at Brundisium? Could you have killed one whom the
conqueror himself, who, as you used to boast, had made
you chief of his robber band, had wished to spare and ordered to return to Italy?[5] Suppose you could have done.
That is the sort of kindness one gets from bandits, Members of the Senate: they can say they granted their lives to
those whose lives they did not take. If that were a kindness,
those who killed the man who had spared them, whom you
yourself often call "illustrious gentlemen," would never
have won so much glory.[6] But where is the kindness in ab-

ing the leaders M. Brutus and C. Cassius, had received pardon
from Caesar when they switched sides in the Civil War.

te abstinueris nefario scelere? Qua in re non tam iucundum mihi videri debuit non interfectum ‹me›[3] a te quam miserum te id impune facere potuisse.

6   Sed sit beneficium, quando quidem maius accipi a latrone nullum potuit: in quo potes me dicere ingratum? An de interitu rei publicae queri non debui, ne in te ingratus viderer? At in illa querela misera quidem et luctuosa, sed mihi pro hoc gradu in quo me senatus populusque Romanus collocavit necessaria, quid est dictum a me cum contumelia, quid non moderate, quid non amice? Quod quidem cuius temperantiae fuit, de M. Antonio querentem abstinere maledicto, praesertim cum tu reliquias rei publicae dissipavisses, cum domi tuae turpissimo mercatu omnia essent venalia, cum leges eas quae numquam promulgatae essent et de te et a te latas confiterere, cum auspicia augur, intercessionem consul sustulisses, cum esses foedissime stipatus armatis, cum omnis impuritates pudica in domo

7 cotidie susciperes vino lustrisque confectus. At ego, tamquam mihi cum M. Crasso contentio esset, quocum multae et magnae fuerunt, non cum uno gladiatore nequissimo, de re publica graviter querens de homine nihil dixi. Itaque hodie perficiam ut intellegat quantum a me beneficium tum acceperit.

---

3 *suppl. Madvig*

---

7 It was illegal to sponsor a law conferring any office or function on the proposer or his family or colleagues (*Leg. agr.* 2.21), and the *Lex Caecilia Didia* of 98 required a bill to be posted publicly for at least three successive market days (falling every eight days).

8 The house that had formerly been Pompey's; cf. §69.

staining from an atrocious crime? In this affair, I could not help but feel not so much pleased at not having been killed by you as unhappy that you could have done this with impunity.

But grant it was a kindness, since none greater could be 6 accepted from a bandit: where can you say I have been ungrateful? Should I have refrained from protesting at the destruction of the Republic for fear of seeming ungrateful to you? And yet, in making that protest, a melancholy, mournful business but a necessary one in view of the rank conferred upon me by the senate and people of Rome, did I say an offensive word, did I speak immoderately, did I speak in an unfriendly fashion? That speech required a good deal of self-restraint—to complain of Marcus Antonius while refraining from personal attack! And that too after you had scattered the last remnants of the Republic to the winds, when everything was up for sale at your house in a shameful market, when you were acknowledging that you were both the beneficiary and author of legislation that was adopted without ever having been promulgated,[7] when as augur you had abolished the auspices and as consul the right of veto, when you were surrounded by your abominable armed bodyguard, when you were daily indulging in every kind of vice in a virtuous house,[8] exhausted by drink and debauchery? And yet, just as though 7 I were in a controversy with Marcus Crassus, with whom I had many notable affrays, and not with the most worthless gladiator, I complained in grave terms on public grounds but said nothing about the man. Very well, today I shall make him realize just how considerable a kindness he had from *me* on that occasion.

[4] At etiam litteras, quas me sibi misisse diceret, recitavit homo et humanitatis expers et vitae communis ignarus. Quis enim umquam, qui paulum modo bonorum
consuetudinem nosset, litteras ad se ab amico missas of-
fensione aliqua interposita in medium protulit palamque
recitavit? Quid est aliud tollere ex vita vitae societatem,
tollere amicorum colloquia absentium? Quam multa ioca
solent esse in epistulis quae, prolata si sint, inepta videantur, quam multa seria neque tamen ullo modo divulganda!
8 Sit hoc inhumanitatis: stultitiam incredibilem videte. Quid
habes quod mihi opponas, homo diserte, ut Mustelae tamen Seio et Tironi Numisio videris—qui cum hoc ipso
tempore stent cum gladiis in conspectu senatus, ego quoque te disertum putabo, si ostenderis quo modo sis eos
inter sicarios defensurus—sed quid opponas tandem, si
negem me umquam ad te istas litteras misisse? Quo me
teste convincas? An chirographo, in quo habes scientiam
quaestuosam? Qui possis? Sunt enim librari manu. Iam in-
video magistro tuo, qui te tanta mercede quantam iam pro-
9 feram nihil sapere doceat. Quid enim est minus non dico
oratoris, sed hominis quam id obicere adversario quod ille
si verbo negarit longius progredi non possit qui obiecerit?
At ego non nego, teque in isto ipso convinco non inhumanitatis solum sed etiam amentiae. Quod enim verbum in

---

9 In reply to Antony's request for Cicero's permission to recall
Sex. Cloelius from exile (cf. 1.3). Both Antony's letter and Cicero's
are extant (*Att.* 14.13A, 14.13B, respectively). Cicero's is fulsome.

10 Allusion to the forging of laws and decrees that Antony
claimed to have discovered among Caesar's papers.

11 The Sicilian rhetorician Sex. Clodius.

[4] Then there is the letter he said I wrote him.[9] In his hopeless ignorance of civilized conduct and the usages of society, he read it aloud. Has anyone possessing the least acquaintance with the behavior of gentlemen ever produced a letter written to him by a friend with whom he had subsequently had a difference and read it aloud in public? That amounts to robbing life of its social foundations, abolishing conversation between absent friends. How many jests find their way into letters which would seem silly if produced in public, along with much that is serious but on no account to be divulged! So much for uncivilized behavior. But look at the crass stupidity. What would you have to say to me in reply, clever orator that you are, or at least appear to be in the eyes of Muṣṭela Sẹius and Tiro Numisius—why, there they are, standing sword in hand in full view of the senate! I too shall call you a clever speaker if you will show me how you intend to defend them in the court that punishes murder and the carrying of a weapon—but I ask you, what would you have to say in reply, if I were to deny ever having sent you that letter? Where is your witness to contradict me? Would you prove it by the handwriting? You have a lucrative knowledge of that subject,[10] but how could you when the letter is in the hand of a secretary? I really envy that coach of yours,[11] seeing that he teaches you to be without any sense in exchange for an enormous fee, which I shall shortly be revealing. To charge an opponent with something that cannot be followed up by the bringer of the charge, if his opponent simply denies it—that is not the act of a rational human being, to say nothing of an orator. But I am not denying it. On this very point I prove you not only lacking in decency but an imbecile. There is not a word in that letter that does not

8

9

63

istis litteris est non plenum humanitatis, offici, benevo-
lentiae? Omne autem crimen tuum est quod de te in his
litteris non male existimem, quod scribam tamquam ad civem, tamquam ad bonum virum, non tamquam ad sceleratum et latronem. At ego tuas litteras, etsi iure poteram a te
lacessitus, tamen non proferam: quibus petis ut tibi per me
liceat quendam de exsilio reducere, adiurasque id te invito
me non esse facturum; idque a me impetras⟨ti⟩.[4] Quid
enim me interponerem audaciae tuae, quam neque auctoritas huius ordinis neque existimatio populi Romani neque
10   leges ullae possent coercere? Verum tamen quid erat quod
me rogares, si erat is de quo rogabas Caesaris lege reduc-
tus? Sed videlicet meam gratiam voluit esse, in quo ne
ipsius quidem ulla esse poterat lege lata.

[5] Sed cum mihi, patres conscripti, et pro me aliquid et
in M. Antonium multa dicenda sint, alterum peto a vobis
ut me pro me dicentem benigne, alterum ipse efficiam ut,
contra illum cum dicam, attente audiatis. Simul illud oro:
si meam cum in omni vita tum in dicendo moderationem
modestiamque cognostis, ne me hodie, cum isti, ut provo-
cavit, respondero, oblitum esse putetis mei. Non tractabo
ut consulem: ne ille quidem me ut consularem. Etsi ille
nullo modo consul, vel quod ita vivit vel quod ita rem publicam gerit vel quod ita factus est, ego sine ulla controver-
sia consularis.

11   Ut igitur intellegeretis qualem ipse se consulem pro-
fiteretur, obiecit mihi consulatum meum. Qui consulatus

⁴ corr. Bake

breathe courtesy, regard for duty, goodwill. All you can say against it is that in this letter I don't think badly of you, I write as though I were writing to a fellow citizen and a gentleman, not to a criminal and a bandit. On my side, however, I shall not produce *your* letter, though after such provocation from you I could quite rightly do so. In it you ask my permission to bring a certain person back from exile and swear that you will not do so against my will. You gained from me your request. Why should I stand in the way of your audacity, which neither the authority of this body nor the opinion of the Roman people nor any laws could check? And yet, why ask me, if the man concerned had been brought back from exile by a law of Caesar's? But I suppose Antonius wanted it to come as a favor from me, whereas it could not even count as a favor from himself given the passage of the law! 10

[5] Members of the Senate, I have something to say on my own behalf and a good deal to say against Marcus Antonius. As to the former, I crave your indulgence when I speak in my defense; as for the latter, I shall myself make sure of your riveted attention when I denounce *him*. And I have another request: if you are acquainted with my moderation and modesty as a man and as a speaker, do not suppose that I am forgetting myself today when I give this man the answer he has provoked. I shall not treat him as a consul any more than he has treated me as a consular—though he, after all, is nothing of a consul, neither in his mode of life nor in his official conduct nor in the manner of his election; whereas I without any question am a consular.

Well then, in order to let you see what kind of consul he professes himself to be, he reproached me with *my* consulship. Members of the Senate, that consulship was 11

verbo meus, patres conscripti, re vester fuit. Quid enim
ego constitui, quid gessi, quid egi nisi ex huius ordinis
consilio, auctoritate, sententia? Haec tu homo sapiens,
non solum eloquens, apud eos quorum consilio sapien-
tiaque gesta sunt ausus es vituperare? Quis autem meum
consulatum praeter te et P. Clodium qui vituperaret inventus est? Cuius quidem tibi fatum, sicuti C. Curioni, manet,
quoniam id domi tuae est quod fuit illorum utrique fatale.

12   Non placet M. Antonio consulatus meus. At placuit
P. Servilio, ut eum primum nominem ex illius temporis
consularibus qui proxime est mortuus; placuit Q. Catulo,
cuius semper in hac re publica vivet auctoritas; placuit
duobus Lucullis, M. Crasso, Q. Hortensio, C. Curioni, C.
Pisoni, M'. Glabrioni, M'. Lepido, L. Vulcatio, C. Figulo,
⟨placuit⟩[5] D. Silano, L. Murenae, qui tum erant consules
designati; placuit idem quod consularibus M. Catoni, qui
cum multa vita excedens providit, tum quod te consulem
non vidit. Maxime vero consulatum meum Cn. Pompeius
probavit qui, ut me primum decedens ex Syria vidit, complexus et gratulans meo beneficio patriam se visurum esse
dixit. Sed quid singulos commemoro? Frequentissimo senatui sic placuit ut esset nemo qui mihi non ut parenti gratias ageret, qui mihi non vitam suam, fortunas, liberos, rem
publicam referret acceptam.

[5] *suppl. SB*

---

[12] Clodius and Curio, the two previous husbands of Antony's
wife Fulvia, had both died violent deaths.
[13] This list of deceased consulars (the living are named below,
§13) is in official order of seniority, except that on that basis Curio
(the elder) should come before the Luculli.

mine only in name; in reality it was yours. Every decision, every official act, everything I did was done by the advice and authority and vote of this body. And now you, as a man of sense and not merely of eloquence, have dared to abuse these measures in front of those whose advice and wisdom determined them! Who was ever heard abusing my consulship except yourself and Publius Clodius, whose fate awaits you, as it awaited Gaius Curio, since you have that in your house which proved fatal to them both?[12]

Marcus Antonius disapproves of my consulship. 12
But Publius Servilius approved of it—to single out first among the consulars of that time the name of him who is the latest to have died. So did Quintus Catulus, a name that will ever live respected in this Republic. So likewise the two Luculli, Marcus Crassus, Quintus Hortensius, Gaius Curio, Gaius Piso, Manius Glabrio, Manius Lepidus, Lucius Vulcatius, Gaius Figulus.[13] So too the two consuls-elect at that time, Decimus Silanus and Lucius Murena. The consulars' approval was shared by Marcus Cato, who in taking leave of life displayed foresight in sparing himself many sorry sights but none sorrier than you as consul. Above all, my consulship was approved by Gnaeus Pompeius, who at our first meeting on his return from Syria embraced me and congratulated me, saying that he owed it to me that he would see his native land again. But why mention individuals? A very full meeting of the senate approved so heartily that every member present thanked me as a son might thank a father, acknowledging himself indebted to me for life, goods, children, and the Republic.

13   [6] Sed quoniam illis quos nominavi tot et talibus viris
res publica orbata est, veniamus ad vivos, qui duo de con-
sularium numero reliqui sunt. L. Cotta, vir summo ingenio
summaque prudentia, rebus eis gestis quas tu reprehendis
supplicationem decrevit verbis amplissimis, eique illi ipsi
quos modo nominavi consulares senatusque cunctus adsensus est; qui honos post conditam hanc urbem habitus
14   est togato ante me nemini. L. Caesar, avunculus tuus, qua
oratione, qua constantia, qua gravitate sententiam dixit in
sororis suae virum, vitricum tuum! Hunc tu cum auctorem
et praeceptorem omnium consiliorum totiusque vitae de-
buisses habere, vitrici te similem quam avunculi maluisti.
Huius ego alienus consiliis consul usus sum: tu, sororis
filius, ecquid ad eum umquam de re publica rettulisti? At
ad quos refert, di immortales? Ad eos scilicet quorum no-
15   bis etiam dies natales audiendi sunt. "Hodie non descendit
Antonius." "Cur?" "Dat nataliciam in hortis." "Cui?" Neminem nominabo: putate tum Phormioni alicui, tum Gna-
thoni, tum etiam Ballioni. O foeditatem hominis flagitiosam, o impudentiam, nequitiam, libidinem non ferendam!
Tu cum principem senatorem, civem singularem tam pro-
pinquum habeas, ad eum de re publica nihil referas, referas ad eos qui suam rem nullam habent, tuam exhauriunt?

Tuus videlicet salutaris consulatus, perniciosus meus.

---

14 The Catilinarian conspirator P. Cornelius Lentulus Sura.

15 *Horti*, usually but misleadingly rendered "gardens," means
a house and grounds near a city, outside the city boundary.

16 Characters from the comic plays of Plautus and Terence.
The first two are parasites, the third a pimp.

[6] But inasmuch as the Republic is now bereft of all   13
the distinguished personages whom I have named, let me
come to the two living consulars out of that roll who are
still with us. There is the extremely wise and gifted Lucius
Cotta. *He* proposed a Thanksgiving in the most flattering
terms for the actions which you reprobate, and the entire
senate, including these same consulars whose names I
have just rehearsed, agreed to the motion. Never before,
since the foundation of Rome, had that honor been
granted to a civilian. There is also Lucius Caesar, your un-   14
cle, who made a most eloquent, resolute, and impressive
speech against his own brother-in-law, your stepfather.[14]
You should have made him your guide and mentor in all
decisions, in your whole life; but you preferred to resem-
ble your stepfather rather than your uncle. As consul I
availed myself of his counsels, though I had no family connection with him: you are his sister's son, but have you ever
once consulted him on public affairs? But good heavens,
whom *does* Antonius consult? Those fellows, I suppose,
whose very birthdays have to be brought to our notice.
"Antonius is not appearing in public today." "Oh, why   15
is that?" "He is giving a birthday party on his suburban
estate."[15] "For whom?" Well, gentlemen, I won't name
names. One day it will be for some Phormio, let us suppose, another for Gnatho, and another for Ballio even.[16]
Foul! Infamous! Oh the intolerable shamelessness, worthlessness, licentiousness! Even though you have a leading
senator, an outstanding member of the community as such
a close relative, are you never to consult him about public
affairs, but rather are you to consult those who have nothing of their own and drain what is yours?

So clearly your consulship is salutary, mine ruinous!

[7] Adeone pudorem cum pudicitia perdidisti ut hoc in eo templo dicere ausus sis in quo ego senatum illum qui quondam florens orbi terrarum praesidebat consulebam,

16 tu homines perditissimos cum gladiis collocavisti? At etiam ausus es—quid autem est quod tu non audeas?— clivum Capitolinum dicere me consule plenum servorum armatorum fuisse, ut illa, credo, nefaria senatus consulta fierent, vim adferebam senatui! O miser, sive illa tibi nota non sunt—nihil enim boni nosti—sive sunt, qui apud talis viros tam impudenter loquare! Quis enim eques Romanus, quis praeter te adulescens nobilis, quis ullius ordinis qui se civem esse meminisset, cum senatus in hoc templo esset, in clivo Capitolino non fuit, quis nomen non dedit? Quam-quam nec scribae sufficere nec tabulae nomina illorum ca-

17 pere potuerunt. Etenim cum homines nefarii de patriae parricidio confiterentur, consciorum indiciis, sua manu, voce paene litterarum coacti se urbem inflammare, civis trucidare, vastare Italiam, delere rem publicam consen-sisse, quis esset qui ad salutem communem defendendam non excitaretur, praesertim cum senatus populusque Ro-manus haberet ducem, qualis si qui nunc esset, tibi idem quod illis accidit contigisset?

Ad sepulturam corpus vitrici sui negat a me datum. Hoc vero ne P. quidem Clodius dixit umquam: quem, quia iure ei inimicus fui, doleo a te omnibus vitiis iam esse

18 superatum. Qui autem tibi venit in mentem redigere in memoriam nostram te domi P. Lentuli esse educatum? An

---

17 The Clivus Capitolinus, part of the Via Sacra, was a street leading from the Forum up to the Capitol, passing the Temple of Concord.

[7] Your tongue must have become as loose as your life, if you dare to say such a thing in the very temple where I used to consult the senate in its greatest days, when it ruled the world, and where you have posted desperados carrying weapons. You have even dared to say—but what don't you dare?—that when I was consul, Capitol Rise[17] was full of armed slaves. I forced the senate to pass those nefarious decrees under threat of violence, is that it? Miserable wretch, whether you don't know what happened—wholesome knowledge does not come your way—or whether you do! Such shameless talk before such an audience! When the senate met in this temple, not one Roman knight, not one young nobleman except you, nobody of any class who remembered he was a Roman, but stood on Capitol Rise and volunteered his services. There were not clerks enough or tablets enough to take the names. For when wicked men were confessing to treason against their native land, when compelled by the evidence of their accomplices, by their own handwriting, and by documents which almost cried aloud, they admitted their plot to set Rome on fire, slaughter her citizens, lay Italy waste, and destroy the Republic, who was there who was not stirred to defend the common well-being, especially since the senate and people of Rome had a true leader, and if any of that sort were a leader now, what happened to the plotters would have happened to you.

He says I refused to give up his stepfather's body for burial. Even Publius Clodius never said that, Clodius, who to my regret (for I had good reason to be his enemy) has now been outdone by you in all his vices. How, I wonder, did it occur to you to remind us that you were brought up in Publius Lentulus' house? Were you perhaps afraid that

16

17

18

verebare ne non putaremus natura te potuisse tam improbum evadere, nisi accessisset etiam disciplina? [8] Tam
autem eras excors ut tota in oratione tua tecum ipse pug-
nares, non modo non cohaerentia inter se diceres sed
maxime diiuncta atque contraria, ut non tanta mecum
quanta tibi tecum esset contentio. Vitricum tuum fuisse in
tanto scelere fatebare, poena adfectum querebare. Ita
quod proprie meum est laudasti; quod totum est senatus
reprehendisti. Nam comprehensio sontium mea, animadversio senatus fuit. Homo disertus non intellegit eum
quem contra dicit laudari a se, eos apud quos dicit vituperari.

19   Iam illud cuius est, non dico audaciae—cupit enim se
audacem—sed, quod minime vult, stultitiae, qua vincit
omnis, clivi Capitolini mentionem facere, cum inter subsellia nostra versentur armati, cum in hac cella Concordiae, di immortales, in qua me consule salutares sententiae dictae sunt, quibus ad hanc diem viximus, cum
gladiis homines collocati stent! Accusa senatum; accusa
equestrem ordinem, qui tum cum senatu copulatus fuit;
accusa omnis ordines, omnis civis, dum confiteare hunc
ordinem hoc ipso tempore ab Ituraeis circumsederi. Haec
tu non propter audaciam dicis tam impudenter, sed quia
tantam rerum repugnantiam non vide[a]s.[6] Nihil profecto
sapis. Quid est enim dementius quam, cum rei publicae
perniciosa arma ipse ceperis, obicere alteri salutaria?

---

[6] *corr. Ernesti*

---

[18] Bedouin Arabs from the Beqa' Valley in modern Leba-
non. Noted for their skill as archers, they were recruited by the
Romans for service in the army.

we might fail to believe that you could have turned out such a rogue by mere nature without the assistance of training? [8] But in your witlessness you were fighting against yourself all through your speech. Not only did what you said lack coherence, but it was also downright out of joint and self-contradictory so that you were more in conflict with yourself than with me. You admitted that your stepfather had been involved in that monstrous crime, but you complained of his punishment, thus praising what is properly mine and blaming what is entirely the senate's. For the arrest of the guilty men was my doing, their punishment was the senate's. Indeed a clever pleader! He does not understand that he is praising the man against whom he is speaking, while he is abusing his audience.

Now what sort of, I do not call it audacity—since he likes to be thought audacious—but rather what sort of unrivaled stupidity (which is the last thing he wants to hear) is it to make mention of Capitol Rise, when armed men are moving among our benches and stand posted sword in hand in this very sanctuary of Concord (o immortal gods) where salutary measures were proposed when I was consul, measures by which we have lived down to this day! Accuse the senate by all means, accuse the order of knights, which on that occasion was united with the senate, accuse all classes, all citizens—so long as you confess that this body is surrounded by Ituraeans[18] at this very moment! It is not audacity that makes you say these shameless things, but your failure to perceive glaring inconsistencies. Obviously you are a fool, for nothing could be more senseless than to reproach another man for using armed force in the public interest when you have resorted to it yourself to the public injury.

19

20   At etiam quodam loco facetus esse voluisti. Quam id te, di boni, non decebat! In quo est tua culpa non nulla; aliquid enim salis a mima uxore trahere potuisti. "Cedant arma togae." Quid? Tum nonne cesserunt? At postea tuis armis cessit toga. Quaeramus igitur utrum melius fuerit libertati populi Romani sceleratorum arma an libertatem nostram armis tuis cedere, nec vero tibi de versibus plura respondebo: tantum dicam breviter, te neque illos neque ullas omnino litteras nosse; me nec rei publicae nec amicis umquam defuisse, et tamen omni genere monumentorum meorum perfecisse operis subsicivis ut meae vigiliae meaeque litterae et iuventuti utilitatis et nomini Romano laudis aliquid adferrent. Sed haec non huius temporis: maiora videamus.

21   [9] P. Clodium meo consilio interfectum esse dixisti. Quidnam homines putarent, si tum occisus esset cum tu illum in foro inspectante populo Romano gladio insecutus es negotiumque transegisses, nisi se ille in scalas tabernae librariae coniecisset eisque oppilatis impetum tuum compressisset? Quod quidem ego favisse me tibi fateor, suasisse ne tu quidem dicis. At Miloni ne favere quidem potui; prius enim rem transegit quam quisquam eum facturum id suspicaretur. At ego suasi. Scilicet is animus erat Milonis ut

---

19 Antony's mistress, the freedwoman Volumnia Cytheris.

20 Part of a line from Cicero's poem on his consulship.

21 Probably in the autumn of 53, when Antony was a candidate for the quaestorship (§49) and Clodius for the praetorship.

At one point you even wanted to be witty. Good gods, 20
how you fell flat on your face! That is partly your own
fault—you could have picked up a little humor from your
mime-actress spouse.[19] "Let arms yield to civilian garb."[20]
Well, and didn't they at that time? Later on, it is true, the
civilian garb yielded to *your* arms. So let us ask a question,
which was better: that the arms of criminals yield to the
freedom of the Roman people or that our freedom yield to
your arms? But I will not make you any further answer
about the verses. I shall merely remark briefly that you
know nothing about them or about any kind of literature. I,
on the other hand, while never failing in my obligations to
the Republic and to my friends, have employed my spare
hours in producing works in a variety of genres that will
preserve my name, in order that what I have written in the
watches of the night may be of some profit to our young
people and bring some credit to the Roman name. But this
is not a time to speak of such things; let us move to greater
matters.

[9] You say that I instigated the killing of Publius 21
Clodius. Now what in the world would people be thinking
if he had lost his life on the memorable occasion[21] when
you chased him with a sword in the Forum before the eyes
of the Roman people and would have finished the job, if he
had not flung himself under the stairs of a bookshop and
barricaded them, thus stopping your assault? I admit that
my sympathies were on your side on that occasion, but
even you don't say that I put you up to it. On the other
hand, I could not even lend Milo encouragement, since he
finished the business before anybody suspected that he
was going to set about it. But, it will be objected, I put him
up to it. No doubt Milo lacked spirit to do the Republic a

CICERO

prodesse rei publicae sine suasore non posset. At laetatus sum. Quid ergo? In tanta laetitia cunctae civitatis me
22   unum tristem esse oportebat? Quamquam de morte Clodi
fuit quaestio, non satis prudenter illa quidem constituta—
quid enim attinebat nova lege quaeri de eo qui hominem
occidisset, cum esset legibus quaestio constituta?—quae-
situm est tamen. Quod igitur, cum res agebatur, nemo in
me dixit, id tot annis post tu es inventus qui diceres.

23   Quod vero dicere ausus es idque multis verbis, opera
mea Pompeium a Caesaris amicitia esse diiunctum ob
eamque causam culpa mea bellum civile esse natum, in eo
non tu quidem tota re sed, quod maximum est, temporibus
errasti. [10] Ego M. Bibulo, praestantissimo cive, consule
nihil praetermisi, quantum facere enitique potui, quin
Pompeium a Caesaris coniunctione avocarem. In quo Caesar felicior fuit; ipse enim Pompeium a mea familiaritate
diiunxit. Postea vero quam se totum Pompeius Caesari tradidit, quid ego illum ab eo distrahere conarer? Stulti erat
24   sperare, suadere impudentis. Duo tamen tempora incide-
runt quibus aliquid contra Caesarem Pompeio suaserim;
ea velim reprehendas, si potes: unum ne quinquenni imperium Caesari prorogaret, alterum ne pateretur ferri ut
absentis eius ratio haberetur. Quorum si utrumvis per-
suasissem, in has miserias numquam incidissemus. Atque
idem ego, cum iam opes omnis et suas et populi Romani
Pompeius ad Caesarem detulisset, seroque ea sentire coepisset quae ego multo ante provideram, inferrique patriae

22 A special court to try Milo for Clodius' murder was set up
under a law sponsored by Pompey.
23 In fact the charge *was* made (see *Mil.* 47).

service without an instigator! Ah, but I rejoiced. So what? Was mine to be the only gloomy face when the whole community was making merry? And yet, that there was an inquiry into Clodius' death, an inquiry not very wisely constituted, it is true—for what was the point of trying a homicide under a new law when a legally constituted court already existed for that purpose?[22]—be that as it may, there was an inquiry. So you turn up all these years later to make an accusation against me which nobody made during the actual proceedings.[23]

You further dared to say, and at great length, that detaching Pompeius from Caesar's friendship was my work and that therefore it was my fault that the Civil War broke out. In this you were not entirely wrong, but you were wrong about the timing, which is all-important. [10] In the consulship of that outstanding citizen Marcus Bibulus I did everything I could, no effort spared, to wean Pompeius from his alliance with Caesar. But Caesar had the better luck: he detached Pompeius from his intimacy with *me*. But after Pompeius had put himself entirely in Caesar's hands, why should I try to draw him away? It would have been folly to hope for that, impertinence to advise it. However, there were two occasions when I advised Pompeius against Caesar's interests, and you may blame me if you can: one when I advised him not to extend Caesar's five-year command, the other when I cautioned him against letting through the proposal that Caesar should be permitted to stand for office in absentia. If he had listened to me on either point, we would never have fallen on these evil times. But after Pompeius had already put all his own resources and those of the Roman people at Caesar's disposal and begun too late to feel the truth of what I had long be-

22

23

24

bellum viderem nefarium, pacis, concordiae, compositio-
nis auctor esse non destiti, meaque illa vox est nota multis:
"Utinam, Cn. Pompei, cum C. Caesare societatem aut numquam coisses aut numquam diremisses! Fuit alterum gravitatis, alterum prudentiae tuae." Haec mea, M. Antoni,
semper et de Pompeio et de re publica consilia fuerunt;
quae si valuissent, res publica staret, tu tuis flagitiis, eges-
tate, infamia concidisses.

25   [11] Sed haec vetera, illud vero recens, Caesarem meo
consilio interfectum. Iam vereor, patres conscripti, ne,
quod turpissimum est, praevaricatorem mihi apposuisse
videar, qui me non solum meis laudibus ornaret sed etiam
oneraret alienis. Quis enim meum in ista societate glorio-
sissimi facti nomen audivit? Cuius autem qui in eo numero
fuisset nomen est occultatum? Occultatum dico? Cuius
non statim divulgatum? Citius dixerim iactasse se aliquos
ut fuisse in ea societate viderentur, cum conscii non fuis-
26 sent, quam ut quisquam celari vellet qui fuisset. Quam veri
simile porro est in tot hominibus partim obscuris, partim
adulescentibus, neminem occultantibus meum nomen la-
tere potuisse? Etenim si auctores ad liberandam patriam
desiderarentur illis a[u]ctoribus,[7] Brutos ego impellerem,
quorum uterque L. Bruti imaginem cotidie videret, alter
etiam Ahalae? Hi igitur his maioribus ab alienis potius

7 *corr. Madvig*

24 M. Brutus was descended through his mother from C.
Servilius Ahala, who as Master of the Horse under the Dictator
Cincinnatus in 439 killed Sp. Maelius, who was suspected of aim-
ing at despotism.

fore foreseen, when I saw that a wicked war was threatening our native land, I never ceased advocating peace, concord, composition. There is a widely known saying of mine: "Gnaeus Pompeius, if only you had either never gone into partnership with Gaius Caesar or never dissolved it! The first course would have befitted you as a man of principle, the second as a man of prudence." Such, Marcus Antonius, was the advice I gave over the years concerning Pompeius and concerning the Republic. Had it prevailed, the Republic would still stand, and you would have been brought low by your scandalous behavior, your poverty and infamy.

[11] All this is old news, but here is something recent: he says I instigated Caesar's killing. Members of the Senate, I really am afraid it may appear I have committed the disgraceful offense of putting up a sham prosecutor against myself, somebody not only to honor me with praise that is rightfully mine but also to load me with credit belonging to other people. Who ever heard my name linked with that partnership in a most glorious deed? And was the name of any member of that company suppressed? Suppressed, do I say? Rather, whose was not broadcast immediately? I would sooner say that some individuals, although they were not in the secret, spoke boastingly so as to make it appear that they belonged to that association than that any man who did belong would wish to be concealed. On top of that, how likely is it that my name could have remained hidden among so many, some of them persons unknown to fame, others quite young, persons who concealed nobody? And if instigators for liberating our native land were needed by those doers of the deed, was I to spur on the two Bruti, both of whom saw Lucius Brutus' portrait every day, and one of them also Ahala's?[24] Sprung

25

26

79

consilium peterent quam a suis et foris potius quam domo?
Quid C. Cassius?[8] In ea familia natus quae non modo dominatum sed ne potentiam quidem cuiusquam ferre potuit
me auctorem, credo, desideravit! Qui etiam sine his clarissimis viris hanc rem in Cilicia ad ostium fluminis Cydni
confecisset, si ille ad eam ripam quam constituerat, non ad
27 contrariam navis appulisset. Cn. Domitium non patris interitus, clarissimi viri, non avunculi mors, non spoliatio
dignitatis ad recuperandam libertatem, sed mea auctoritas
excitavit? An C. Trebonio ego persuasi? Cui ne suadere
quidem ausus essem. Quo etiam maiorem ei res publica
gratiam debet, qui libertatem populi Romani unius amicitiae praeposuit depulsorque dominatus quam particeps
esse maluit. An L. Tillius Cimber me est auctorem secutus? Quem ego magis fecisse illam rem sum admiratus
quam facturum putavi, admiratus autem ob eam causam
quod immemor beneficiorum, memor patriae fuisset.
Quid duo Servilii[9]—Cascas dicam an Ahalas? Et hos auctoritate mea censes excitatos potius quam caritate rei publicae? Longum est persequi ceteros, idque rei publicae
praeclarum, fuisse tam multos, ipsis gloriosum.

---

8 *dist.* SB: Quid? C. Cassius *vulgo*
9 *corr.* SB: duos Servilios *codd.*

---

25 According to one tradition, Sp. Cassius Vicellinus (cos. 502,
494, 486) was put to death in 485 either by his father, or with
the help of his father's testimony, on the charge of aiming at tyranny. Here Cicero may be thinking rather of L. Cassius Longinus
Ravilla, consul in 127, a strong-minded figure, famous for his se-
verity as a judge.
26 This is the only authority for an attempt by Cassius to assas-
sinate Caesar at Tarsus, when Caesar was returning in 47 from
Egypt, shortly before the Battle of Zela on 2 Aug.

from such ancestors, would they seek inspiration from out-
siders rather than from their own blood, abroad rather
than at home? What of Gaius Cassius? Born in a family that
could tolerate no man's superior power, to say nothing of
despotism,[25] he had need of me, I suppose, to prompt him!
Even without these most illustrious men, he would have
finished this business in Cilicia, at the mouth of the river
Cydnus, if Caesar had moored his ships to the bank originally determined, instead of the one opposite.[26] Was   27
Gnaeus Domitius[27] roused to recover freedom by my influence and not by the slaying of his illustrious father, the
death of his uncle, the deprivation of his status? Or did I
persuade Gaius Trebonius? I should not have ventured
even to offer him advice. The Republic, therefore, owes
him gratitude all the greater for placing the freedom of the
Roman people above the friendship of an individual and
choosing to be an overthrower of despotism rather than a
partner in it. Or did Lucius Tillius Cimber follow me as his
prompter? I rather admired him for doing that deed than
expected it of him—admired because he forgot favors and
was mindful of his native land. And then the two Servilii—
Cascas shall I call them, or Ahalas?[28] Do you suppose they
too were spurred by advice from me rather than by patriotism? It would take me too long to go through the rest of the
list; happy for the Republic that there were so many, and
glorious for themselves!

[27] Son of L. Domitius Ahenobarbus (cos. 54), who was killed
at Pharsalia, and a nephew of Cato.

[28] P. Servilius Casca (tr. pl. 43) struck the first blow against
Caesar and called out to his brother to help him finish the job
(Plut. *Caes*. 66.4–5). On Servilius Ahala, see above, n. 24.

28   [12] At quem ad modum me coarguerit homo acutus recordamini. "Caesare interfecto" inquit "statim cruentum alte extollens Brutus pugionem Ciceronem nominatim exclamavit atque ei recuperatam libertatem est gratulatus." Cur mihi potissimum? Qui⟨a⟩[10] sciebam? Vide ne illa causa fuerit appellandi mei quod, cum rem gessisset consimilem rebus eis quas ipse gesseram, me potissimum testatus est se aemulum mearum laudum exstitisse.

29   Tu autem, omnium stultissime, non intellegis, si, id quod me arguis, voluisse interfici Caesarem crimen sit, etiam laetatum esse morte Caesaris crimen esse? Quid enim interest inter suasorem facti et probatorem? Aut quid refert utrum voluerim fieri an gaudeam factum? Ecquis est igitur exceptis eis qui illum regnare gaudebant qui illud aut fieri noluerit aut factum improbarit? Omnes ergo in culpa. Etenim omnes boni, quantum in ipsis fuit, Caesarem occiderunt: aliis consilium, aliis animus, aliis occasio defuit; voluntas nemini.

30   Sed stuporem hominis vel dicam pecudis attendite. Sic enim dixit: "M. Brutus, quem ego honoris causa nomino, cruentum pugionem tenens Ciceronem exclamavit: ex quo intellegi debet eum conscium fuisse." Ergo ego sceleratus appellor a te quem tu suspicatum aliquid suspicaris; ille qui stillantem prae se pugionem tulit, is a te honoris causa nominatur. Esto; sit in verbis tuis hic stupor: quanto in rebus sententiisque maior! Constitue hoc, consul, aliquando,

<hr />

[10] *corr. Graevius*

[12] However, do remember how the clever fellow   28
proved his point against me. "The moment Caesar was
killed," says he, "Brutus raised his bloodstained dagger
high, called on Cicero by name, and congratulated him on
the recovery of freedom." Now why me in particular? Because I knew? Quite possibly the reason he called my
name was just this: after an achievement similar to my own
he called on me rather than another to witness that he was
now my rival in glory.

You utter fool! Don't you see that if it is a crime to have   29
wished Caesar killed, which is the charge you bring against
me, it is also a crime to have been glad of Caesar's death?
What difference is there between one who advises an action and one who approves of it? Or what does it matter
whether I wanted it done or rejoice at the doing? Well
then, is there anyone, apart from those who were happy
to see Caesar king of Rome, who did not want this to happen or disapproved of the act? So we are all guilty. And so,
all decent men killed Caesar so far as it was in them to do
so: some lacked design, some courage, some opportunity;
none lacked the will.

Observe the stupidity of the man, or of the brute, I   30
should rather say. For this is what he said: "Marcus Brutus,
whose name I mention with respect, called on Cicero as he
held his bloodstained dagger: hence it ought to be inferred
that Cicero was in the plot." So then: you call *me* a criminal
because you suspect that I suspected something, whereas
Brutus, who brandished his dripping weapon, is named by
you with respect! Very good; so much for the stupidity in
your words: how much greater the stupidity in your actions
and opinions! Make up your mind, consul, at long last: decide what you want the status of the Bruti, Gaius Cassius,

Brutorum, C. Cassi, Cn. Domiti, C. Treboni, reliquorum
quam velis esse causam; edormi crapulam, inquam, et ex-
hala. An faces admovendae sunt quae excitent tantae
causae indormientem? Numquamne intelleges statuen-
dum tibi esse utrum illi qui istam rem gesserunt homici-
31 daene sint an vindices libertatis? [13] Attende enim paulis-
per cogitationemque sobrii hominis punctum temporis
suscipe. Ego, qui sum illorum, ut ipse fateor, familiaris, ut
a te arguor, socius, nego quicquam esse medium: confiteor
eos, nisi liberatores populi Romani conservatoresque rei
publicae sint, plus quam sicarios, plus quam homicidas,
plus etiam quam parricidas esse, si quidem est atrocius
patriae parentem quam suum occidere. Tu, homo sapiens
et considerate, quid dicis? Si parricidas, cur honoris causa
a te sunt et in hoc ordine et apud populum Romanum
semper appellati? Cur M. Brutus referente te legibus est
solutus, si ab urbe plus quam decem dies afuisset? Cur
ludi Apollinares incredibili M. Bruti honore celebrati? Cur
provinciae Bruto, Cassio datae, cur quaestores additi, cur
legatorum numerus auctus? Atqui[11] haec acta per te.
Non igitur homicidas. Sequitur ut liberatores tuo iudicio,
32 quando quidem tertium nihil potest esse. Quid est? Num
conturbo te? Non enim fortasse satis quae diiunctius dicuntur intellegis. Sed tamen haec summa est conclusionis

11 *Jahn*: atque *codd.*

29 *Parens patriae*, a formal title granted to Caesar.
30 The duties of Brutus' office as city praetor required him to
be available to administer justice.   31 See 1.36, n. 58.
32 Presumably the number was increased from one to three
when Brutus and Cassius received proconsular *imperium* to gov-

Gnaeus Domitius, Gaius Trebonius, and the rest to be.
Rouse yourself from your intoxication, I say, and blow it all
out. Will it take lighted torches to rouse you from your
slumbers over an issue like this? Will you never understand
that you have to make up your mind whether the authors of
that deed are murderers or champions of freedom? [13]
Pay attention for a little while, and just for a moment try to   31
think like a sober man. I, who am their close friend, as I
myself acknowledge—their partner, as you accuse me of
being—state that there is no middle ground: if they are
not liberators of the Roman people and preservers of the
Republic, I confess them to be worse than assassins, worse
than murderers, worse even than parricides, if indeed it
is a more atrocious crime to kill the "father of the fatherland"[29] than one's own parent. Well, what do you say in
your pensive wisdom? If you regard them as parricides,
why have you always named them with respect both in this
body and before the Roman people? Why was Marcus
Brutus on your motion granted dispensation from the laws,
if he should be absent from Rome more than ten days?[30]
Why were the Apollinarian Games celebrated with exceptional honor to Marcus Brutus?[31] Why were provinces
given to Brutus and Cassius, why were quaestors assigned,
why was the number of legates increased?[32] And yet all of
this was done through you. Therefore you do not take them
for murderers. It follows that in your judgment they are
liberators, since there can be no third possibility. What is   32
it? Can it be that I am confusing you? Perhaps you don't
quite understand a logical dilemma. However, this in sum

ern their provinces, after serving earlier as special commissioners
for grain.

meae: quoniam scelere a te liberati sunt, ab eodem amplissimis praemiis dignissimos iudicatos.

Itaque iam retexo orationem meam. Scribam ad illos ut, si qui forte, quod a te mihi obiectum est, quaerent sitne verum, ne cui negent. Etenim vereor ne aut celatum me illis ipsis non honestum aut invitatum refugisse mihi sit turpissimum. Quae enim res umquam, pro sancte Iuppiter, non modo in hac urbe sed in omnibus terris est gesta maior, quae gloriosior, quae commendatior hominum memoriae sempiternae? In huius me tu consili societatem tamquam

33   in equum Troianum cum principibus includis? Non recuso; ago etiam gratias, quoquo animo facis. Tanta enim res est ut invidiam istam quam tu in me vis concitare cum laude non comparem. Quid enim beatius illis quos tu expulsos a te praedicas et relegatos? Qui locus est aut tam desertus aut tam inhumanus qui illos, cum[12] accesserint, non adfari atque appetere videatur? Qui homines tam agrestes qui se, cum eos aspexerint, non maximum cepisse vitae fructum putent? Quae vero tam immemor posteritas, quae tam ingratae litterae reperientur quae eorum gloriam non immortalitatis memoria prosequantur? Tu vero ascribe me talem in numerum.

34   [14] Sed unam rem vereor ne non probes: si enim ‹in eo›[13] fuissem, non solum regem sed etiam regnum de re publica sustulissem; et, si meus stilus ille fuisset, ut dicitur, mihi crede, non solum unum actum sed totam fabulam confecissem.

---

12 *ed. Cratandrina*: quo *codd.*
13 *suppl. C. F. W. Müller*

---

33 I.e., insisted upon the murder of Antony, as well as Caesar.

is my conclusion: inasmuch as you have absolved them of crime, you have consequently judged them deserving of the highest rewards.

So I now take back what I just said. I shall write to them and tell them, if anyone should inquire whether your charge against me is true, not to deny it to anyone at all. Frankly, I am afraid that they may be criticized themselves for keeping me in the dark, or else that the refusal on my part to accept an invitation to join may be highly discreditable to me. For never, holy Jupiter, was a greater deed done in Rome or anywhere else in the world; none more glorious, none more sure to live forever in the memory of mankind. Do you make me a partner in that enterprise, shutting me inside with the leaders as in a Trojan Horse? I 33 do not decline, I even thank you, no matter what your motive. It is so great a matter that this odium which you want to stir up against me is in my eyes minor in comparison with the praise I shall receive. Is there anything happier than these men whom you boast of having driven out and banished? Is there a region either so uninhabited or so uncivilized that it will not seem to speak words of welcome when they approach? Are there any human beings so uncouth as not to rate the sight of them the greatest experience of their lives? No future age will be found so unmindful, no literature so ungrateful as not to preserve their glory in everlasting remembrance. Yes, indeed, add my name to such a roll.

[14] However, there is one item which I fear may not 34 meet with your approval: if I had had a hand in the matter, I would have removed monarchy from the Republic, and not merely the monarch; and if the pen had been mine, as it is alleged, believe me, I would have finished the whole play, not just one act.[33]

Quamquam si interfici Caesarem voluisse crimen est,
vide, quaeso, Antoni, quid tibi futurum sit, quem et Narbone hoc consilium cum C. Trebonio cepisse notissimum
est et ob eius consili societatem, cum interficeretur Caesar, tum te a Trebonio vidimus sevocari. Ego autem—vide
quam tecum agam non inimice—quod bene cogitasti aliquando, laudo; quod non indicasti, gratias ago; quod non
35 fecisti, ignosco. Virum res illa quaerebat. Quod si te in
iudicium quis adducat usurpetque illud Cassianum, "cui
bono fuerit," vide, quaeso, ne haereas. Quamquam illud
fuit, ut tu dicebas quidem, omnibus bono qui servire nole-
bant, tibi tamen praecipue, qui non modo non servis sed
etiam regnas; qui maximo te aere alieno ad aedem Opis
liberavisti; qui per easdem tabulas innumerabilem pecuniam dissipavisti; ad quem e domo Caesaris tam multa
delata sunt; cuius domi quaestuosissima est falsorum com-
mentariorum et chirographorum officina, agrorum, oppi-
dorum, immunitatium, vectigalium flagitiosissimae nun-
36 dinae. Etenim quae res egestati et aeri alieno tuo praeter
mortem Caesaris subvenire potuisset? Nescio quid con-
turbatus esse videris: num quid subtimes ne ad te hoc crimen pertinere videatur? Libero te metu: nemo credet umquam. Non est tuum de re publica bene mereri. Habet
istius pulcherrimi facti clarissimos viros res publica auctores. Ego te tantum gaudere dico, fecisse non arguo.

Respondi maximis criminibus: nunc etiam reliquis re-
37 spondendum est. [15] Castra mihi Pompei atque illud

---

34 In the spring/summer of 45, during Caesar's Spanish campaign. The story is doubtless Cicero's invention.
35 Cassius Ravilla (see n. 25 above).

But after all, Antonius, if it is a crime to have wished Caesar to be killed, consider, please, what is to become of *you*, since it is common knowledge that you plotted his death at Narbo with Gaius Trebonius;[34] and it was because of your association with him in that plan that when Caesar was being killed we saw Trebonius take you aside. For my own part—do note how far I am from treating you as an enemy—I applaud the salutary thought you once entertained. I thank you for not turning informer. I forgive you for not taking action; that enterprise needed a *man*. But if someone should take you to court and quote that watchword of Cassius,[35] "Who stood to gain?", please be on your guard against getting caught. And yet, as you yourself used to say, everybody who did not want to be a slave gained thereby, but particularly you, who are not only no slave but even a monarch. You took a vast load of debt off your shoulders at the Temple of Ops. You used the same records to squander more money than is able to be counted. So many things have been transferred from Caesar's house to yours; and there a most lucrative factory of false memoranda and handwritten documents is in operation, and a scandalous market in lands, towns, exemptions, revenues. After all, what but Caesar's death could have relieved your poverty and debt? You seem a trifle agitated. Can it be that deep down inside you are afraid that this charge may appear to have something to do with you? I free you of your fear: nobody will ever believe it. Service to the Republic is not your style. As authors of that magnificent exploit the Republic has illustrious men. I say only that you are glad of it; I don't charge you with having done it.

I have answered the most serious charges. Now I must answer the rest as well. [15] You brought up against me

35

36

37

omne tempus obiecisti. Quo quidem tempore si, ut dixi, meum consilium auctoritasque valuisset, tu hodie egeres, nos liberi essemus, res publica non tot duces et exercitus amisisset. Fateor enim me, cum ea quae acciderunt providerem futura, tanta in maestitia fuisse quanta ceteri optimi cives, si idem providissent, fuissent. Dolebam, dolebam, patres conscripti, rem publicam vestris quondam meisque consiliis conservatam brevi tempore esse perituram. Nec vero eram tam indoctus ignarusque rerum ut frangerer animo propter vitae cupiditatem, quae me manens conficeret angoribus, dimissa molestiis omnibus liberaret. Illos ego praestantissimos viros, lumina rei publicae, vivere volebam, tot consularis, tot praetorios, tot honestissimos senatores, omnem praeterea florem nobilitatis ac iuventutis, tum optimorum civium exercitus; qui si viverent, quamvis iniqua condicione pacis—mihi enim omnis pax cum civibus bello civili utilior videbatur—rem publicam 38 hodie teneremus. Quae sententia si valuisset ac non ei maxime mihi quorum ego vitae consulebam spe victoriae elati obstitissent, ut alia omittam, tu certe numquam in hoc ordine vel potius numquam in hac urbe mansisses. At vero Cn. Pompei voluntatem a me alienabat oratio mea. An ille quemquam plus dilexit, cum ullo aut sermones aut consilia contulit saepius? Quod quidem erat magnum, de summa re publica dissentientis in eadem consuetudine amicitiae permanere. Sed et ego quid ille et contra ille quid ego sentirem et spectarem videbat. Ego incolumitati civium pri-

Pompeius' camp and that whole period. As I have said, if my advice and influence had prevailed at that time, you would be a pauper today, we would be free men, and the Republic would not have lost so many leaders and armies. I admit that, foreseeing the things that have happened, I was as sad as other good patriots would have been, if they had seen as far. I grieved, indeed I grieved, Members of the Senate, at the imminent dissolution of the Republic, which your counsels and mine had once preserved. I was not so unschooled, however, or so ignorant of the world as to be plunged in dismay because of any clinging to life—a life which while it lasted would plague me with sufferings but once let go would free me from all troubles. But I wanted those distinguished gentlemen to live, luminaries of the Republic, all those consulars and praetorians, so many highly respected senators, and, besides these, all the flower of our younger nobility, as well as the armies of patriotic citizens. If they were alive, however unfair the terms of peace—and I regarded any peace with fellow countrymen more advantageous than civil war—we would retain today a Republic. If my opinion had prevailed and if 38 those whose lives I was anxious to preserve had not in their confidence of victory been foremost to oppose me, well, to mention only one thing, *you* would assuredly never have remained in this body, or rather in this city. You say that the way I talked lost me Pompeius' friendship. Was there a man for whom he had more regard, with whom he talked and conferred more often? That was no small thing, that two men, though holding divergent views on the great question affecting the Republic, remained on their old friendly footing. But each of us saw what the other felt and was taking into consideration. My concern was for the sur-

mum, ut postea dignitati possemus, ille praesenti dignitati
potius consulebat. Quod autem habebat uterque quid se-
39 queretur, idcirco tolerabilior erat nostra dissensio. Quid
vero ille singularis vir ac paene divinus de me senserit
sciunt qui eum de Pharsalia fuga Paphum persecuti sunt.
Numquam ab eo mentio de me nisi honorifica, nisi plena
amicissimi desideri, cum me vidisse plus fateretur, se spe-
ravisse meliora. Et eius viri nomine me insectari audes
cuius me amicum, te sectorem esse fateare? [16] Sed omit-
tatur bellum illud in quo tu nimium felix fuisti. Ne ‹de›[14]
iocis quidem respondebo quibus me in castris usum esse
dixisti: erant quidem illa castra plena curae; verum tamen
homines, quamvis in turbidis rebus sint, tamen, si modo
40 homines sunt, interdum animis relaxantur. Quod autem
idem maestitiam meam reprehendit, idem iocum, magno
argumento est me in utroque fuisse moderatum.

Hereditates mihi negasti venire. Utinam hoc tuum verum crimen esset! Plures amici mei et necessarii viverent.
Sed qui istuc tibi venit in mentem? Ego enim amplius sestertium ducentiens acceptum hereditatibus rettuli. Quamquam in hoc genere fateor feliciorem esse te. Me nemo
nisi amicus fecit heredem, ut cum illo commodo, si quod
erat, animi quidam dolor iungeretur; te is quem tu vidisti
41 numquam, L. Rubrius Casinas [fecit heredem].[15] Et qui-

---

14 *suppl. Wesenberg*   15 *del. Madvig*

---

36 Pompey's last stopping point before his fateful crossing to
Egypt, where he was treacherously murdered.   37 A *sector*
bought *en bloc* property that was confiscated by the state and sold
at auction. Such speculators, who had a lowly reputation (§65),
then resold the holdings piecemeal so as to turn a profit.

vival of our countrymen first and foremost; dignity could be considered later. He cared rather for dignity in the present. The fact that each of us had a reasonable aim made our disagreement easier to bear. What that emi- 39 nent, almost superhuman man thought of me is known to those who accompanied him in his flight from Pharsalia to Paphos.[36] He never mentioned me except in terms of honor, full of affection and the wish that I were by his side, acknowledging that mine had been the surer vision, his a hope for a better outcome. Do you dare to attack me in the name of that man, whose friend you acknowledge I was, whereas you confess yourself to be the liquidator of his confiscated property?[37] [16] But let us say no more about that war, in which you were all too fortunate. Nor shall I make any reply about the joking you claimed I did in Pompey's camp. That camp was full of anxiety; but human beings sometimes let their minds relax, even in the most troubled of times, if human they be. But the fact that one 40 minute he censures my gloom, the next my jesting, is a pretty good indication that I did not overdo either.

You said that bequests do not come my way. I only wish this taunt of yours were true! In that case, more of my friends and connections would still be alive. But what put that into your head? Actually my account books show that I have received more than twenty million sesterces in bequests. I must admit, though, that you have better luck in this area. Nobody ever made me his heir unless he was a friend, so that any benefit there was came along with a certain amount of grief; whereas Lucius Rubrius of Casinum made you his heir, a man you never set eyes on. And see 41

dem vide quam te amarit is qui albus aterne fuerit ignoras.
Fratris filium praeterit, Q. Fufi, honestissimi equitis Romani suique amicissimi; quem palam heredem semper
factitarat, ne nominat quidem: te, quem numquam viderat
⟨a⟩ut[16] cer⟨t⟩e[17] numquam salutaverat, fecit heredem.
Velim mihi dicas, nisi molestum est, L. Turselius qua facie
fuerit, qua statura, quo municipio, qua tribu. "Nihil scio,"
inquies, "nisi quae praedia habuerit." Igitur fratrem exhe-
redans te faciebat heredem. In multas praeterea pecunias
alienissimorum hominum vi eiectis veris heredibus, tam-
42   quam heres esset, invasit. Quamquam hoc maxime admiratus sum, mentionem te hereditatum ausum esse facere,
cum ipse hereditatem patris non adisses.

[17] Haec ut colligeres, homo amentissime, tot dies in
aliena villa declamasti? Quamquam tu quidem, ut tui fami-
liarissimi dictitant, vini exhalandi, non ingeni acuendi causa declamitas. At vero adhibes ioci causa magistrum suffra-
gio tuo et compotorum tuorum rhetorem, cui concessisti
ut in te quae vellet diceret, salsum omnino hominem, sed
materia facilis in te et in tuos dicta dicere. Vide autem quid
intersit inter te et avum tuum. Ille sensim dicebat quod
43   causae prodesset; tu cursim dicis aliena. At quanta merces
rhetori data est! Audite, audite, patres conscripti, et cognoscite rei publicae vulnera. Duo milia iugerum campi

16   V2
17   *corr. Faërnus*

---

38   Because it was encumbered with debts.
39   The villa at Tibur that had formerly belonged to Pompey's
father-in-law, Metellus Scipio.
40   M. Antonius, consul in 99 and a famous advocate.

how fond he was of you, this person who may have been white or black for all you know! He passed over the son of his brother, Quintus Fufius, a much respected Roman knight with whom he was on very good terms, and did not even mention in his will the one he had always made his heir in open declaration; whereas you, on whom he had never set eyes, or at any rate had never spoken to, he made his heir. Tell me please, if you don't mind, what Lucius Turselius looked like, what was his height, his home town, his tribe. "I know nothing about him," you will say, "except what farms he owned." Therefore, he disinherited his brother and made you his heir. Besides these, Antonius has seized many sums of money belonging to total strangers, claiming to be their heir and forcibly ejecting the real heirs. And yet this is what most surprised me, that you   42 dared to mention bequests when you yourself had refused to accept your father's estate.[38]

[17] Was it to rake this stuff together, you addle-brain, that you spent all these days declaiming in a country house that does not belong to you?[39] Though, to be sure, you do that to clear your head of intoxication from wine, not to sharpen your wits; that's what your closest friends claim. Ah, but then for sport, you and your drinking companions voted to set up as the master of ceremonies a professional rhetorician, and you gave him permission to say whatever he liked against you—a witty fellow, no doubt, but you and your crowd make easy targets for satire. Observe, however, the contrast between you and your grandfather:[40] he spoke with deliberate care words that advanced his case; you speak in contradictions, helter-skelter. But what a fee our   43 rhetorician received! Hear, hear, Members of the Senate, and learn the blows dealt to the Republic. You allocated

Leontini Sex. Clodio rhetori adsignasti et quidem immunia, ut populi Romani tanta mercede nihil sapere disceres. Num etiam hoc, homo audacissime, ex Caesaris commentariis? Sed dicam alio loco et de Leontino agro et de Campano, quos iste agros ereptos rei publicae turpissimis possessoribus inquinavit. Iam enim, quoniam criminibus eius satis respondi, de ipso emendatore et correctore nostro quaedam dicenda sunt. Nec enim omnia effundam, ut, si saepius decertandum sit, ut erit, semper novus veniam: quam facultatem mihi multitudo istius vitiorum peccatorumque largitur.

44   [18] Visne igitur te inspiciamus a puero? Sic opinor; a principio ordiamur. Tenesne memoria praetextatum te decoxisse? "Patris," inquies, "ista culpa est." Concedo. Etenim est pietatis plena defensio. Illud tamen audaciae tuae quod sedisti in quattuordecim ordinibus, cum esset lege Roscia decoctoribus certus locus constitutus, quamvis quis fortunae vitio, non suo decoxisset. Sumpsisti virilem, quam statim muliebrem togam reddidisti. Primo vulgare scortum; certa flagiti merces nec ea parva; sed cito Curio intervenit, qui te a meretricio quaestu abduxit et, tamquam stolam dedisset, in matrimonio stabili et certo collo-
45   cavit. Nemo umquam puer emptus libidinis causa tam fuit in domini potestate quam tu in Curionis. Quotiens te pater

---

41 Nearly two square miles. A *iugerum* was a little less than two-thirds of an acre.   42 At §§101–102.   43 Passed in 67, it reserved the first fourteen rows of the *cavea* in the theater for knights.   44 The toga (generally a male garb) was worn by female prostitutes, and so Cicero insinuates that Antony sold sexual favors to men, playing the passive (feminine) role in these illicit relationships.

two thousand *iugera*[41] in the plain of Leontini to Sextus
Clodius, professor of rhetoric, and tax-free at that; such
a great price the Roman people had to pay for you to learn
to be a fool! Did this too come from Caesar's memoranda,
you insolent wretch? But I shall be speaking elsewhere
both of the Leontine and the Campanian lands,[42] the lands
Antonius snatched from the Republic and befouled with
disgraceful tenants. For now, having sufficiently answered
his charges, there are certain things I have to say about this
censorious corrector of mine. But I shall not pour out everything so I may come always fresh to the fray, if there are
to be further bouts, as doubtless there will be. The multitude of his vices and misdeeds affords me ample scope.

[18] Are you in favor, then, of having us examine your   44
record from boyhood? Yes, I think that is best. Let us begin
from the beginning. Do you recollect that you went bankrupt before you came of age? "That," you will say, "was my
father's fault." I grant this; your defense drips with a son's
devotion to his father! But it was your own insolence that
made you sit in the fourteen rows, although bankrupts had
their place assigned to them under the Roscian law,[43] even
those whose plight was due to bad luck and no fault of their
own. You put on the toga of manhood and promptly turned
it into the badge of a harlot.[44] You started out as a common
whore. Your shame had a fixed price, and no mean one. But
quite soon, along came Curio, who took you out of the
prostitute's trade, gave you a married lady's robe as it were,
and settled you down in steady wedlock. No slave boy   45
bought to satisfy lust was ever so completely in his master's
power as you were in Curio's. How many times did his fa-

eius domu sua eiecit, quotiens custodes posuit ne limen
intrares! Cum tu tamen nocte socia, hortante libidine, co-
gente mercede, per tegulas demitterere. Quae flagitia domus illa diutius ferre non potuit. Scisne me de rebus mihi
notissimis dicere? Recordare tempus illud cum pater Curio maerens iacebat in lecto; filius se ad pedes meos pro-
sternens, lacrimans, te mihi commendabat; orabat ut se[18]
contra suum patrem, si sestertium sexagiens peteret, de-
fenderem; tantum enim se pro te intercessisse dicebat.
Ipse autem amore ardens confirmabat, quod desiderium
tui discidi ferre non posset, se in exsilium iturum. Quo
tempore ego quanta mala florentissimae familiae sedavi
vel potius sustuli! Patri persuasi ut aes alienum fili dissolveret, redimeret adulescentem, summa spe et animi et ingeni praeditum, rei familiaris facultatibus eumque non
modo tua familiaritate sed etiam congressione patrio iure
et potestate prohiberet. Haec tu cum per me acta meminisses, nisi illis quos videmus gladiis confideres, maledictis
me provocare ausus esses?

47   [19] Sed iam stupra et flagitia omittamus: sunt quaedam quae honeste non possum dicere; tu autem eo liberior
quod ea in te admisisti quae a verecundo inimico audire
non posses. Sed reliquum vitae cursum videte, quem quidem celeriter perstringam. Ad haec enim quae in civili bello, in maximis rei publicae miseriis fecit, et ad ea quae

46

_____

[18] te *bcst (prob. SB)*

_____

45 Curio junior had guaranteed loans made to Antony totaling
six million sesterces, which Curio had no way of paying off without
his father's resources.

ther throw you out of his house, how many times did he post guards to stop you from crossing the threshold! While you, with night to befriend you, lust to encourage you, gain to drive you, used to have yourself let down through the roof tiles. Such shameful acts that house could bear no longer. You know, do you not, that I speak of matters with which I am fully familiar? Recall that time when the elder Curio lay in bed, eating his heart out. The son fell at my feet in tears, asked me to take care of you, begged me to shield him from his own father's wrath in case he asked for six million sesterces[45]—that being the sum for which he said he had gone surety for you. For himself, in his lover's fever the young man assured me that he would go into self-imposed exile because he could not bear the pain of separation from you. It was I who at this point eased the grave troubles of a flourishing family, or rather removed them. I persuaded Curio's father to settle his son's debt, to use his family's financial resources to save the credit of a young man whose disposition and talents promised so well, and further, to use his right and authority as a father to forbid his son to associate with you or even meet you. Remembering what happened then through my intervention, would you have dared to challenge me with insults, if you had not put your trust in those weapons which we see before our eyes?

[19] But let us say no more of shame and debauchery. There are some things of which I cannot decently speak. You have greater freedom because you have committed offenses too shameful to be spoken of by an enemy with a sense of decorum. Let me pass on to the rest of the career, which I shall only touch upon rapidly, for I am impatient to get on to what he did in the Civil War, that time of greatest

46

47

cotidie facit, festinat animus. Quae peto ut, quamquam
multo notiora vobis quam mihi sunt, tamen, ut facitis, attente audiatis. Debet enim talibus in rebus excitare animos
non cognitio solum rerum sed etiam recordatio; etsi inci-
damus, opinor, media ne nimis sero ad extrema veniamus.

48   Intimus erat in tribunatu Clodio qui sua erga me
beneficia commemorat; eius omnium incendiorum fax,
cuius etiam domi iam tum quiddam molitus est. Quid dicam ipse optime intellegit. Inde iter Alexandriam contra
senatus auctoritatem, contra rem publicam et religiones;
sed habebat ducem Gabinium, quicum quidvis rectissime
facere posset. Qui tum inde reditus aut qualis? Prius in ultimam Galliam ex Aegypto quam domum. Quae autem domus? Suam enim quisque domum tum obtinebat nec erat
usquam tua. Domum dico? Quid erat in terris ubi in tuo
pedem poneres praeter unum Misenum, quod cum sociis
49   tamquam Sisaponem tenebas? [20] Venis e Gallia ad
quaesturam petendam. Aude dicere te prius ad parentem

46 No doubt a hint at an intrigue with Fulvia, later Antony's
wife, but in 58 married to Clodius.

47 Antony was an officer in the army of A. Gabinius, the governor of Syria, when in 55 Gabinius restored the deposed king of
Egypt, Ptolemy Auletes. Gabinius' action violated a decree of the
senate, a law (forbidding governors to leave their provinces without authorization), and a Sibylline oracle (*religio*). Hence, on his
return to Rome in 54, Gabinius succumbed to criminal prosecution.   48 Lit. "furthest Gaul" (i.e., Gaul beyond the old
Roman province of Narbonensis), territory conquered by Caesar
in 58–51.   49 A hit at the later disruption of the ownership
of property caused in 47–45 by confiscations in the Civil War and
in 44 by the seizure of land by the Agrarian Board of Seven created
by Antony and his consular colleague.

national misery, and to what he is doing every day. You gentlemen know all that much better than I, but still I beg you to listen closely, as you are doing. In matters such as these we should be stirred not only by learning of them but even by remembering them. However, I think I had best cut short the middle of the story lest it take me too long to reach the final stages.

This fellow who is reminding me of the favors he   48 has done me was intimate with Clodius during the latter's tribunate. Antonius was the torch that set light to all Clodius' conflagrations, and even at that period, he was up to something in Clodius' house. He himself knows very well what I mean.[46] Then his journey to Alexandria, in defiance of the senate's authority, of the Republic, of religious bars[47]—but he served under Gabinius, and anything he did in Gabinius' company could not but be right and proper. So what was the manner of his return at that time? First, he traveled from Egypt to Outer Gaul[48] instead of coming home. And what home? In those days everybody's home was his own,[49] and yours did not exist anywhere. Home, do I say? Nowhere on earth was there a place where you could set foot on your own ground, excepting only your property at Misenum,[50] which you held with partners like a property at Sisapo.[51] [20] You come back   49 from Gaul to stand for the quaestorship.[52] I challenge you

[50] This country estate on the Bay of Naples had belonged to Antony's paternal grandfather (*De or.* 2.60).

[51] Location of mines in southern Spain, exploited by a Roman company made up of shareholders, just as Antony's property was not his outright, but the title was encumbered by debts.

[52] *c.* Aug./Sept. 53.

CICERO

tuam venisse quam ad me. Acceperam iam ante Caesaris
litteras ut mihi satis fieri paterer a te: itaque ne loqui quidem sum te passus de gratia. Postea sum cultus a te, tu
a me observatus in petitione quaesturae; quo quidem
tempore P. Clodium approbante populo Romano in foro es
conatus occidere, cumque eam rem tua sponte conarere,
non impulsu meo, tamen ita praedicabas, te non existimare, nisi illum interfecisses, umquam mihi pro tuis in me
iniuriis satis esse facturum. In quo demiror cur Milonem
impulsu meo rem illam egisse dicas, cum te ultro mihi
idem illud deferentem numquam sim adhortatus. Quamquam, si in eo perseverares, ad tuam gloriam rem illam re-
50 ferri malebam quam ad meam gratiam. Quaestor es factus:
deinde continuo sine senatus consulto, sine sorte, sine lege
ad Caesarem cucurristi. Id enim unum in terris egestatis,
aeris alieni, nequitiae perditis vitae rationibus perfugium
esse ducebas. Ibi te cum et illius largitionibus et tuis rapi-
nis explevisses, si hoc est explere, ⟨haurire⟩[19] quod statim
effundas, advolasti egens ad tribunatum, ut in eo magistra-
tu, si posses, viri tui similis esses.

[21] Accipite nunc, quaeso, non ea quae ipse in se atque
in domesticum [de]decus[20] impure et intemperanter, sed
quae in nos fortunasque nostras, id est in universam rem
publicam, impie ac nefarie fecerit. Ab huius enim scelere

---

[19] *suppl. Faërnus*   [20] *corr. Madvig*

---

53 Elected in 52 for 51, Antony hastened in the late summer,
or early autumn, of 52 to join Caesar in Gaul to aid him in putting
down the violent insurrection of Vercingetorix.
54 Curio, allegedly Antony's former lover (§§44–45), was active on Caesar's behalf as tribune in 50.

to say that you went to your mother before coming to see me. I had previously received a letter from Caesar asking me to accept your apologies, and so I did not so much as let you speak about making your peace. Afterwards, you paid me some attentions, and I treated you with respect when you were a candidate for the quaestorship. It was at that time you tried to kill Publius Clodius in the Forum with the approval of the Roman people. And although the attempt was made on your own initiative, without any prompting on my part, still, you let it be known that you felt you would never make amends for the injuries you had done me unless you killed Clodius. I wonder why, therefore, you say I prompted Milo to do that deed, seeing that when you offered me the same service of your own accord I never encouraged you. To be sure, I preferred the exploit, if you persevered, to stand to your credit rather than be regarded as a favor to me. Well, you were elected 50 quaestor; then, straightaway, without a decree of the senate or a drawing of lots or any legal justification, you dashed off to Caesar.[53] You thought that there lay the one refuge on earth for your poverty, debt, and worthlessness after squandering your means of livelihood. When you had glutted yourself there with Caesar's largess and your own plunderings—if glut is the word for gobbling down one minute to throw up the next—impoverished you swooped down on the tribunate, with the intention, if you could, of performing in that office like your—husband.[54]

[21] Now, gentlemen, please hear an account not of vile excesses committed against himself and his private good name, but of his impious crimes against ourselves and our fortunes, that is to say against the entire Republic. You will

51 omnium malorum principium natum reperietis. Nam cum
L. Lentulo C. Marcello consulibus Kalendis Ianuariis la-
bentem et prope cadentem rem publicam fulcire cuperetis
ipsique C. Caesari, si sana mente esset, consulere velletis,
tum iste venditum atque emancipatum tribunatum consiliis vestris opposuit cervicesque suas ei subiecit securi qua
multi minoribus in peccatis occiderunt. In te, M. Antoni,
id decrevit senatus et quidem incolumis, nondum tot lumi-
nibus exstinctis, quod in hostem togatum decerni est soli-
tum more maiorum. Et tu apud patres conscriptos contra
me dicere ausus es, cum ab hoc ordine ego conservator essem, tu hostis rei publicae iudicatus? Commemoratio illius
tui sceleris intermissa est, non memoria deleta. Dum genus hominum, dum populi Romani nomen exstabit—quod
quidem erit, si per te licebit, sempiternum—tua illa pesti-
52 fera intercessio nominabitur. Quid cupide a senatu, quid
temere fiebat, cum tu unus adulescens universum ordinem
decernere de salute rei publicae prohibuisti, neque id semel sed saepius, neque tu tecum de senatus auctoritate agi
passus es? Quid autem agebatur nisi ne delere et evertere
rem publicam funditus velles? Cum te neque principes
civitatis rogando neque maiores natu monendo neque frequens senatus agendo de vendita atque addicta sententia

---

55 Consuls in 49.   56 The so-called Ultimate Decree
(*senatus consultum ultimum*), tantamount to a declaration of mar-
tial law, empowering the consuls and the other magistrates "to see
that no harm befall the Republic."   57 About 33 years old
when he took up his tribunate on 10 Dec. 50. To portray Antony as
the sole culprit, Cicero ignores the supporting role played by Antony's fellow tribune Q. Cassius Longinus.

58 *Senatus auctoritas* is the term given to a decree that has
been blocked by a veto.

find that all our calamities have their origin in a wicked act of his. When, on the first of January, in the consulship of 51 Lucius Lentulus and Gaius Marcellus,[55] you gentlemen were anxious to shore up a tottering, almost collapsing Republic, and when you were ready to consider the interests of Gaius Caesar himself, if he kept his sanity, at that point Antonius placed in opposition to your decisions the office which he had sold and given up as his own; he put his own neck under the axe by which many have lost their lives for lesser offenses. The senate, a body still intact before so many of its shining lights had been put out, passed against you, Marcus Antonius, the decree that has traditionally been passed against a public enemy in our midst.[56] And you have dared to attack me before the assembled senate, despite the fact that this body had judged me the savior and you the enemy of the Republic? For a time that crime of yours has not been mentioned, but the memory of it has not been erased. So long as the human race and the name of the Roman people survive—a name that will last for ever, if you do not prevent it—that ruinous veto of yours will be on the lips of men. What was the senate doing un- 52 fairly or rashly, when you, a single youth,[57] prevented the entire body from passing decrees concerning the safety of the Republic? Not once, but again and again you did this, refusing to allow negotiations to be conducted with you concerning the senate's expressed intention.[58] Moreover, what was the object of the negotiation except to talk you out of wanting to destroy and utterly overthrow the Re- public? But since neither the requests of Rome's leading men, nor the warnings of your seniors, nor the representa- tions of a full senate could move you from your corrupt,

movere potui‹sse›t,[21] tum illud multis rebus ante temptatis necessario tibi vulnus inflictum est quod paucis ante te,

53 quorum incolumis fuit nemo: tum contra te dedit arma hic ordo consulibus reliquisque imperiis et potestatibus: quae non effugisses, nisi te ad arma Caesaris contulisses.

[22] Tu, tu, inquam, M. Antoni, princeps C. Caesari omnia perturbare cupienti causam belli contra patriam inferendi dedisti. Quid enim aliud ille dicebat, quam causam sui dementissimi consili et facti adferebat, nisi quod intercessio neglecta, ius tribunicium sublatum, circumscriptus a senatu esset Antonius? Omitto quam haec falsa, quam levia, praesertim cum omnino nulla causa iusta cuiquam esse possit contra patriam arma capiendi. Sed nihil de Caesare: tibi certe confitendum est causam perniciosissimi

54 belli in persona tua constitisse. O miserum te, si haec intellegis, miseriorem, si non intellegis hoc litteris mandari, hoc memoriae prodi, huius rei ne posteritatem quidem omnium saeculorum umquam immemorem fore, ‹propter unum te›[22] consules ex Italia expulsos, cumque eis Cn. Pompeium, quod imperi populi Romani decus ac lumen fuit, omnis consularis qui per valetudinem exsequi cladem illam fugamque potuissent, praetores, praetorios, tribunos plebis, magnam partem senatus, omnem subolem iuventutis, uno[que][23] verbo rem publicam expulsam atque exterminatam suis sedibus! Ut igitur in seminibus est causa

55 arborum et stirpium, sic huius luctuosissimi belli semen

21 *corr. Madvig*
22 *suppl. SB*
23 *corr. Ferrarius*

bought decision, then after much unsuccessful effort to resolve the impasse, it was inevitable for you to suffer that
blow which few before you have experienced and none
survived unscathed. Then it was that this body put weap-   53
ons in the hands of the consuls and the other holders of official authority and power, for use against you; weapons
you would not have escaped, if you had not gone off to join
Caesar's armed forces.

[22] You, yes, you, Marcus Antonius, were the first one
to give Gaius Caesar, who desired to throw everything into
confusion, a pretext for making war upon his native land.
What else did Caesar say, what pretext did he offer for
his absolutely mad design and deed except that the veto
had been ignored, the tribunician prerogative annulled,
Antonius curtailed of his rights by the senate? I refrain
from saying how false and frivolous these pretexts were,
especially since no excuse whatsoever can justify any man
in taking up arms against his native land. But leave Caesar
out of it: *you* at least must admit that your person constituted the occasion of that most terrible war. Oh you   54
wretched fellow, if you realize this! More wretched still, if
you do not realize that it is being recorded by historians,
that it is being handed down to memory, that even all ages
to come will never cease to recall this fact, namely, that on
your sole account the consuls were driven from Italy, and
with them Gnaeus Pompeius, the pride and ornament of
the Roman people's empire, as well as all consulars whose
health allowed them to follow that disastrous exodus, the
praetors, the praetorians, the tribunes of the plebs, a large
part of the senate, all our rising youth—that in a word the
Republic was driven out, banished from its home. Thus,   55
just as the cause of trees and shrubs is in their seeds, so

107

tu fuisti. Doletis tris exercitus populi Romani interfectos:
interfecit Antonius. Desideratis clarissimos civis: eos quoque vobis eripuit Antonius. Auctoritas huius ordinis ad-
flicta est: adflixit Antonius. Omnia denique, quae postea
vidimus—quid autem mali non vidimus?—si recte ratioci-
nabimur, uni accepta referemus Antonio. Ut Helena Troia-
nis, sic iste huic rei publicae causa belli, causa pestis atque
exiti fuit.

Reliquae partes tribunatus principi similes. Omnia per-
fecit quae senatus salva re publica ne fieri possent perfece-
56 rat. Cuius tamen scelus in scelere cognoscite. [23] Resti-
tuebat multos calamitosos: in eis patrui nulla mentio. Si
severus, cur non in omnis? Si misericors, cur non in suos?
Sed omitto ceteros: Licinium Denticulum[24] de alea condemnatum, collusorem suum, restituit, quasi vero ludere
cum condemnato non liceret; sed ⟨id egit⟩[25] ut quod in
alea perdiderat beneficio legis dissolveret. Quam attulisti rationem populo Romano cur eum restitui oporteret?
Absentem, credo, in reos relatum; rem indicta causa iudi-
catam; nullum fuisse de alea lege iudicium; vi oppressum
et armis; postremo, quod de patruo tuo dicebatur, pecunia

---

[24] *corr. Heusinger*: denticulam *Vbct*: lenticulam *nsv*
[25] *suppl. SB*

---

[59] In the Civil War, at the battles of Pharsalia (in 48), Thapsus
(in 46), and Munda (in 45).   [60] C. Antonius, called Hybrida,
Cicero's colleague in the consulship of 63, subsequently exiled in
59 for misgovernment in his province of Macedonia. He was not
recalled under Antony's law in 49 but brought back later, in either
46 or 45.   [61] Otherwise unknown. "Rehabilitated," not "recalled," because the penalty for gambling in public appears to

you were the seed of this most lamentable war. You grieve, gentlemen, over the slaughter of three Roman armies;[59] the slaughterer was Antonius. You mourn the loss of our most illustrious fellow countrymen; Antonius robbed you of them too. The authority of this body was shattered; Antonius shattered it. In short, all calamities that we have seen since that time—and what calamity have we *not* seen?—if we reckon correctly, we shall put it down to one man, Antonius. As Helen was to the Trojans, so this fellow was to this Republic, the cause of war, the cause of ruinous destruction.

The remaining episodes of his tribunate resembled its beginning. He accomplished all that the senate had managed to prevent from being done so long as the Republic survived. But learn of his crime within a crime. [23] He brought many banished men back home, but among them there was no mention of his uncle.[60] If he is severe, why not to all? If compassionate, why not to members of his own family? To say nothing of others, he rehabilitated Licinius Denticulus,[61] his gaming partner who had been condemned for gambling—as though it were not permissible to play with a convicted gambler. Ah, but his object was to pay his gambling losses by conferring a favor through legislation. What reason did you give to the Roman people as to why it was proper to rehabilitate him? I suppose because he had been charged in his absence, or because the case had been decided without a hearing, or because gambling was not an indictable offense, or because he had been a victim of armed force, or, finally, because the jury had been

56

have been not exile but a fine and loss of civic rights, which Antony's law restored to Denticulus.

iudicium esse corruptum! Nihil horum. At vir bonus et
re publica dignus. Nihil id quidem ad rem; ego tamen,
quoniam condemnatum esse pro nihilo est, si ita esset,
ignoscerem. Hominem omnium nequissimum, qui non
dubitaret vel in foro alea ludere, lege quae est de alea
condemnatum qui in integrum restituit, is non apertissime
studium suum ipse profitetur?

57   In eodem vero tribunatu, cum Caesar in Hispaniam
proficiscens huic conculcandam Italiam tradidisset, quae
fuit eius peragratio itinerum, lustratio municipiorum! Scio
me in rebus celebratissimis omnium sermone versari, eaque
quae dico dicturusque sum notiora esse omnibus qui in
Italia tum fuerunt quam mihi qui non fui: notabo tamen
singulas res, etsi nullo modo poterit oratio mea satis facere
vestrae scientiae. Etenim quod umquam in terris tantum
flagitium exstitisse auditum est, tantam turpitudinem, tan-
58 tum dedecus? [24] Vehebatur in essedo tribunus plebis;
lictores laureati antecedebant, inter quos aperta lectica
mima portabatur, quam ex oppidis municipales homines
honesti, obviam necessario prodeuntes, non noto illo et
mimico nomine, sed Volumniam consalutabant. Sequebatur raeda cum lenonibus, comites nequissimi; reiecta
mater amicam impuri fili tamquam nurum sequebatur. O

---

62 Cicero, in fact, remained in Italy for two months after
Caesar's departure for Spain in early April 49, and Antony's extrav-
agances are mentioned in his letters. But Cicero wished it forgotten that he had taken so long to make up his mind to join Pompey.

63 Caesar had made Antony propraetor in 49, which entitled
him to lictors. The laurel wound around their rods (*fasces*) were
for Caesar's victories in Gaul (58–51 B.C.).

bribed, as used to be said about your uncle's conviction? None of these. But rather on the grounds of his decency and worthiness to exercise his rights as a citizen. That is beside the point; but still, inasmuch as a conviction counts for nothing, if it were indeed so, I would let the matter rest. But seeing that he is an utterly worthless fellow, the sort that did not hesitate to gamble in the very Forum and was condemned under the gaming law, does not the author of his rehabilitation make his own proclivities unmistakable?

But in that same tribunate, when Caesar, upon setting out for Spain, handed over Italy to be trodden under Antony's boots, just think of his progress along the highways, his circuit of the towns! I know I am dealing with matters that are generally known and universally talked about, and that what I say and am about to say is better known to all who were in Italy at that time than to me, who was elsewhere.[62] I will, however, mention some particulars, although my words cannot possibly match your knowledge. Where in the world has the existence of anything so shocking, so scandalous, so disgraceful, ever been heard of? [24] As tribune of the plebs, he used to ride about in a two-wheeled carriage; lictors decked with laurel led the way,[63] and in their midst a mime actress[64] was carried in an open litter. Respectable folk from the country towns, who were obliged to come out and meet the cortege, greeted her not by her well-known stage name but as "Volumnia." Then followed a carriage full of pimps, Antonius' utterly worthless entourage. His mother, relegated to the rear, followed her worthless son's mistress as if a daughter-in-law. Poor

57

58

---

[64] Cytheris; see n. 19 above.

miserae mulieris fecunditatem calamitosam! Horum flagitiorum iste vestigiis omnia municipia, praefecturas, colonias, totam denique Italiam impressit.

59   Reliquorum factorum eius, patres conscripti, difficilis est sane reprehensio et lubrica. Versatus in bello est; saturavit se sanguine dissimillimorum sui civium: felix fuit, si potest ulla in scelere esse felicitas. Sed quoniam veteranis cautum esse volumus, quamquam dissimilis est militum causa et tua—illi secuti sunt, tu quaesisti ducem—tamen, ne apud illos me in invidiam voces, nihil de genere belli dicam. Victor e Thessalia Brundisium cum legionibus revertisti. Ibi me non occidisti. Magnum beneficium! Potuisse enim fateor. Quamquam nemo erat eorum qui tum tecum

60   fuerunt qui mihi non censeret parci oportere. Tanta est enim caritas patriae ut vestris etiam legionibus sanctus essem, quod eam a me servatam esse meminissent. Sed fac id te dedisse mihi quod non ademisti, meque a te habere vitam, quia non a te sit erepta: licuitne mihi per tuas contumelias hoc tuum beneficium sic tueri ut tuebar, praesertim

61   cum te haec auditurum videres? [25] Venisti Brundisium, in sinum quidem et in complexum tuae mimulae. Quid est? Num mentior? Quam miserum est id negare non posse quod sit turpissimum confiteri! Si te municipiorum non pudebat, ne veterani quidem exercitus? Quis enim miles fuit qui Brundisi illam non viderit? Quis qui nescierit

---

65   Antony's. Cicero suddenly switches from the third to the second person in referring to Antony.

66   See §§5–6.

unfortunate woman, to be mother of that brood! He left the traces of these infamies in every town, prefecture, and colony, in fact throughout Italy.

To censure his remaining deeds, Members of the Senate, is a matter of some difficulty and delicacy. He took part in the war. He saturated himself with the blood of fellow countrymen who resembled him not at all. He was fortunate, if there can be good fortune in any crime. But since we do not wish to upset the veterans—not that the soldiers' case and yours[65] is the same; they followed their general, you sought him out—I shall say nothing about the kind of war to prevent you from bringing me into their disfavor. You returned victorious from Thessaly to Brundisium with the legions. There you did not kill me.[66] Mighty kind of you! I admit you had the power, even though there was no one of those who were with you at that time who did not think that I ought to be spared. Love of one's native land is such a potent force that it made my person sacred even to Caesar's legions because they remembered that I had been Rome's preserver. But granted that you gave me what you did not take from me and that I owe you my life because you did not deprive me of it, did your insults permit me to show proper appreciation of this kindness of yours, as I used to do, especially since you were well aware that you would hear this response? [25] Anyway, you arrived in Brundisium, into the bosom and arms, that is to say, of your little mime actress—What's the matter? Am I not telling the truth? What a sorry predicament to be unable to deny what it is most disgraceful to admit! If you felt no shame before the eyes of the country towns, did you not do so even before the eyes of the veteran army? Was there a soldier who did not see her at Brundisium? Which of them

59

60

61

venisse eam tibi tot dierum viam gratulatum? Quis qui non
indoluerit tam sero se quam nequam hominem secutus es-
62 set cognoscere? Italiae rursus percursatio eadem comite
mima; in oppida militum crudelis et misera deductio; in
urbe auri, argenti maximeque vini foeda direptio. Accessit ut Caesare ignaro, cum esset ille Alexandriae, beneficio amicorum eius magister equitum constitueretur. Tum
existimavit se suo iure cum Hippia vivere et equos vectiga-
lis Sergio mimo tradere; tum sibi non hanc quam nunc
male tuetur, sed M. Pisonis domum ubi habitaret legerat.
Quid ego istius decreta, quid rapinas, quid hereditatum
possessiones datas, quid ereptas proferam? Cogebat eges-
tas; quo se verteret non habebat: nondum ei tanta a L. Ru-
brio, non a L. Turselio hereditas venerat; nondum in Cn.
Pompei locum multorumque aliorum qui aberant repentinus heres successerat. Erat vivendum latronum ritu, ut
tantum haberet quantum rapere potuisset.
63   Sed haec quae robustioris improbitatis sunt, omittamus: loquamur potius de nequissimo genere levitatis. Tu
istis faucibus, istis lateribus, ista gladiatoria totius corporis
firmitate tantum vini in Hippiae nuptiis exhauseras ut tibi

67 The name means "horsey," inviting the pun on the name of
Antony's office, which in Greek (Hipparchos) happens to be the
name of the brother of another Hippias, who was a son of the
sixth-century Athenian tyrant Pisistratus.

68 The contracts were for race horses at public games (Ascon.
p. 93C), but the facts are otherwise unknown.

69 Pompey's house; precariously occupied because negotiations were under way in 44 to restore it to Pompey's son Sextus,
who had an army in Spain. Piso is probably the praetor of 44, son
of M. Pupius Piso (cos. 61). Given Piso's ties of friendship with Antony in 44 (3.25), it is entirely possible that Antony was invited by

did not know that she had traveled so many days' journey to congratulate you? Which of them was not grieved to learn so late what a worthless wretch he had been following? Then once again a junket through Italy in the 62 same mime actress's company. Soldiers were billeted in the towns, a cruel, distressful operation. In Rome there was an ugly pillaging of gold, silver, and, most of all, wine. On top of all, he was appointed Master of the Horse by favor of Caesar's friends without Caesar's knowledge, since he was in Alexandria. After that, he felt fully entitled to live with Hippias[67] and hand over the state contract for horses[68] to Sergius the mime actor. At that time, Antonius had chosen Marcus Piso's house as his residence, not the house that he is now precariously occupying.[69] Need I bring up his orders, his plunderings, the estates of deceased persons bestowed by him or taken away? Poverty drove him; he had no place to turn. Not yet had he come into those fat bequests from Lucius Rubrius and Lucius Turselius,[70] not yet as a sudden heir had he moved into the place of Gnaeus Pompeius and many other absentees.[71] He had to live as robbers do, possessing as much as he had been able to steal.

But let us leave aside such acts of sturdy wickedness, 63 and speak rather of the lowest kind of irresponsibility. With that gullet of yours, that chest, that robust physique befitting a gladiator, you engulfed such a quantity of wine at Hippias' wedding that the following day you found it

Piso to use his house in 48 and may even have (nominally) rented it from him. Cicero stops short of asserting that Antony appropriated the property.   [70] Cf. §§40–41.

[71] Properties confiscated by Caesar in 47 and sold at auction.

necesse esset in populi Romani conspectu vomere postridie. O rem non modo visu foedam sed etiam auditu! Si
inter cenam in ipsis tuis immanibus illis poculis hoc tibi accidisset, quis non turpe duceret? In coetu vero populi Romani negotium publicum gerens, magister equitum, cui
ructare turpe esset, is vomens frustis esculentis vinum re-
dolentibus gremium suum et totum tribunal implevit. Sed
haec ipse fatetur esse in suis sordibus: veniamus ad splen-
dida.

64   [26] Caesar Alexandria se recepit, felix, ut sibi quidem
videbatur, mea autem sententia, qui rei publicae sit infelix,
felix esse nemo potest. Hasta posita pro aede Iovis Stato-
ris bona subiecta Cn. Pompei—miserum me! consumptis
enim lacrimis tamen infixus animo haeret dolor—bona,
inquam, Cn. Pompei Magni voci acerbissimae subiecta
praeconis. Una in illa re servitutis oblita civitas ingemuit
servientibusque animis cum omnia metu tenerentur, ge-
mitus tamen populi Romani liber fuit. Exspectantibus omnibus quisnam esset tam impius, tam demens, tam dis hominibusque hostis qui ad illud scelus sectionis auderet
accedere, inventus est nemo praeter Antonium, praesertim cum tot essent circum hastam illam qui alia omnia au-
derent: unus inventus est qui id auderet quod omnium fu-
65   gisset et reformidasset audacia. Tantus igitur te stupor
oppressit vel, ut verius dicam, tantus furor ut primum,
cum sector sis isto loco natus, deinde cum Pompei sector,

---

72 A *hasta* was the symbol of a public auction (recalling the
disposal of booty captured in war).

73 See n. 37 above.

necessary to vomit in full view of the Roman people. Disgusting to witness, disgusting even to hear tell of! Had this happened to you at dinner in those same monstrous cups of yours, who would not think it a shameful exhibition? But while conducting public business, in a gathering of the Roman people in his role as Master of the Horse, for whom it would be disgraceful to burp, he vomited, filling his lap and the whole platform with morsels of food stinking of wine! Ah well, he admits himself that this was one of his less creditable performances. Let us proceed to his shining deeds.

[26] Caesar returned from Alexandria, a fortunate man, as he considered himself; but in my opinion, no man can be fortunate who brings misfortune upon the Republic. A lance[72] was planted in front of the Temple of Jupiter Stator, and the property of Gnaeus Pompeius—dear me; tears may have run dry, but the pain clings deep in my heart—the property, I say, of Gnaeus Pompeius Magnus was subjected to the harsh voice of an auctioneer. In that single instance did the community forget its bondage and groan aloud, and though their spirits were enslaved, since fear dominated everything, nevertheless the groaning of the Roman people was free. While all waited in suspense to learn what impious madman, what enemy to gods and men would dare to commit the heinous crime of a bid, nobody came forward except Antonius, even though there stood around that lance so many who dared all else. Yes, he alone was found to dare an act from which the audacity of all the rest recoiled in consternation. Have you become so insensate, or, to use a more apt word, so insane as to serve as the liquidator of confiscated goods[73] (a man of your birth!), and those goods Pompeius' goods, without knowing that

64

65

non te exsecratum populo Romano, non detestabilem, non
omnis tibi deos, non omnis homines et esse inimicos et fu-
turos scias? At quam insolenter statim helluo invasit in eius
viri fortunas cuius virtute terribilior erat populus Romanus
exteris gentibus, iustitia carior! [27] In eius igitur viri copias cum se subito ingurgitasset, exsultabat gaudio, persona de mimo, "modo egens, repente dives." Sed, ut est apud
poetam nescio quem, "male parta male dilabuntur." Incredibile ac simile portenti est quonam modo illa tam multa
quam paucis non dico mensibus sed diebus effuderit.
Maximus vini numerus fuit, permagnum optimi pondus
argenti, pretiosa vestis, multa et lauta supellex et magnifica
multis locis, non illa quidem luxuriosi hominis, sed tamen
abundantis. Horum paucis diebus nihil erat. Quae Charybdis tam vorax? Charybdim dico? Quae si fuit, animal
unum fuit: Oceanus, me dius fidius, vix videtur tot res tam
dissipatas, tam distantibus in locis positas tam cito absor-
bere potuisse. Nihil erat clausum, nihil obsignatum, nihil
scriptum. Apothecae totae nequissimis hominibus condo-
nabantur; alia mimi rapiebant, alia mimae; domus erat
aleatoribus referta, plena ebriorum; totos dies potabatur
atque id locis pluribus; suggerebantur etiam saepe—non
enim semper iste felix—damna aleatoria; conchyliatis Cn.
Pompei peristromatis servorum in cellis lectos stratos videres. Quam ob rem desinite mirari haec tam celeriter
esse consumpta. Non modo unius patrimonium quamvis

66

67

74 Possibly quoted from some mime given its proximity to
"like a character in a farce (mime)." 75 Cn. Naevius of the
third century. 76 A mythical monster taking the form of a
whirlpool. In Cicero's day, it was pictured as lying on the Sicilian
side of the straits separating Italy from Sicily.

118

you are on that account abominable and accursed in the sight of the Roman people and that all gods and all men are your enemies, now and for ever more? But how insolently the good-for-nothing laid hasty hands on the possessions of the man whose valor made the Roman people more feared by foreign nations, whose justice made them more loved! [27] Thus, having plunged suddenly into the wealth of such a man, he wildly rejoiced like a character in a farce, "beggar one day, rich the next."[74] But, as some playwright[75] has it, "ill gotten is ill squandered." It is unbelievable, like a 66 prodigy, how he dissipated so much within a few, I do not say months, but days. There was a great quantity of wine, a very large weight of the finest silver plate, costly draperies, much elegant and magnificent furniture, variously located, the appointments not indeed of a luxurious man, but of an affluent one. Within a few days, nothing of this remained. Was ever a Charybdis[76] so ravenous? Charybdis, do I say? 67 If it ever existed, it was a single creature. So help me god, it hardly seems possible that the Ocean could have swallowed up so many objects so rapidly, scattered as they were in places wide apart. Nothing was closed, nothing sealed, nothing written down. Whole storerooms were given away to the dregs of society. Mime actors snatched this, mime actresses that. The house was crammed full with gamblers and drunks. Drinking went on all day long and in a variety of places too. Often gambling losses would add to the wastage, for Antonius was not always blessed with good luck. In the slaves' cubicles, you might see couches spread with Gnaeus Pompeius' purple coverlets. Consequently, cease to wonder at the amazing speed of the consumption. Such prodigality could quickly have devoured cities and king-

amplum, ut illud fuit, sed urbis et regna celeriter tanta nequitia devorare potuisset. At idem aedis etiam et hortos—
68 o audaciam immanem!—tu etiam ingredi illam domum
ausus es, tu illud sanctissimum limen intrare, tu illarum aedium dis penatibus os impurissimum ostendere? Quam
domum aliquamdiu nemo aspicere poterat, nemo sine lacrimis praeterire, hac te in domo tam diu deversari non pudet? In qua, quamvis nihil sapias, tamen nihil tibi potest
esse iucundum. [28] An tu illa in vestibulo rostra [spolia]²⁶
cum aspexisti, domum tuam te introire putas? Fieri non
potest. Quamvis enim sine mente, sine sensu sis, ut es, tamen et te et tua et tuos nosti. Nec vero te umquam neque
vigilantem neque in somnis credo posse mente consistere.
Necesse est, quamvis sis, ut es, violentus et furens, cum
tibi obiecta sit species singularis viri, perterritum te de
69 somno excitari, furere etiam saepe vigilantem. Me quidem
miseret parietum ipsorum atque tectorum. Quid enim
umquam domus illa viderat nisi pudicum, quid nisi ex optimo more et sanctissima disciplina? Fuit enim ille vir,
patres conscripti, sicuti scitis, cum foris clarus tum domi
admirandus, neque rebus externis magis laudandus quam
institutis domesticis. Huius in sedibus pro cubiculis stabu-
la, pro conclavibus popinae [tricliniis]²⁷ sunt. Etsi iam
negat. Nolite quaerere; frugi factus est: illam suam suas
res sibi habere iussit, ex duodecim tabulis clavis ademit,
exegit. Quam porro spectatus civis, quam probatus, cuius

²⁶ *del. Orelli*   ²⁷ *del. Halm*

---

⁷⁷ Trophies commemorating Pompey's naval victories over
the pirates in 67.
⁷⁸ Cytheris.

doms, let alone one individual's patrimony, however ample—and ample it was. Likewise, even the house and suburban estate—oh the monstrous audacity!—did you 68 actually dare to enter that house, to cross that most hallowed threshold, to show your debauched face to the household gods of that dwelling? Are you not ashamed to be lodging for such a long time in a house that for quite some time no man could behold, no man pass by without tears? Dull though you are, nothing can be pleasant to you there. [28] Or when you see those ships' beaks in the forecourt,[77] do you imagine it is *your* house you are entering? That is impossible. You may be, indeed you are, mindless and insensate, but you recognize yourself and your own possessions and the members of your own family. I do not believe you can have a tranquil moment awake or asleep. You may be, indeed you are, a man of violence and fury, but when the likeness of that matchless man is set before you, it is inevitable that you be roused from your sleep in terror, and even in your waking hours you must often rave. For my part, I pity the very walls and ceilings. What had 69 that house ever seen that was not decorous, what that was not in accord with the highest and strictest moral code? For as you know, Members of the Senate, the great man of whom I speak was as admirable at home as he was renowned abroad, and his achievements in foreign lands were no more praiseworthy than his domestic life. Now in this man's dwelling there are brothels in place of bedrooms, cheap eateries in place of dining rooms. Oh, but he now denies it! Don't ask questions; he has become frugal. He has told that mistress of his[78] to get her own things together, he has taken away her keys according to the provisions of the Twelve Tables, he has put her out of doors. What a respectable citizen he is, what an upright one, out

ex omni vita nihil est honestius quam quod cum mima fecit
70 divortium! At quam crebro usurpat: "et consul et Antonius!" Hoc est dicere, et consul et impudicissimus, et consul et homo nequissimus. Quid est enim aliud Antonius?
Nam si dignitas significaretur in nomine, dixisset, credo,
aliquando avus tuus se et consulem et Antonium. Numquam dixit. Dixisset etiam collega meus, patruus tuus, nisi
si tu es solus Antonius.

Sed omitto ea peccata quae non sunt earum partium
propria quibus tu rem publicam vexavisti: ad ipsas tuas
partis redeo, id est ad civile bellum, quod natum, con-
71 flatum, susceptum opera tua est. [29] Cui bello ‹iam›[28]
cum propter timiditatem tuam tum propter libidines de-
fuisti. Gustaras civilem sanguinem vel potius exsorbue-
ras; fueras in acie Pharsalica; antesignanus L. Domitium,
clarissimum et nobilissimum virum, occideras multosque
praeterea qui e proelio effugerant, quos Caesar, ut non
nullos, fortasse servasset, crudelissime persecutus truci-
daras. Quibus rebus tantis ‹et›[29] talibus gestis quid fuit
causae cur in Africam Caesarem non sequerere, cum praesertim belli pars tanta restaret? Itaque quem locum apud
ipsum Caesarem post eius ex Africa reditum obtinuisti?
Quo numero fuisti? Cuius tu imperatoris quaestor fueras,
dictatoris magister equitum, belli princeps, crudelitatis

---

[28] *suppl. SB*   [29] *suppl. Eberhard*

---

[79] Lit. *antesignanus* (an elite, mobile fighter who operated in
front of the legions), a term that must be used metaphorically
in reference to Antony's role in pursuing fugitives because during the battle itself Antony commanded Caesar's left wing (Caes.
BCiv. 3.89.2).

of whose whole life the most creditable action is to have divorced a mime actress! But how frequently he employs 70
the phrase "both consul and an Antonius," which is to
say "both consul and an utterly shameless fellow," "both
consul and a completely worthless fellow." What else is
Antonius? If the name indicated worth, I imagine your
grandfather would now and then have called himself "consul and an Antonius"; but he never did. So would my former colleague, your uncle—unless you are the one and
only Antonius.

However, I leave aside misdemeanors which have nothing to do with the political activity with which you plagued
the Republic, and I return to that particular activity of
yours, that is to the Civil War, which was engendered,
stirred up, undertaken by your doing. [29] Both your cow- 71
ardice and your lusts now kept you out of it. You had tasted
the blood of your fellow countrymen, or rather drained it.
You had a place in the battle line at Pharsalia. As a commando,[79] you had slain the illustrious and highborn Lucius Domitius; and many besides, who had escaped from
the battlefield and whose lives Caesar might perhaps have
spared as he spared some others, had been cruelly pursued
and butchered by you. After such important and distinguished exploits, what was your reason for not following
Caesar to Africa, especially when so large a part of the war
had still to be fought? So what post did you occupy on
Caesar's staff after his return from Africa? What was your
rating? You had been quaestor to him as commander-in-chief, Master of the Horse to him as dictator, the prime
mover of his war, instigator of his cruelty, partner in his

auctor, praedae socius, testamento, ut dicebas ipse, filius, appellatus es de pecunia quam pro domo, pro hortis, pro

72 sectione debebas. Primo respondisti plane ferociter et, ne omnia videar contra te, prope modum aequa et iusta dicebas: "A me C. Caesar pecuniam? Cur potius quam ego ab illo? An sine me ille vicit? At ne potuit quidem. Ego ad illum belli civilis causam attuli; ego leges perniciosas rogavi; ego arma contra consules imperatoresque populi Romani, contra senatum populumque Romanum, contra deos patrios arasque et focos, contra patriam tuli. Num sibi soli vicit? Quorum facinus est commune, cur non sit eorum praeda communis?" Ius postulabas, sed quid ad rem? Plus

73 ille poterat. Itaque excussis tuis vocibus et ad te et ad praedes tuos milites misit, cum repente a te praeclara illa tabula prolata <e>s<t>.[30] Qui risus hominum, tantam esse tabulam, tam varias, tam multas possessiones, ex quibus praeter partem Miseni nihil erat quod is qui auctionaretur posset suum dicere. Auctionis vero miserabilis aspectus: vestis Pompei non multa eaque maculosa; eiusdem quaedam argentea vasa collisa, sordidata mancipia, ut doleremus quicquam esse ex illis reliqui[s][31] quod videre posse-

74 mus. Hanc tamen auctionem heredes L. Rubri decreto Caesaris prohibuerunt. Haerebat nebulo: quo se verteret non habebat. Quin his ipsis temporibus domi Caesaris percussor ab isto missus deprehensus dicebatur esse cum sica: de quo Caesar in senatu aperte in te invehens questus est.

---

30 *corr. Halm*   31 *corr. Pluygers*

---

80 Pompey's properties purchased a year earlier, in the autumn of 47 (§64).

81 Details unknown; cf. §§40–41.

plunder, and under his will (so you used to say yourself) his adopted son: and yet you were called upon to pay up the money you owed on the house, on the suburban estate, and on the properties earmarked for liquidation.[80] At first you 72 retorted with undisguised defiance—and, not to appear to be always against you, what you said was almost fair and reasonable: "Gaius Caesar demand money from *me*? Why not I rather from him? Did he win without me? Indeed he couldn't. I brought him his pretext for civil war, I sponsored pernicious laws, I bore arms against consuls and commanders of the Roman people, against the senate and the people of Rome, against our ancestral gods and altars and hearths, against our native land. Did he win only for himself? Why shouldn't those who share the guilt share the loot?" You were asking for your right, but what of that? He was the stronger. And so, shrugging aside your protests, 73 he sent soldiers to you and your sureties; at which point you suddenly posted that magnificent notice announcing a sale. Loud was the laughter to see so long a list of properties so many and various, of which (except for a share in the Misenum estate) there was not one that the person putting them up for sale could call his own. Ah, but the auction itself was a sorry spectacle. Some tapestries of Pompeius', just a few and stained at that; certain dented articles of silver, also his; some squalid slaves. It made us sad that anything remained for us to see. However, the heirs of Lucius 74 Rubrius halted the auction by means of a decree issued by Caesar.[81] Our prodigal was stuck; he had nowhere to turn. Indeed, at that very time, the story circulated that an assassin sent by Antonius had been arrested in Caesar's house with a dagger; Caesar complained about it and railed against you openly in the senate.

Proficiscitur in Hispaniam Caesar paucis tibi ad solvendum propter inopiam tuam prorogatis diebus. Ne tum quidem sequeris. Tam bonus gladiator rudem tam cito? Hunc igitur quisquam qui in suis partibus, id est in suis fortunis, tam timidus fuerit pertimescat? [30] Profectus est aliquando tandem in Hispaniam; sed tuto, ut ait, pervenire non potuit. Quonam modo igitur Dolabella pervenit? Aut non suscipienda fuit ista causa, Antoni, aut, cum suscepisses, defendenda usque ad extremum. Ter depugnavit Caesar cum civibus, in Thessalia, Africa, Hispania. Omnibus adfuit his pugnis Dolabella; in Hispaniensi etiam vulnus accepit. Si de meo iudicio quaeris, nollem; sed tamen consilium a primo reprehendendum, laudanda constantia. Tu vero quid es? Cn. Pompei liberi tum primum patriam repetebant. Esto, fuerit haec partium causa communis. Repetebant praeterea deos patrios, aras, focos, larem suum familiarem, in quae tu invaseras. Haec cum peterent armis ei quorum erant legibus—etsi in rebus iniquissimis quid potest esse aequi?—tamen quem erat aequissimum contra Cn. Pompei liberos pugnare? Quem? Te sectorem. An ut tu Narbone mensas hospitum convomeres Dolabella pro te in Hispania dimicaret?

Qui vero Narbone reditus! Etiam quaerebat cur ego ex ipso cursu tam subito revertissem. Exposui nuper, patres conscripti, causam reditus mei. Volui, si possem, etiam

82 Lit. "wooden sword" (*rudis*), a symbol of a gladiator's discharge.
83 I.e., Antony had a personal stake in defeating the sons of Pompey in the Spanish campaign so that he could continue to occupy Pompey's confiscated holdings.
84 See 1.7–10.

Caesar left for Spain after granting you a few days' grace in which to pay in consideration of your lack of means. You did not follow him on this occasion either. Should so good a gladiator have taken his discharge[82] so soon? Would anyone fear this fellow who was so cowardly in supporting his own side, that is, his own fortunes?[83] [30] At long last he did leave for Spain; but he could not get   75 there safely, so he says. Then how did Dolabella get there? You should either not have enlisted under that banner, Antonius, or having done so, you should have fought for it to the end. Three times Caesar met his countrymen in decisive battle, in Thessaly, Africa, and Spain. Dolabella took part in all these engagements; in the Spanish one he was actually wounded. If you ask my opinion, I would wish he had not. All the same, while his original choice is censurable, his constancy is nevertheless praiseworthy. But what sort of fellow are *you*? In that campaign, the sons of Gnaeus Pompeius were first of all trying to reclaim their native land. Very well, let us grant that this was the common cause of their side. Furthermore, they were trying to reclaim their ancestral gods, altars, hearths, their family home, which you had invaded. When the legal owners claimed their property by resorting to arms, who—I know there can be no justice in such iniquity, but still, *who* could most justly be expected to fight against Gnaeus Pompeius' sons? Who but you, the liquidator of those confiscated assets? Or was Dolabella to fight on your behalf in Spain so   76 that you might vomit over your hosts' dinner tables at Narbo?

But what a return he made from Narbo—and he was asking why I turned back so suddenly, abandoning my journey! Members of the Senate, I explained the reason for my return not long ago.[84] I wanted, if possible, to be of

ante Kalendas Ianuarias prodesse rei publicae. Nam quod quaerebas quo modo redissem, primum luce, non tenebris; deinde cum calceis et toga, nullis nec gallicis nec lacerna. At etiam aspicis me et quidem, ut videris, iratus. Ne tu iam mecum in gratiam redeas, si scias quam me pudeat nequitiae tuae, cuius te ipsum non pudet. Ex omnium omnibus flagitiis nullum turpius vidi, nullum audivi. Qui magister equitum fuisse tibi viderere, in proximum annum consulatum peteres vel potius rogares, per municipia coloniasque Galliae, a qua nos tum cum consulatus petebatur, non rogabatur, petere consulatum solebamus, cum gallicis et lacerna cucurristi.

77 [31] At videte levitatem hominis. Cum hora diei decima fere ad Saxa Rubra venisset, delituit in quadam cauponula atque ibi se occultans perpotavit ad vesperam; inde cisio celeriter ad urbem advectus domum venit capite obvoluto. Ianitor: "Quis tu?" "A Marco tabellarius." Confestim ad eam cuius causa venerat, eique epistulam tradidit. Quam cum illa legeret flens—erat enim scripta amatorie; caput autem litterarum sibi cum illa mima posthac nihil futurum; omnem se amorem abiecisse illim atque in hanc transfudisse—cum mulier fleret uberius, homo misericors ferre

---

85 Cicero now addresses Antony directly.

86 I.e., Antony could not in good conscience remain at enmity with a man who feels shame for his (Antony's) conduct as one friend would do for another.

87 Sc. from Caesar.

88 A town on the Via Flaminia, about nine miles north of Rome.

89 Lit. the "tenth hour": the Romans divided into twelve equal

some use to the Republic even before the first of January. As for your question,[85] *how* did I return, to begin with, it was by daylight, not darkness; secondly, it was in boots and a toga, not in Gaulish slippers and a cloak. Ah, you are giving me a look, and you appear to be enraged indeed. I assure you, if you knew the shame I feel at your depravity, which *you* are not ashamed of, you would be friends by now with me again.[86] Of all the outrages in the world, none have I seen, none have I heard of that was more disgraceful. You who looked upon yourself as a former Master of the Horse, who were standing for the consulship, or rather requesting it[87] for the following year, dressed in Gaulish slippers and a cloak, you rushed through the towns and colonies of Gaul, the region where we used to canvass for the consulship when that office was stood for and not asked for!

[31] But note the frivolity of the fellow! Arriving at Saxa   77
Rubra[88] about three o'clock in the afternoon,[89] he kept out of sight in a little tavern and stayed in hiding there until sunset, drinking steadily. From that tavern he was brought swiftly to Rome in a two-wheeled carriage and came to his house with his face muffled. Doorman: "Who's there?" "A courier from Marcus." Straightaway he is conducted to the lady[90] on whose account he had come and hands her a letter. She wept as she read—it was a love letter, and the main point of it was that he would have nothing to do with the actress in the future; he had jettisoned all love from that relationship and transferred it to this lady. When she wept

parts the period of daylight, which extended from *c.* 6 a.m. to *c.* 6 p.m. at the time of this incident (*c.* mid-March).
    90 His wife Fulvia.

non potuit, caput aperuit, in collum invasit. O hominem nequam! Quid enim aliud dicam? Magis proprie nihil possum dicere. Ergo, ut te catamitum, nec opinato cum te ostendisses, praeter spem mulier aspiceret, idcirco urbem terrore nocturno, Italiam multorum dierum metu perturbasti? Et domi quidem causam amoris habui⟨s⟩t⟨i⟩,[32] foris etiam turpiorem, ne L. Plancus praedes tuos venderet. Productus autem in contionem a tribuno plebis cum respondisses te rei tuae causa venisse, populum etiam dicacem in te reddidisti. Sed nimis multa de nugis: ad maiora veniamus.

[32] C. Caesari ex Hispania redeunti obviam longissime processisti. Celeriter isti redisti, ut cognosceret te, si minus fortem, at tamen strenuum. Factus es ei rursus nescio quo modo familiaris. Habebat hoc omnino Caesar: quem plane perditum aere alieno egentemque, si eundem nequam hominem audacemque cognorat, hunc in familiaritatem libentissime recipiebat. His igitur rebus praeclare commendatus iussus es renuntiari consul et quidem cum ipso. Nihil queror de Dolabella qui tum est impulsus, in-

78

79

---

[32] *corr. Ferrarius*

---

[91] One of six (or eight?) city prefects (*praefecti urbi*) appointed by Caesar to assist M. Lepidus, his Master of the Horse, to manage affairs during his absence in 45 (Cass. Dio 43.28.2). Here, Plancus carries out a function normally assigned to the city praetor, an office not filled until Caesar returned from Spain in Sept.

[92] Like the English word "affair," *res* (lit. "thing") can refer to business or amorous relations.

[93] From Narbo (in southern Gaul, *c.* 50 miles from the border with Spain) to Rome (in March 45) and back (in the summer) to intercept Caesar on his return journey to Italy.

all the more, the softhearted fellow could bear it no longer and, revealing his face, he threw his arms passionately around her neck. What a good-for-nothing!—What else am I to call him? I can find no term more appropriate. Well then, just so that your wife might be surprised to see you, her pretty boy, when you revealed yourself unexpectedly, was it for this reason that you caused alarm in Rome during the night, and caused fear and turmoil in Italy for days on end? Well, at home you had a lover's reason; out of doors 78 your reason was still more discreditable: you were afraid Lucius Plancus[91] would sell the property of your sureties. When you were brought before a public meeting by a tribune of the plebs and said in reply to questioning that you had come to Rome on an affair that was personal, you made even the common folk witty at your expense.[92] But that's more than enough about trifles. Let us get to matters of greater moment.

[32] You traveled a great distance to meet Gaius Caesar on his way home from Spain—a rapid round trip[93] so that he should see that if your courage left something to be desired, you were at least a man of energy. Somehow or other you again became one of his cronies. It was a way that Caesar had: if he saw a man head over heels in debt, without a penny to his name, then, provided he knew that the man was of a bold worthless sort, Caesar was delighted to welcome him into his circle of friends. Since you were 79 admirably commended by these qualities, Caesar gave orders for you to be declared elected consul, and with himself as your colleague. I make no complaint about Dolabella, who was prompted to stand, led on, and then made a

ductus, elusus. Qua in re quanta fuerit uterque vestrum perfidia in Dolabellam quis ignorat? Ille induxit ut peteret, promissum et receptum intervertit ad seque transtulit; tu eius perfidiae voluntatem tuam ascripsisti. Veniunt Kalendae Ianuariae; cogimur in senatum: invectus est copiosius multo in istum et paratius Dolabella quam nunc ego.

80 Hic autem iratus quae dixit, di boni! Primum cum Caesar ostendisset se, prius quam proficisceretur, Dolabellam consulem esse iussurum—quem negant regem, qui et faceret semper eius modi aliquid et diceret—sed cum Caesar ita dixisset, tum hic bonus augur eo se sacerdotio praeditum esse dixit ut comitia auspiciis vel impedire vel vitiare posset, idque se facturum esse adseveravit. In quo primum incredibilem stupiditatem hominis cognoscite.

81 Quid enim? Istud quod te sacerdoti iure facere posse dixisti, si augur non esses et consul esses, minus facere potuisses? Vide ne etiam facilius. Nos enim nuntiationem solum habemus, consules et reliqui magistratus etiam spectionem. Esto: hoc imperite; nec enim est ab homine numquam sobrio postulanda prudentia. Sed videte impudentiam. Multis ante mensibus in senatu dixit se Dolabellae comitia aut prohibiturum auspiciis aut id facturum esse quod fecit. Quisquamne divinare potest quid viti in auspi-

---

94 I.e., nullify the results of the election after the assembly voted (§83).

fool of. Who does not know how perfidiously you both behaved toward Dolabella? Caesar led him on to stand for
the office, and then, after it had been promised and guaranteed, snatched it away and transferred it to himself. You
cloaked your own desire to block Dolabella's consulship by
placing the blame on Caesar's treachery. The first of January arrived. We were summoned to a meeting of the senate, where Dolabella delivered a much more copious and
studied invective against Antonius than I am delivering
now. Good gods, what a speech Antonius made in anger!   80
To begin with, Caesar had made it clear that before leaving
Rome he would order the consulship to be conferred on
Dolabella—Caesar was always doing and saying that sort
of thing, and yet they deny that he was a monarch!—anyway, Caesar having so pronounced, this fine augur of ours
then stated that he was invested with a priestly office which
enabled him to hold up or invalidate the elections by
means of auspices, and he emphatically declared that this
was his intention. First, note the unbelievable stupidity of
the man. What do I mean? Well, if you were *not* an augur   81
and were truly a consul, would you have been any the less
able to do what you said you could do by your priestly prerogative? Surely you could have done it even more easily.
We augurs only possess the right to report an unfavorable
omen, whereas consuls and the rest of the magistrates also
have the right to look for omens. So be it; he made this
statement incompetently—after all, we cannot demand
expertise from a man who is never sober. But consider his
impudence: many months before the event, he stated in
the senate that he would either use the auspices to block
the assembly called to elect Dolabella, or do what in fact he
did.[94] Can anyone foretell a flaw in the auspices unless he

ciis futurum sit, nisi qui de caelo servare constituit? Quod
neque licet comitiis per leges et si qui servavit, non comitiis habitis sed prius quam habeantur, debet nuntiare. Verum implicata inscientia impudentia est: nec scit quod
augurem nec facit quod pudentem decet.

82   Itaque ex illo die recordamini eius usque ad Idus Martias consulatum. Quis umquam apparitor tam humilis, tam
abiectus? Nihil ipse poterat; omnia rogabat; caput in aver-
sam lecticam inserens, beneficia quae venderet a collega
petebat. [33] Ecce Dolabellae comitiorum dies. Sortitio
praerogativae: quiescit. Renuntiatur: tacet. Prima classis
vocatur [renuntiatur],[33] deinde, ita ut adsolet, suffragia,
tum secunda classis, quae omnia sunt citius facta quam

83   dixi. Confecto negotio bonus augur—C. Laelium diceres—"alio die" inquit. O impudentiam singularem! Quid
videras, quid senseras, quid audieras? Neque enim te de
caelo servasse dixisti nec hodie dicis. Id igitur obvenit vitium quod tu iam Kalendis Ianuariis futurum esse provi-
deras et tanto ante praedixeras. Ergo hercule magna, ut
spero, tua potius quam rei publicae calamitate ementitus
es auspicia; obstrinxisti religione populum Romanum; augur auguri, consul consuli obnuntiasti. Nolo plura, ne acta

---

[33] *del. Garatoni*

---

[95] One of the 35 centuries of *iuniores* in the first class was
selected by lot to cast its vote first.   [96] Twelve of the eigh-
teen centuries of knights voted with the first class, but the remaining six voted afterwards and recalled an earlier period when there
were only six centuries of knights in all, two from each of the old
clan tribes.   [97] C. Laelius Sapiens (cos. 140), friend of the
younger Scipio Africanus and a famous augur.

invalidating Dolabella's official acts, which one day will
have to be referred to our College. But look at the arro-   84
gance, the insolence of the fellow! So long as *you* wish,
Dolabella's consulship is flawed; then, the moment your
wishes change,[99] he was elected with the auspices in order.
If it means nothing when an augur makes an announcement in the terms in which you made yours, admit that you
were not sober when you said "Meeting adjourned." On
the other hand, if those terms have any force, as one augur
to another I ask you to tell me what it is.

So that my account does not inadvertently skip over the
single most brilliant of Marcus Antonius' many exploits, let
us come to the Feast of Lupercal. [34] He doesn't disguise
it, Members of the Senate; his agitation is evident; he
sweats, turns pale. Anything, as long as he doesn't do what
he did[100] in the Colonnade of Minucius! What possible defense can be offered for such disgraceful conduct? I am
anxious to hear it, to see where the plain of Leontini comes
into view.[101] Your colleague sat on the Rostra, wearing his   85
purple toga, on his golden chair, a garland on his head. Up
you come, you approach the chair, as a Lupercus—you
were a Lupercus, but you should have remembered that
you were a consul[102]—you display a diadem. Groans all
over the Forum! Where did the diadem come from? You
had not picked one up that had been cast aside, but you
had brought it with you from home, a planned, premedi-
tated crime. You tried to place the diadem on Caesar's
head amid the lamentations of the people: he kept refusing
it, and the people applauded. You had been urging Caesar

naked (§86) because priests on the board of Luperci wore nothing
but an apron or girdle made from the skin of a sacrificial goat.

Tu ergo unus, scelerate, inventus es qui, cum auctor regni
esses eumque quem collegam habebas dominum habere
velles, idem temptares quid populus Romanus ferre et pati
86 posset. At etiam misericordiam captabas: supplex te ad pedes abiciebas. Quid petens? Ut servires? Tibi uni peteres,
qui ita a puero vixeras ut omnia paterere, ut facile servires;
a nobis populoque Romano mandatum id certe non habebas. O praeclaram illam eloquentiam tuam cum es nudus
contionatus! Quid hoc turpius, quid foedius, quid suppli-
ciis omnibus dignius? Num exspectas dum te stimulis fo-
diamus? Haec te, si ullam partem habes sensus, lacerat,
haec cruentat oratio. Vereor ne imminuam summorum
virorum gloriam; dicam tamen dolore commotus: quid indignius quam vivere eum qui imposuerit diadema, cum
87 omnes fateantur iure interfectum esse qui abiecerit? At
etiam ascribi iussit in fastis ad Lupercalia C. CAESARI, DIC-
TATORI PERPETUO, M. ANTONIUM CONSULEM POPULI
IUSSU REGNUM DETULISSE, CAESAREM UTI NOLUISSE.
Iam iam minime miror te otium perturbare; non modo
urbem odisse sed etiam lucem; cum perditissimis latronibus non solum de die sed etiam in diem bibere. Ubi enim
tu in pace consistes? Qui locus tibi in legibus et in iudiciis esse potest, quae tu, quantum in te fuit, dominatu regio sustulisti? Ideone L. Tarquinius exactus, Sp. Cassius,

---

103 Cf. §§44–46.

104 A punishment fit for slaves.

105 Instead of "what is more unseemly than that he . . . is
alive?" (*quid indignius quam vivere eum*), Atticus suggested "it is
most unseemly that this man is alive" (*indignissimum est hunc
vivere*), and Cicero approved (*Att*. 16.11.2). However, the change
has not been made in the transmitted text.

to make himself king, you wanted him as a master instead
of a colleague, so you and only you, you criminal, were
found to make trial of what the Roman people could bear
and suffer. Why, you even tried pathos, throwing yourself 86
as a suppliant at his feet. What was your petition? To be
a slave? You should have petitioned for yourself alone,
who had lived in such a fashion from boyhood that you
were prepared to endure anything and happily accept servitude.[103] Assuredly you had no such commission from
us and from the Roman people. What a marvelously eloquent public speech you made—in the nude! What could
be more disgraceful, more loathsome, more worthy of all
manner of punishment than this? Are you waiting for us to
dig your flesh with goads?[104] If you have a trace of feeling,
these words of mine tear you, make you bleed. I fear that
what I am about to say may detract from the glory of our
greatest heroes, but indignation moves me to say it none
the less: what is more unseemly than that he who put on
the diadem is alive,[105] when all admit that he who thrust it
aside was rightly done to death! Why, he even gave orders 87
that the following notation be added to the calendar beside
the date of the Lupercalia: "To Gaius Caesar, dictator for
life, Marcus Antonius, consul, offered royal power by order of the people: Caesar declined." I am not the least bit
surprised any longer that quiet times unnerve you, that you
hate the city, even the light of day, that you not only drink
from early in the day with your crew of utterly wicked robbers but drink day after day. Where can you maintain your
footing in peacetime? What place for you can there be
among laws and law courts, which you, so far as in you lay,
abolished under monarchical rule? Was Lucius Tarqui-

⟨Sp. ⟩[37] Maelius, M. Manlius necati ut multis post saeculis
a M. Antonio, quod fas non est, rex Romae constitueretur?

88   [35] Sed ad auspicia redeamus, de quibus [rebus][38] Idibus Martiis fuit in senatu Caesar acturus. Quaero: tum
tu quid egisses? Audiebam equidem te paratum venisse,
quod me de ementitis auspiciis, quibus tamen parere necesse erat, putares esse dicturum. Sustulit illum diem Fortuna rei publicae. Num etiam tuum de auspiciis iudicium
interitus Caesaris sustulit? Sed incidi in id tempus quod eis
rebus in quas ingress⟨ur⟩a[39] erat oratio praevertendum
est. Quae tua fuga, quae formido praeclaro illo die, quae
propter conscientiam scelerum desperatio vitae, cum ex
illa fuga beneficio eorum qui te, si sanus esses, salvum esse

89   voluerunt, clam te domum recepisti! O mea frustra semper verissima auguria rerum futurarum! Dicebam illis in
Capitolio liberatoribus nostris, cum me ad te ire vellent ut
ad defendendam rem publicam te adhortarer, quoad me-
tueres, omnia te promissurum; simul ac timere desisses, similem te futurum tui. Itaque cum ceteri consulares irent
redirent, in sententia mansi: neque te illo die neque poste-
ro vidi neque ullam societatem optimis civibus cum impor-
tunissimo hoste foedere ullo confirmari posse credidi.

    Post diem tertium veni in aedem Telluris et quidem in-
90   vitus, cum omnis aditus armati obsiderent. Qui tibi dies
ille, Antoni, fuit! Quamquam mihi inimicus subito exstitis-

---

37 *n*²: *om. VD*   38 *del. Halm*: rebus Idibus *om. V*
39 *corr. SB*

---

106 On Cassius and Maelius, see §26, nn. 24–25; on Manlius,
1.32, n. 52.

nius driven out, were Spurius Cassius, Spurius Maelius, Marcus Manlius put to death,[106] in order that centuries later a king (blasphemous thought!) should be set up by Marcus Antonius in Rome?

[35] Let us, however, get back to the auspices, concern- 88 ing which Caesar was going to consult the senate on the fifteenth of March. I ask you: what would you have done then? I was indeed told that you had come prepared, because you thought that I would speak about the falsified auspices—which nonetheless had to be obeyed. The Fortune of the Republic cancelled the meeting that day. Did Caesar's death also cancel your judgment concerning the auspices? But I have come to a period of time that must be given precedence over the topics I was about to take up in my speech. You fled in panic on that glorious day, and in the consciousness of guilt you despaired of your life; but by favor of those who wished you to survive if you were of sound mind, you turned back from your flight and secretly retreated to your house. Ah, my prophecies of things to 89 come! Always true to the letter, always in vain! I told our liberators there in the Capitol, when they wanted me to go to you in order to urge you to defend the Republic, that you would promise anything as long as you were afraid, but as soon as you had lost your fear, you would be like your old self. So while other consulars went back and forth, I held to my opinion. I did not see you that day or the next, nor did I believe that any pact could cement an alliance between loyal citizens and a relentless public enemy.

Two days later I came into the Temple of Tellus, against my own inclination since armed men stood guarding every entrance. What a day that was for you, Antonius! Though 90 you have suddenly become my enemy, I pity you for being

ti, tamen me tui miseret quod tibi invideris. [36] Qui tu vir,
di immortales, et quantus fuisses, si illius diei mentem servare potuisses! Pacem haberemus, quae erat facta per ob-
sidem puerum nobilem, M. Bambalionis nepotem. Quamquam bonum te timor faciebat, non diuturnus magister
offici; improbum fecit ea quae, dum timor abest, a te non
discedit, audacia. Etsi tum, cum optimum te ‹multi›[40]
putabant me quidem dissentiente, funeri tyranni, si illud
91 funus fuit, sceleratissime praefuisti. Tua illa pulchra laudatio, tua miseratio, tua cohortatio; tu, tu, inquam, illas faces
incendisti, et eas quibus semustilatus ille est et eas quibus
incensa L. Bellieni domus deflagravit. Tu illos impetus
perditorum et ex maxima parte servorum quos nos vi
manuque reppulimus in nostras domos immisisti. Idem tamen quasi fuligine abstersa reliquis diebus in Capitolio
praeclara senatus consulta fecisti, ne qua post Idus Martias
immunitatis tabula neve cuius benefici figeretur. Meminis-
ti ipse de exsulibus, scis de immunitate quid dixeris. Optimum vero quod dictaturae nomen in perpetuum de re publica sustulisti: quo quidem facto tantum te cepisse odium
regni videbatur ut eius omnem [propter proximum dic-
92 tatorem][41] metum tolleres. Constituta res publica videbatur aliis, mihi vero nullo modo, qui omnia te gubernante

40 *suppl. SB*
    41 *del. SB*

---

    107 M. Fulvius Bambalio was the boy's maternal grandfather,
whom Cicero describes at 3.16 as "a person of no consequence."

    108 *Audacia* connotes lack of moral scruple.

    109 According to Suetonius (*Iul.* 84.2), Antony spoke only a
very few (*perpauca*) words of his own, but Cicero's statement sug-

your own worst enemy. [36] Immortal gods, what a man, and how great a man you would have been, if you could have maintained the frame of mind you were in that day! We would have peace, the peace made through a hostage, a boy of high descent, Marcus Bambalio's grandson.[107] But fear made you honest, and fear as the counselor of duty is short-lived; recklessness,[108] which never deserts you so long as fear is absent, made you disloyal. And yet even at that time, when many thought very well of you (I did not agree), you presided at the tyrant's funeral, if funeral it was, in a most criminal manner. That beautiful trib-   91
ute to the deceased, the pathos, the incitement—they were yours.[109] It was you, yes, you, who set light to the firebrands, both those with which Caesar was half-cremated, and those others which set fire to Lucius Bellienus' house and burned it down. It was you who directed those onslaughts of desperate characters, mostly slaves, against our houses, which we repelled by force of arms. And yet, in the days following, wiping off the soot as it were, you carried some admirable decrees of the senate in the Capitol, providing that after the fifteenth of March no record of an exemption or of any special grant be posted.[110] You yourself remember what you said about exiles, you know what you said about grants of exemption. Best of all, you removed the office of dictator from the Republic for all time. Thus it appeared that you had developed such a hatred of monarchy that you removed all fear of it. Oth-   92
ers thought the Republic had been reestablished, but I thought nothing of the kind, for I feared all manner of

gesting the contrary is supported by *Att*. 14.10.1 and later historians.   110 Cf. 1.3.

naufragia metuebam. Num igitur me fefellit, aut num
diutius sui potuit dissimilis esse? Inspectantibus vobis
toto Capitolio tabulae figebantur, neque solum singulis
veni[e]bant[42] immunitates sed etiam populis universis: civitas non iam singillatim, sed provinciis totis dabatur.
Itaque si haec manent, quae stante re publica manere non
possunt, provincias universas, patres conscripti, perdidistis, neque vectigalia solum sed etiam imperium populi Romani huius domesticis nundinis deminutum est.

93b[43]   [37] Sunt ea quidem innumerabilia quae a tuis eme-
bantur non insciente te, sed unum egregium de rege Deiotaro, populi Romani amicissimo, decretum in Capitolio
fixum: quo proposito nemo erat qui in ipso dolore risum
94 posse⟨t⟩[44] continere. Quis enim cuiquam inimicior quam
Deiotaro Caesar? Aeque atque huic ordini, ut equestri,
ut Massiliensibus, ut omnibus quibus rem publicam populi Romani caram esse sentiebat. Igitur a quo vivo nec
praesens nec absens rex Deiotarus quicquam aequi boni
impe⟨t⟩ravit,[45] apud mortuum factus est grat⟨ios⟩us.[46]
Compellarat hospitem praesens, computarat pecuniam

---

111 Cf. 1.24.
112 §§93b–96 dropped out of an ancestor of all our extant
manuscripts and was later restored to the branch of the tradition from which V is descended slightly out of order, displacing
three sentences (§93a) that should logically come after §96, while
§§93b–96 make a natural sequel to §92.

shipwreck with you at helm. Well, was I wrong? Could he be unlike himself for any length of time? Before your very eyes, gentlemen, official notices were put up all over the Capitol, and not only to individuals but to whole peoples exemptions from taxes were sold; citizenship was given no longer to one person at a time but to whole provinces.[111] If these measures stand, as stand they cannot unless the Republic falls, you, Members of the Senate, have lost entire provinces; not revenues only but the very empire of the Roman people has been whittled down in Antonius' private market.

[37] There is no counting the items bought from persons close to you[113] not without your knowledge, but one stands out: the decree posted on the Capitol concerning King Deiotarus, that faithful friend of the Roman people. When it was put up, nobody could help laughing in the midst of his indignation. For who ever had a worse enemy than Caesar was to Deiotarus, who was hated as much as Caesar hated this body, or the order of knights, or the people of Massilia,[114] or all those to whom he felt the Republic of the Roman people was precious. And so King Deiotarus came into favor with a dead man from whom, when that man was alive, Deiotarus obtained no justice or fair treatment either when he was with Caesar or apart from him. When Deiotarus was his host, Caesar had rebuked him in person, had reckoned a sum, had planted one of his Greek

93b[112]

94

---

113 Fulvia: cf. the reference to the women's apartments (*gynaecium*) below, §95.   114 The Greek colony of Massilia (Marseilles), which wished to remain neutral in the Civil War, was taken by Caesar's forces in October 49 and subjected to sanctions and the loss of territory (8.18–19; 13.32).

CICERO

[impetrarat],[47] in eius tetrarchia unum ex Graecis comiti-
bus suis collocarat, Armeniam abstulerat a se‹na›tu[48] da-
95 tam. Haec vivus eripuit, reddit mortuus. At quibus verbis!
Modo aequum sibi videri, modo non iniquum. Mira verbo-
rum comple‹xio›![49] At ille ‹n›umquam[50]—semper enim
absenti adfui Deiotaro—quicquam sibi quod nos pro illo
postularemus aequum dixit videri. Syngrapha sesterti cen-
tiens per legatos, viros bonos sed timidos et imperitos, sine
‹no›stra,[51] sine reliquorum hospitum regis ‹sententia›[52]
facta in gynaecio est, quo in loco plurimae res venierunt et
veneunt. Qua ex syngrapha quid sis acturus meditere censeo: rex enim ipse sua sponte, nullis commentariis Caesaris, simul atque audivit eius interitum, suo Marte res suas
96 recuperavit. Sciebat homo sapiens ius semper hoc fuisse
ut, quae tyranni eripuissent, ea tyrannis interfectis ei quibus erepta essent recuperarent. Nemo igitur iure[is][53]
consultus, ne iste quidem, qui tibi uni est iure consultus,
per quem haec agis, ex ista syngrapha deberi dicet pro eis
rebus quae erant ante syngrapham recuperatae. Non enim
a te emit, sed prius quam tu suum sibi vendere‹s›[54] ipse

47 *del. Clark*   48 *corr. Poggius*   49 *corr. Poggius*
50 *corr. Poggius*   51 *corr. Muretus*
52 *add.* V[2]   53 *corr. Poggius*   54 *corr. Poggius*

115 Mithridates of Pergamum, an adventurer to whom Caesar
granted territory in eastern Galatia, a tetrarchy Deiotarus had
managed to seize temporarily during the confusion caused by the
Civil War.
116 I.e., Armenia Minor, a region south of the eastern end of
the Black Sea (in mod. Turkey).

146

companions in Deiotarus' tetrarchy,[115] had deprived him of Armenia,[116] which had been given by the senate. All this he took away in his lifetime and returns after his death! And in what terms! Sometimes "it seems fair" to him, sometimes "it seems not unfair." A remarkable turn of phrase! But Caesar never said that anything *we* asked of him on Deiotarus' behalf "seemed fair"—I know, for I always appeared for Deiotarus in his absence. A bond for ten million sesterces was signed by envoys, worthy men but timid and inexperienced, without my approval or that of the king's other friends in Rome. The document was signed in the women's apartments, where a great many things have been sold and are being sold. I advise you[117] to consider well what action you are going to take on that bond. For the king himself, of his own volition and without any memoranda of Caesar's, recovered his possessions with his own military might as soon as he heard the news of Caesar's death. He knew in his wisdom that it has ever been lawful for those whose possessions have been seized by tyrants to recover them after the tyrants have been killed. No jurist, not even that person[118] whom only you believe to be a jurist, through whom you are conducting this business, will say that payment is due on that bond for items which had been recovered before the bond was signed. Deiotarus did not buy from you, but before you could sell him his own property, he took possession him-

95

96

---

[117] Cicero suddenly addresses Antony.
[118] Possibly P. Alfenus Varus (suff. cos. 39), a pupil of the jurist Ser. Sulpicius, and a prominent figure in assisting the Triumvirs in settling veterans on confiscated land.

possedit. Ille vir fuit; nos quidem contemnendi, qui auctorem odimus, acta defendimus.

93a⁵⁵   Ubi est septiens miliens quod est in tabulis quae sunt ad Opis? Funestae illius quidem pecuniae, sed tamen quae nos, si eis quorum erat non redderetur, a tributis posset vindicare. Tu autem quadringentiens sestertium quod Idibus Martiis debuisti quonam modo ante Kalendas Aprilis debere desisti?

97   [38] Quid ego de commentariis infinitis, quid de innumerabilibus chirographis loquar? Quorum etiam institores sunt qui ea tamquam gladiatorum libellos palam venditent. Itaque tanti acervi nummorum apud istum construuntur ut iam expendantur, non numerentur pecuniae. At quam caeca avaritia est! Nuper fixa tabula est qua civitates locupletissimae Cretensium vectigalibus liberantur, statuiturque ne post M. Brutum pro consule sit Creta provincia. Tu mentis compos, tu non constringendus? An Caesaris decreto Creta post M. Bruti decessum potuit liberari, cum Creta nihil ad Brutum Caesare vivo pertineret? At huius venditione decreti, ne nihil actum putetis, provinciam Cretam perdidistis. Omnino nemo ullius rei fuit emptor cui defuerit hic venditor.

98   Et de exsulibus legem quam fixisti Caesar tulit? Nullius insector calamitatem: tantum queror, primum eorum redi-

---

⁵⁵ ubi est . . . desisti *(2.93a) post 2.96 transp. Nägelsbach*

---

¹¹⁹ Strictly speaking, of course, Caesar was not the "author" of the acts just discussed, but because Antony alone had access to Caesar's private papers (1.16–18), it was impossible to impugn the authorship.   ¹²⁰ See n. 112 above.   ¹²¹ Cf. 1.17, n. 34.

¹²² Roman citizens had not been required to pay tribute since

self. He behaved like a man; but we deserve contempt, who hate the author but defend his acts.[119]

Where is the seven hundred million which is recorded in the account books kept at the Temple of Ops? That money has an evil history to be sure,[121] but if it was not going to be returned to its owners it could save us from having to pay levies.[122] As for you, how was it that before the first of April you ceased to owe the forty million sesterces that you owed on the fifteenth of March? 93a[120]

[38] What am I to say about the endless memoranda, the innumerable handwritten documents? There are actually peddlers who sell them openly like programs for the gladiators. Such great heaps of coin are built up at Antonius' house that the money is no longer counted but weighed. But how blind avarice is! An official notice was lately posted exempting the richest communities in Crete from taxation and decreeing that after the proconsulship of Marcus Brutus, Crete shall cease to be a province. Are you in your right mind? Should you not be in a straitjacket? Could Crete be freed at the end of Marcus Brutus' term as governor by an order of Caesar's, when Crete had nothing to do with Brutus in Caesar's lifetime? By the sale of this order, in case you gentlemen imagine that nothing has happened, you have lost the province of Crete. To sum it up, Antonius has been ready to sell anything to anybody who was ready to buy. 97

Again, did Caesar pass the law that you posted up concerning exiles? I do not seek to add to the misery of any man's misfortune. I merely complain, first, that a taint has 98

its suspension in 167, but the growing financial crisis caused it to be reinstated in 43.

CICERO

tus inquinatos quorum causam Caesar dissimilem iudicarit; deinde nescio cur non reliquis idem tribuas: neque enim plus quam tres aut quattuor reliqui sunt. Qui simili in calamitate sunt, cur tua misericordia non simili fruuntur, cur eos habes in loco patrui? De quo ferre, cum de reliquis ferres, noluisti: quem etiam ad censuram petendam impulisti, eamque petitionem comparasti quae et risus hominum et querelas moveret. Cur autem ea comitia non habuisti? An quia tribunus plebis sinistrum fulmen nuntiabat? Cum tua quid interest, nulla auspicia sunt; cum tuorum, tum fis religiosus. Quid? Eundem in septemviratu nonne destituisti? Intervenit enim cui metuisti, credo, ne salvo capite negare non posses! Omnibus eum contumeliis onerasti quem patris loco, si ulla in te pietas esset, colere debebas. Filiam eius, sororem tuam, eiecisti, alia condicione quaesita et ante perspecta. Non est satis: probri insimulasti pudicissimam feminam. Quid est quod addi possit? Contentus eo non fuisti: frequentissimo senatu Kalendis Ianuariis sedente patruo hanc tibi esse cum Dolabella causam odi dicere ausus es quod ab eo sorori et uxori tuae stuprum esse oblatum comperisses. Quis interpretari

99

---

123 Nothing came of this candidacy in 44, but the Triumvirs later caused C. Antonius (Hybrida) to be elected censor for 42.

124 Lightning from any direction automatically caused an assembly to be dissolved. By specifying "on the left" (normally a favorable quarter), Cicero may be implying that Antony is not a very skilled augur.

125 Set up by Antony and Dolabella to distribute land among Caesar's veterans and needy citizens. Cicero implies that C. Antonius was led to expect appointment to this board but then was cast aside in favor of another.

been placed upon the returns of those whose cases Caesar judged to be dissimilar; second, I don't know why you are not doing as much for the rest—for not more than three or four exiles still remain. Why should persons in like misfortune not benefit alike from your compassion? Why do you treat them as you treated your uncle? You chose to leave him out when you put through your law about the others. You also prompted him to stand for the censorship, getting up a candidature that evoked general mirth and general protest.[123] And why did you not hold that election? Was it because a tribune of the plebs announced lightning on the left?[124] When it is you whose interests are concerned, the auspices mean nothing, but when it is your relations, then you develop religious scruples. Well? Did you not also let him down in the matter of the Board of Seven?[125] Somebody unexpectedly came along to whom, I suppose, it was more than your life was worth to say no? You have heaped all manner of insults on your uncle, whom you should have treated like a surrogate father, if you had any family feeling. You turned his daughter, your cousin,[126] out of your house after you had looked for and investigated in advance another match. That wasn't enough for you: you accused her, a lady of the utmost propriety, of immoral conduct. How much further could you go? Still not satisfied, at a full meeting of the senate, on the first of January, in your uncle's presence, you dared to allege as the reason for your hatred of Dolabella that you had discovered his adultery with your cousin and wife. Who can decide which was the

99

126 Antony's first wife Antonia, whom he divorced to marry Fulvia, with whom Cicero implies that Antony was already carrying on an affair.

potest, impudentiorne qui in senatu, an improbior qui in
Dolabellam, an impurior qui patre audiente, an crudelior
qui in illam miseram tam spurce, tam impie dixeris?

100   [39] Sed ad chirographa redeamus. Quae tua fuit cognitio? Acta enim Caesaris pacis causa confirmata sunt a
senatu: quae quidem Caesar egisset, non ea quae egisse
Caesarem dixisset Antonius. Unde ista erumpunt, quo
auctore proferuntur? Si sunt falsa, cur probantur? Si vera,
cur veneunt? At sic placuerat ut ex Kalendis Iuniis de Caesaris actis cum consilio cognosceretis. Quod fuit consilium,
quem umquam advocasti, quas Kalendas Iunias exspectas-
ti? An eas ad quas te peragratis veteranorum coloniis stipa-
tum armis rettulisti?

    O praeclaram illam percursationem tuam mense Aprili
atque Maio, tum cum etiam Capuam coloniam deducere
conatus es! Quem ad modum illim abieris vel potius paene
101 non abieris scimus. Cui tu urbi minitaris. Utinam conere,
ut aliquando illud "paene" tollatur! At quam nobilis est tua
illa peregrinatio! Quid prandiorum apparatus, quid furio-
sam vinolentiam tuam proferam? Tua ista detrimenta sunt,
illa nostra: agrum Campanum, qui cum de vectigalibus

127 *Att*. 16.16C.2 (of July 44) indicates that an advisory board
was in fact formed and assisted the consuls in deciding which of
Caesar's intended acts were worthy of being implemented.

128 From *c*. 25 April until late May, Antony was engaged in settling Caesar's veterans on land in Campania so as to remove them
from Rome, where they posed a threat to stable conditions.

129 Antony tried to plant a colony at Capua that would have
encroached on the territory of an existing colony. Cicero had been
consulted by Antony and advised against it (§102). Antony and his
new colonists were roughly handled (12.7).

more extraordinary, your impudence in saying such a thing in the senate, your rascality in accusing Dolabella, your caddishness in doing so in your uncle's hearing, or your cruelty in making such a filthy, outrageous charge against the unfortunate woman?

[39] But to get back to the handwritten documents: 100 what review did you conduct? Caesar's acts were confirmed by the senate for the sake of peace—that is, what Caesar had actually done, not what Antonius claimed Caesar had done. Where do these handwritten documents spring from, on whose authority are they produced? If they are forgeries, why are they approved? If genuine, why are they being sold? But it had been decided that you and your colleague with a board of assessors should scrutinize Caesar's acts, commencing the first of June. What was the board; whom did you ever summon as an advisor; which first of June did you wait for?[127] Was it the one on which you returned with a bodyguard of armed men after your tour of the veterans' colonies?[128]

What a marvelous junket you made in April and May, at which time you attempted to establish a colony at Capua! We know how you got away from that place, or rather almost failed to get away.[129] Now you make threats against 101 Capua. If only you'd make the attempt so that the word "almost" might be eliminated! But how glorious is your traveling about! Why should I bring up the finery of your luncheons, your frenzied drunkenness? All that was at your expense, but it was at ours when you went about dividing the Campanian land between your lunch companions and gaming partners. Why, when that land was taken

eximebatur ut militibus daretur, tamen infligi magnum rei publicae vulnus putabamus, hunc tu compransoribus tuis et collusoribus dividebas. Mimos dico et mimas, patres conscripti, in agro Campano collocatos. Quid iam querar de agro Leontino? Quoniam quidem hae quondam arationes Campana et Leontina in populi Romani patrimonio grandiferae et fructuosae ferebantur. Medico tria milia iugerum: quid si te sanasset? Rhetori duo: quid si te disertum facere potuisset? Sed ad iter Italiamque redeamus.

102 [40] Deduxisti coloniam Casilinum, quo Caesar ante deduxerat. Consuluisti me per litteras de Capua tu quidem, sed idem de Casilino respondissem: possesne, ubi colonia esset, eo coloniam novam iure deducere. Negavi in eam coloniam quae esset auspicato deducta, dum esset incolumis, coloniam novam iure deduci: colonos novos ascribi posse rescripsi. Tu autem insolentia elatus omni auspiciorum iure turbato Casilinum coloniam deduxisti, quo erat paucis annis ante deducta, ut vexillum tolleres, ut aratrum circumduceres; cuius quidem vomere portam Capuae paene perstrinxisti, ut florentis coloniae territorium minueretur.

103 Ab hac perturbatione religionum advolas in M. Varronis, sanctissimi atque integerrimi viri, fundum Casinatem. Quo iure, quo ore? "Eodem," inquies, "quo in heredum L.

---

130 By Caesar in 59 and again in 45.   131 Antony's doctor was perhaps Antonius Musa (so John D. Morgan per litteras), famous later for curing Augustus in 23; the rhetorician is Sex. Clodius (cf. §43). These two grants accounted for nearly one-sixth of the whole Leontine Plain.   132 A *vexillum* served as the traditional marker of a new colony, recalling an earlier period when colonies were founded for defensive purposes.

out of the revenues in order to give it to the soldiers,[130] even that we thought a serious wound inflicted on the Republic. I tell you, Members of the Senate, that mime actors and mime actresses have been settled on Campanian land. Why should I protest concerning the plain of Leontini? Because, of course, these arable lands of Campania and Leontini were once considered part of the patrimony of the Roman people, heavy-yielding and highly profitable. Three thousand *iugera* for your doctor: what would have been his reward, if he had made you sane? Two for your teacher of rhetoric: what if he had been able to make you a good public speaker?[131] But let us return to your journey and to Italy. [40] You founded a colony at Casilinum, where Caesar had founded one previously. You wrote asking my opinion—about Capua, it is true, whether you could legally found a new colony where there was one already; but I would have given the same answer about Casilinum. I informed you it was not legal for a new colony to be founded where there was a previous foundation, duly established with auspices, so long as it was still intact; but new colonists could be enrolled. However, in your insolent euphoria you swept aside regulations governing the auspices and founded a colony at Casilinum, where one had been founded a few years previously, so that you might erect a military banner[132] and mark out the boundaries with the plow. Indeed, you almost grazed the town gate of Capua with that plowshare so as to diminish the territory of that thriving colony.

After this disruption of religious principle, you dash off to a country estate near Casinum belonging to Marcus Varro, a gentleman of unblemished life and character. By what right? With what effrontery? "Why, the same," you

102

103

155

Rubri, quo in heredum L. Turseli praedia, quo in reliquas innumerabilis possessiones." Et si ab hasta, valeat hasta, valeant tabulae, modo Caesaris, non tuae, quibus debuisti, non quibus tu te liberavisti. Varronis quidem Casinatem fundum quis venisse dicit, quis hastam istius venditionis vidit, quis vocem praeconis audivit? Misisse te dicis Alexandriam qui emeret a Caesare; ipsum enim exspectare magnum fuit. Quis vero audivit umquam—nullius autem salus curae pluribus fuit—de fortunis Varronis rem ullam esse detractam? Quid? Si etiam scripsit ad te Caesar ut redderes, quid satis potest dici de tanta impudentia? Remove gladios parumper illos quos videmus: iam intelleges aliam causam esse hastae Caesaris, aliam confidentiae et temeritatis tuae. Non enim te dominus modo illis sedibus sed quivis amicus, vicinus, hospes, procurator arcebit. [41] At quam multos dies in ea villa turpissime es perbacchatus! Ab hora tertia bibebatur, ludebatur, vomebatur. O tecta ipsa misera, "quam dispari domino"—quamquam quo modo iste dominus?—sed tamen quam ab dispari tenebantur! Studiorum enim suorum ‹receptaculum›⁵⁶ M. Varro voluit illud, non libidinum deversorium. Quae in illa villa antea dicebantur, quae cogitabantur, quae litteris

104

105

---

⁵⁶ *suppl. SB*

---

¹³³ The text incorporates a revision recommended to Cicero by Atticus (*Att*. 16.11.2). In an earlier draft, Cicero had compared the seizure of Varro's property with Antony's occupation of Metellus Scipio's villa at Tibur, but Scipio's property was a much less apt example because it had been confiscated by Caesar and sold to Antony at auction. On Rubrius and Turselius, cf. §§40–41.

¹³⁴ Cf. §64, n. 72.

will say, "as when I invaded the lands of Lucius Rubrius'
heirs, and of Lucius Turselius' heirs, and countless other
properties."[133] And if you got it at a public auction, let that
stand, let the records stand: but let them be Caesar's, not
yours, records of what you owed, not those by which you
got out of debt. But as for Varro's property near Casinum,
who says that it was sold? Who saw the lance[134] at such a
sale or heard the voice of an auctioneer? You say you sent
an agent to Alexandria to buy it from Caesar—it would
have been too inconvenient, no doubt, to wait for Caesar in
person. But who ever heard—and no man had a larger   104
number of concerned well-wishers—that any of Varro's
possessions was taken away from him? What if Caesar actually wrote to you directing you to return the property?
What can be said to match such colossal impudence? Remove for a few minutes those weapons which we behold,
and you will soon realize that the status of Caesar's auctions is one thing, your rash assurance another. Not only
the property owner but any friend or neighbor or guest or
agent will keep you away from that residence. [41] But how
many days did you spend disgracefully carousing in that
villa! From eight o'clock in the morning there was drinking, gambling, vomiting. I pity the very building. "How different an owner"[135]—not that Antonius *was* the owner—
but still, how different was the man who occupied that
property! Marcus Varro intended it to be a retreat for his   105
studies, not a den of vice. Think of what previously used to
be spoken and thought and committed to writing in that

---

135 From an unknown play, quoted at greater length in *Off.*
1.139: "O ancient house, alas how different an owner owns you
now!"

mandabantur! Iura populi Romani, monumenta maiorum,
omnis sapientiae ratio omnisque doctrinae. At vero te in-
quilino—non enim domino—personabant omnia vocibus
ebriorum, natabant pavimenta vino, madebant parietes,
ingenui pueri cum meritoriis, scorta inter matres familias
versabantur. Casino salutatum veniebant, Aquino, Interamna: admissus est nemo. Iure id quidem; in homine
enim turpissimo obsolefiebant dignitatis insignia.

106   Cum inde Romam proficiscens ad Aquinum accederet,
obviam ei processit, ut est frequens municipium, magna
sane multitudo. At iste operta lectica latus per oppidum est
ut mortuus. Stulte Aquinates: sed tamen in via habitabant.
Quid Anagnini? Qui, cum essent devii, descenderunt ut
istum, tamquam si esset consul, salutarent. Incredibile
dictu, sed †cum vinus† inter omnis constabat neminem
esse resalutatum, praesertim cum duos secum Anagninos
haberet, Mustelam et Laconem, quorum alter gladiorum
107   est princeps, alter poculorum. Quid ego illas istius minas
contumeliasque commemorem quibus invectus est in Si-
dicinos, vexavit Puteolanos, quod C. Cassium et Brutos
patronos adoptassent? Magno quidem studio, iudicio, benevolentia, caritate, non, ut te et Basilum, vi et armis, et
alios vestri similis quos clientis nemo habere velit, non
modo illorum cliens esse.

[42] Interea dum tu abes, qui dies ille collegae tuo fuit,

---

136 In an earlier draft shared with Atticus, Cicero had failed to
specify these two names, prompting Atticus to ask who they were
(*Att.* 16.11.3).
137 *Patronus* of Picenum and of the Sabines, and looked upon
with scorn by Cicero (*Off.* 3.74).

villa: the laws of the Roman people, the achievements of our ancestors, a systematic treatment of all philosophy, of all learning. But when *you* were its tenant—not its owner—every room echoed with the shouts of drunkards, the pavements swam with wine, the walls were wet with it, boys of free birth mingled with child prostitutes, harlots with married ladies. From Casinum and Aquinum and Interamna people came to pay their respects, but nobody was let inside—properly enough, for the symbols of rank were degraded in so utterly disgraceful a person.

When he departed from there for Rome and approached Aquinum, a pretty large crowd came out to meet him, as might be expected from a populous town. But he was carried through the streets in a closed litter like a dead man. It was foolish of the people of Aquinum, but they did live on the highway. What about the inhabitants of Anagnia? Although they were at a distance from Antony's route, nonetheless, they came down to pay their respects as though he were a consul. It is amazing to report, but it is agreed by all that nobody's greeting was returned—even though he had two native sons of Anagnia with him, Mustela and Laco, one a master swordsman, the other a master drinker.[136] I need not relate the threats and insults with which he spoke harshly against the people of Sidicinum and persecuted the people of Puteoli because they had chosen Gaius Cassius and the Bruti as their patrons. This they did out of their great liking, approval, goodwill, and affection, not under pressure of armed force, as this honor has been conferred on you and Basilus[137] and others like you, whom nobody would want to have as clients, let alone to be a client of theirs.

[42] Meanwhile in your absence, what a glorious day

106

107

cum illud quod venerari solebas bustum in foro evertit!
Qua re tibi nuntiata, ut constabat inter eos qui una fuerunt,
concidisti. Quid evenerit postea nescio; metum credo va-
luisse et arma; collegam quidem de caelo detraxisti effecis-
tique non tu quidem etiam nunc ut similis tui, sed certe ut
dissimilis esset sui.

108   Qui vero inde reditus Romam, quae perturbatio totius
urbis! Memineramus Cinnam nimis potentem, Sullam
postea dominantem, modo Caesarem regnantem videra-
mus. Erant fortasse gladii, sed absconditi nec ita multi.
Ista vero quae et quanta barbaria est! Agmine quadrato
cum gladiis sequuntur; scutorum lecticas portari videmus. Atque his quidem iam inveteratis, patres conscripti,
consuetudine obduruimus. Kalendis Iuniis cum in senatum, ut erat constitutum, venire vellemus, metu perterriti
109   repente diffugimus. At iste, qui senatu non egeret, neque
desideravit quemquam et potius discessu nostro laetatus
est statimque illa mirabilia facinora effecit. Qui chirographa Caesaris defendisset lucri sui causa, is leges Caesaris easque praeclaras, ut rem publicam concutere posset, evertit. Numerum annorum provinciis prorogavit;
idemque, cum actorum Caesaris defensor esse deberet, et
in publicis et in privatis rebus acta Caesaris rescidit. In publicis nihil est lege gravius; in privatis firmissimum est testamentum. Leges alias sine promulgatione sustulit, alias
ut tolleret promulgavit. Testamentum irritum fecit, quod

that was for your colleague when he demolished the tomb in the Forum, which you used to revere! When that was reported to you, according to the general agreement of those who were with you at the time, you collapsed. What happened later I do not know; I imagine fear and weapons prevailed. At any rate you dragged your colleague down from the heights and made him—not indeed like yourself even now, but certainly unlike himself.

Then there was your return to Rome: the whole city 108 turned upside down! We remembered the excessive power of Cinna, and the despotism of Sulla which followed, latterly we had seen Caesar's monarchy. There were weapons perhaps, but hidden and not so numerous. But what an uncivilized, monstrous display yours is—men armed with swords follow you in battle order; we see litters full of shields being carried about. All this has become a thing of habit, Members of the Senate. Custom has made us callous. On the first of June, when we wished to enter the senate as it had been arranged, we took sudden flight in terror. Antonius, since he had no need of the senate, re- 109 gretted nobody's absence; rather he was pleased to see us disperse and immediately carried out those amazing deeds of his. Having defended Caesar's handwritten documents for his own gain, he proceeded to overturn Caesar's laws, excellent laws, in order to undermine the Republic. He extended the tenure of provincial office; and though he ought to have been the defender of Caesar's acts, he actually rescinded Caesar's acts in matters both public and private. In public affairs, nothing has greater weight than a law. In private life, the thing with the greatest validity is a will. As for laws, he annulled some without notice and gave notice of his intention to annul others; and he nullified

etiam infimis civibus semper obtentum est. Signa, tabulas, quas populo Caesar una cum hortis legavit, eas hic partim in hortos Pompei deportavit, partim in villam Scipionis.

110   [43] Et tu in Caesaris memoria diligens, tu illum amas mortuum? Quem is honorem maiorem consecutus erat quam ut haberet pulvinar, simulacrum, fastigium, flaminem? Est ergo flamen, ut Iovi, ut Marti, ut Quirino, sic divo Iulio M. Antonius. Quid igitur cessas? Cur non inauguraris? Sume diem, vide qui te inauguret: collegae sumus; nemo negabit. O detestabilem hominem, sive quod tyranni sacerdos es sive quod mortui! Quaero deinceps num hodiernus dies qui sit ignores. Nescis heri quartum in circo diem ludorum Romanorum fuisse, te autem ipsum ad populum tulisse ut quintus praeterea dies Caesari tribueretur? Cur non sumus praetextati? Cur honorem Caesaris tua lege datum deseri patimur? An supplicationes addendo diem contaminari passus es, pulvinaria contaminari noluisti? Aut undique religionem tolle aut usque quaque

111 conserva. Quaeris placeatne mihi pulvinar esse, fastigium, flaminem. Mihi vero nihil istorum placet: sed tu, qui acta Caesaris defendis, quid potes dicere cur alia defendas, alia non cures? Nisi forte vis fateri te omnia quaestu tuo, non illius dignitate metiri. Quid ad haec tandem? Exspecto

---

138 At the ceremony of the *lectisternium*, images of the gods were borne on couches (*pulvinaria*). As part of his recognition as "Divus Iulius," Caesar was granted all the trappings of godhead enumerated in this passage.

139 On his house, his official residence as Pontifex Maximus, as regularly on temples.   140 I.e. an augur.

141 The final stage of the *Ludi Romani*, lasting from 15 to 18 September in Cicero's time.   142 Cf. 1.12–13.

Caesar's will, yet a will traditionally has always kept its validity even for the humblest. The statues and paintings which Caesar bequeathed to the people along with his suburban estate, those objects Antonius removed, partly to Pompeius' estate, partly to Scipio's villa.

[43] And are *you* looking after Caesar's memory, do 110 you love him in his grave? What greater honor had Caesar attained than to have a sacred couch,[138] an image, a gable,[139] a special priest? Just as Jupiter and Mars and Quirinus have their priests, so the divine Julius has Marcus Antonius. Why do you delay then? Why are you not inaugurated? Choose a date, choose someone[140] to inaugurate you. We are your colleagues, nobody will refuse. Abominable creature, whether because you are the priest of a tyrant or of a dead man! Next I ask whether you are unaware what day it is today. Don't you know that yesterday was the fourth day of the chariot races at the Roman Games[141] and that you yourself put a law through an assembly of the people providing for a fifth day to be added in Caesar's honor? Why are we not in our holiday clothes? Why do we let the honor granted Caesar by your law be omitted? Perhaps you allowed public thanksgivings to be polluted by adding a day[142] but did not want pollution to sully the sacred couches? Either abolish religion altogether or preserve it in every possible respect. You ask whether I approve of the 111 sacred couch, the gable, the special priest. Certainly not, none of it has my approval. But you, who are the defender of Caesar's acts, how can you explain your defense of some acts and indifference to others? Unless perhaps you are willing to admit that you measure everything by your own profit, not Caesar's honor. Well, what have you to say to all

enim eloquentiam. Disertissimum cognovi avum tuum, at te etiam apertiorem in dicendo. Ille numquam nudus est contionatus: tuum hominis simplicis pectus vidimus. Respondebisne ad haec, aut omnino hiscere audebis? Ecquid reperies ex tam longa oratione mea cui te respondere posse confidas?

112   [44] Sed praeterita omittamus: hunc unum diem, unum, inquam, hodiernum diem, hoc punctum temporis, quo loquor, defende, si potes. Cur armatorum corona senatus saeptus est, cur me tui satellites cum gladiis audiunt, cur valvae Concordiae non patent, cur homines omnium gentium maxime barbaros, Ituraeos, cum sagittis deducis in forum? Praesidi sui causa se facere dicit. Non igitur miliens perire est melius quam in sua civitate sine armatorum praesidio non posse vivere? Sed nullum est istuc, mihi crede, praesidium: caritate te et benevolentia civium saep-

113 tum oportet esse, non armis. Eripiet et extorquebit tibi ista populus Romanus, utinam salvis nobis! Sed quoquo modo nobiscum egeris, dum istis consiliis uteris, non potes, mihi crede, esse diuturnus. Etenim ista tua minime avara coniunx, quam ego sine contumelia describo, nimium diu debet populo Romano tertiam pensionem. Habet populus Romanus ad quos gubernacula rei publicae deferat: qui ubicumque terrarum sunt, ibi omne est rei publicae praesidium vel potius ipsa res publica, quae se adhuc tantum modo ulta est, nondum recuperavit. Habet quidem certe

---

143 *Apertum pectus* (lit. "an open breast or heart"), a proverbial term for candor, is used here in its literal sense to allude to Antony's scant clothing when he appeared at the Lupercalia (cf. §86).

144 Allusion to the violent deaths of Fulvia's two previous husbands; cf. §11.

this? I await a display of eloquence. I knew your grandfather to be eloquent in speaking, but I know you to be
even more *open*. He never addressed a public meeting in
the nude, whereas you, plain honest fellow that you are,
have let us see your torso.[143] Will you reply to all this, will
you dare so much as to open your mouth? Will you find any
point in this long speech of mine which you will feel confident of being able to answer?

[44] But let us leave aside what is past. This one day, this
day that is now present, this point of time in which I speak:
defend it if you can. Why is the senate surrounded by a circle of armed men, why do your henchmen hear me with
their swords in hand, why are the doors of the Temple of
Concord not open, why do you bring into the Forum the
most barbarous men of all nations, Ituraeans, with arrows?
He says he does it for his protection. Is it not better to die a
thousand deaths than to be unable to live in one's own
community without an armed guard? But believe me, that
is no protection. You should be fenced around by the love
and goodwill of your countrymen, not by weapons. The
Roman people will take those weapons of yours from you,
wrench them out of your hands; I pray that we do not perish in the process. But however you deal with us, believe
me, so long as you continue in your present course, you
cannot last long. And indeed, that least acquisitive of ladies, your wife, whom I depict without insult, for too long
has been owing her third installment to the Roman people.[144] The Roman people has men to whom it can commit
the helm of the Republic. Wherever in the world they are,
there is the entire defense of the Republic, or rather, there
is the Republic itself, which so far has only avenged itself,
not regained itself. Yes, assuredly the Republic has cham-

112

113

res publica adulescentis nobilissimos paratos defensores. Quam volent illi cedant otio consulentes; tamen a re publica revocabuntur.

Et nomen pacis dulce est et ipsa res salutaris; sed inter pacem et servitutem plurimum interest. Pax est tranquilla libertas, servitus postremum malorum omnium, non modo bello sed morte etiam repellendum. Quod si se ipsos illi nostri liberatores e conspectu nostro abstulerunt, at exemplum facti reliquerunt. Illi quod nemo fecerat fecerunt. Tarquinium Brutus bello est persecutus, qui tum rex fuit cum esse Romae regem licebat; Sp. Cassius, Sp. Maelius, M. Manlius propter suspicionem regni appetendi sunt necati: hi primum cum gladiis non in regnum appetentem, sed in regnantem impetum fecerunt. Quod cum ipsum factum per se praeclarum est atque divinum, tum expositum ad imitandum est, praesertim cum illi eam gloriam consecuti sint quae vix caelo capi posse videatur. Etsi enim satis in ipsa conscientia pulcherrimi facti fructus erat, tamen mortali immortalitatem non arbitror esse contemnendam.

[45] Recordare igitur illum, M. Antoni, diem quo dictaturam sustulisti; pone ante oculos laetitiam senatus populique Romani, confer cum hac nundinatione tua tuorumque: tum intelleges quantum inter lucrum et laudem intersit. Sed nimirum, ut quidam morbo aliquo et sensus stupore suavitatem cibi non sentiunt, sic libidinosi, avari, facinerosi verae laudis gustatum non habent. Sed si te laus adlicere ad recte faciendum non potest, ne metus quidem

---

145 Cf. n. 106 above.
146 Cf. n. 113 above.

even fear deter you from the foulest offenses? You do not
fear the courts. Fine, if innocence is the reason; but if you
rely on violence, don't you realize what must be feared by a
person who neutralizes his fear of the courts in that way? If   116
you do not fear brave men and loyal citizens because they
are kept away from your person by weapons, your own followers, believe me, will not put up with you for long.[147]
And what sort of a life is that, day and night to be afraid
of one's own followers? Unless, of course, you have men
bound to you by greater acts of kindness than Caesar did in
the case of some of those who killed him; or unless you are
to be compared to him in any way. Caesar had talent, the
ability to reason, a retentive memory, literary talent, con-
centration, reflection, industry. His military achievements,
even though disastrous to the Republic, had been great.
Aiming at monarchy for many years, he had accomplished
his intention by means of hard work and great risks. He
had cajoled the naive populace with shows, with buildings,
with gifts and with feasts. He had bound his own followers
by means of rewards, his adversaries by a show of clemency. In short, he had already succeeded in habituating a
free community to servitude, partly through its fears,
partly through its passivity. [46] In your lust for despotic   117
power I can compare you with him, but in all other respects, there is no comparison. But out of the very many
evils that Caesar branded on the Republic this much good
has nonetheless come, namely that the Roman people
learned how much reliance to place on each person, whom
to trust, whom to beware of.[148] Do you not reflect on this
and understand that for brave men it is enough to have
learned what a beautiful thing it is to slay a tyrant, what
gratitude such a benefaction inspires, what fame and glory

118 lum homines non tulerint, te ferent? Certatim posthac,
mihi crede, ad hoc opus curretur neque occasionis tarditas
exspectabitur.

Respice, quaeso, aliquando rem publicam, M. Antoni;
quibus ortus sis, non quibuscum vivas considera. Mecum,
ut voles: redi cum re publica in gratiam, sed de te tu videris; ego de me ipse profitebor. Defendi rem publicam adulescens, non deseram senex: contempsi Catilinae gladios,
non pertimescam tuos. Quin etiam corpus libenter obtule-
rim, si repraesentari morte mea libertas civitatis potest,
ut aliquando dolor populi Romani pariat quod iam diu
119 parturit! Etenim si abhinc annos prope viginti hoc ipso in
templo negavi posse mortem immaturam esse consulari,
quanto verius nunc negabo seni! Mihi vero, patres conscripti, iam etiam optanda mors est, perfuncto rebus eis
quas adeptus sum quasque gessi, duo modo haec opto,
unum ut moriens populum Romanum liberum relin-
quam—hoc mihi maius ab dis immortalibus dari nihil potest—alterum ut ita cuique eveniat ut de re publica quisque
mereatur.

it brings? Will men put up with you, when they did not put up with Caesar? Believe me, from now on it will be a race   118
to get to the job; there will be no waiting for an opportunity which might be slow in coming.

Be so kind as to look back at last upon the Republic, Marcus Antonius. Think of the men from whom you sprang, not of those with whom you associate. Make your peace with me or not, just as you please; but make your peace with the Republic. However, as for you, it is for you to determine. As for me, out of my own mouth I will make this declaration: I defended the Republic when I was young; I shall not desert it now that I am old. I despised Catiline's blades; I shall not fear yours. Yes, and I should be happy to offer my body if my death can bring into reality the freedom of our state so that the suffering of the Roman people at length brings to birth what has so long been in the womb. In this very temple almost twenty years ago I   119
said that death could not be untimely for a consular; with how much greater truth shall I now say, "for an old man"! For me, Members of the Senate, death is now something even to be wished for after the offices I have attained and the services I have rendered. I make only these two prayers: the first, that when I die, I leave the Roman people free—the immortal gods can grant me no greater favor than this—the second, that each man's fate match his deserts as a patriot.

PHILIPPIC 3

INTRODUCTION

After the meeting of the senate on 28 November 44, at which Mark Antony caused a public thanksgiving (*supplicatio*) to be decreed for M. Aemilius Lepidus and the praetorian provinces to be distributed, he left Rome during the night of 28/29 November for the remainder of his consular year (3.19–26). Although Antony's departure (on top of the earlier departure of his consular colleague Dolabella) gave more freedom of action to the remaining magistrates in Rome, no decisive measures were taken. Everything stood suspended in expectation of 1 January 43, when A. Hirtius and C. Vibius Pansa, the new consuls appointed by Caesar, were to take office. Cicero returned to Rome on 9 December 44 (cf. *Fam*. 11.5.1), somewhat earlier than originally intended because of political developments (cf. *Att*. 16.11.6).

On 20 December 44, the new board of tribunes of the plebs convened the senate to discuss security measures for the inauguration of the consuls on 1 January 43 (cf. *Fam*. 11.6a.1). Cicero had planned not to come to that meeting, but to attend the senate only from 1 January 43 onwards (cf. *Fam*. 11.6a.1). Yet on the same day (20 Dec.) a dispatch of D. Iunius Brutus arrived in Rome, in which Brutus stated that he would retain the province of Cisalpine Gaul under the control of the senate and the people of Rome (3.8, 37–38; 4.7–8; 5.28, 36–37).

INTRODUCTION TO PHILIPPIC 3

Cicero realized the need and the favorable opportunity for intervention and came to the meeting on 20 December, his attendance allegedly causing a high turnout of senators (3.32; *Fam.* 11.6a.2). After the introductory report of the tribunes of the plebs, Cicero was the first consular to be asked for his opinion, and he delivered the *Third Philippic*, thereby initiating the open fight against Antony. Cicero praised the tribunes of the plebs for their initiative (3.13, 25, 37), but he primarily used the speech to define the positions of Antony, of Antony's opponents, and of the senate in the present struggle as he described the outrageous behavior of Antony, the beneficial deeds of his opponents, and the steps that must necessarily and immediately follow.

At the end of the speech, Cicero moved that D. Iunius Brutus' actions in Gaul be confirmed, that the present provincial governors continue to hold their provinces at the disposal of the senate and the people of Rome until such time as the senate might appoint successors, and that Octavian, the veterans who had followed him, and the legions who had defected from Antony to Octavian be honored for their opposition to Antony (3.37–39). The senate passed Cicero's motion (cf. 4.1–9; 5.3–5, 28–29, 30; 6.1; 10.23; *Fam.* 12.22a.1; 12.25.2), and according to Cicero, no senator supported Antony except L. Varius Cotyla (5.5; cf. 5.7).

This senatorial decree effectively annulled Antony's law on the assignment of consular provinces to Dolabella and himself passed in June 44 and the allotment of the praetorian provinces in the senate on 28 November 44 (cf. 3.24–26) and also authorized private initiatives of resistance against Antony. Therefore Cicero viewed the *Third Philippic* as laying the foundation for further actions against Antony and for his policy of preserving the Republican system (cf. 4.1; 5.30; 6.2; 14.20; *Fam.* 10.28.2; 12.25.2). Hence Cicero claimed to have recalled a weak and weary senate to its traditional vigor and customs on that day and to have brought to the Roman people the hope of recovering freedom (cf. *Fam.* 10.28.2).

STRUCTURE

Exordium

(1–2) Plea for hurry because of the need for immediate action

Argumentatio

(3–27) Praise of initiatives against Antony and condemnation of his conduct
  (3–14) Private initiatives against Antony by various people
    (3–5) Octavian
    (6–7) *Legio Martia* and *legio quarta*
    (8–12) D. Iunius Brutus
    (13a) The province of Gaul
    (13b–14) Conclusion: call for authorization and honors from the senate
  (15–27) Outrageous behavior of Antony
    (15–18) Insulting edicts
    (19–26) Activities in late November 44
    (27) Threats to Rome

Peroratio

(28–36) Appeal to senate for immediate action against Antony

Sententia

(37–39) Initiatives against Antony should be sanctioned; current governors should retain provinces in support of the Republic

M. TULLI CICERONIS
IN M. ANTONIUM
ORATIO PHILIPPICA TERTIA

1   [1] Serius omnino, patres conscripti, quam tempus rei
publicae postulabat, aliquando tamen convocati sumus;
quod flagitabam equidem cotidie, quippe cum bellum nefarium contra aras et focos, contra vitam fortunasque nostras ab homine profligato ac perdito non comparari, sed
geri iam viderem. Exspectantur Kalendae Ianuariae; quas
non exspectat Antonius, qui in provinciam D. Bruti, summi et singularis viri, cum exercitu impetum facere conatur;
ex qua se instructum et paratum ad urbem venturum esse
2   minitatur. Quae est igitur exspectatio aut quae vel minimi
dilatio temporis? Quamquam enim adsunt Kalendae Ianuariae, tamen breve tempus longum est imparatis. Dies
enim adfert vel hora potius, nisi provisum est, magnas
saepe clades; certus autem dies non ut sacrifici, sic consili
exspectari solet. Quod si aut Kalendae Ianuariae fuissent
eo die quo primum ex urbe fugit Antonius, aut eae non essent exspectatae, bellum iam nullum haberemus. Auctoritate enim senatus consensuque populi Romani facile
hominis amentis fregissemus audaciam. Quod confido

---

1 Probably referring to the sacrifice to Jupiter offered on the
Capitol on 1 Jan. each year by the incoming consuls.

MARCUS TULLIUS CICERO'S THIRD PHILIPPIC ORATION AGAINST MARCUS ANTONIUS

[1] Members of the Senate, we have been called together later than the crisis of the Republic demanded; but
we meet at last. I was pressing every day for a meeting, inasmuch as I saw a wicked war not in preparation but in actual conduct by a profligate and desperate man against our
altars and hearths, against our lives and property. We are
waiting for the first of January: but Antonius does not wait
for this date. He is attempting to invade the province of
our noble and distinguished fellow countryman Decimus
Brutus with an army, and from that province he threatens,
when equipped and ready, to march on the city. Why then
the waiting, or why a moment's delay? Although the first of
January is nearly at hand, nevertheless even a short time is
long for the unready. For a day, or rather an hour, often
brings great disasters if precautions have not been taken.
Yet a decision is not like a sacrifice,[1] not to be made before
a particular day. But if the day when Antonius fled from the
city had been the first of January, or if we had not waited
for this date, we would not now have a war on our hands.
For we should easily have quelled the madman's insolence
by the authority of the senate and the consensus of the Roman people. I am confident that the consuls-elect will do

1

2

179

equidem consules designatos, simul ut magistratum inierint, esse facturos; sunt enim optimo animo, summo
consilio, singulari concordia. Mea autem festinatio non
victoriae solum avida est sed etiam celeritatis.

3   Quo enim usque tantum bellum, tam crudele, tam nefarium privatis consiliis propulsabitur? Cur non quam primum publica accedit auctoritas? [2] C. Caesar adulescens,
paene potius puer, incredibili ac divina quadam mente
atque virtute, cum maxime furor arderet Antoni cumque
eius a Brundisio crudelis et pestifer reditus timeretur, nec
postulantibus nec cogitantibus, ne[c]¹ optantibus quidem
nobis, quia non posse fieri videbatur, firmissimum exercitum ex invicto genere veteranorum militum comparavit
patrimoniumque suum effudit: quamquam non sum usus
eo verbo quo debui; non enim effudit: in salute rei pu-
4   blicae collocavit. Cui quamquam gratia referri tanta non
potest quanta debetur, habenda tamen est tanta quantam
maximam animi nostri capere possunt. Quis enim est tam
ignarus rerum, tam nihil de re publica cogitans qui hoc
non intellegat, si M. Antonius a Brundisio cum eis copiis
quas se habiturum putabat, Romam, ut minabatur, venire
potuisset, nullum genus eum crudelitatis praeteriturum
fuisse? Quippe qui in hospitis tectis Brundisi fortissimos
viros optimosque civis iugulari iusserit; quorum ante pedes eius morientium sanguine os uxoris respersum esse
constabat. Hac ille crudelitate imbutus, cum multo nobis²

---

¹ *Lambinus*: nec *codd.*   ² *Christ*: bonis *codd.*, *SB*

---

² By Octavian and D. Iunius Brutus.
³ Octavian was born on 23 Sept. 63 and thus had just turned 19
in autumn 44.   ⁴ Antony tried to settle the unrest prior to

that as soon as they take office; for they are men of the best intentions, of excellent judgment, and agree remarkably well with one another. But I am in a hurry. I am eager, not merely for victory, but for quick victory.

So, how long will a war of such magnitude, a cruel 3 and wicked war, be beaten back by private initiatives? Why does not public authority come to their support without delay? [2] When Antonius' fury was at its height and we dreaded his return from Brundisium, cruel and baneful as it would have been, without our asking or thinking or even praying for such a thing because it seemed impossible of accomplishment, a young man, or rather hardly more than a boy,[3] Gaius Caesar, showed incredible and superhuman spirit and energy: he raised a very strong army of veteran soldiers who had never known defeat and lavished his patrimony—no, I have not used the appropriate word; he did not lavish it, he invested it in the salvation of the Republic. We cannot repay all we owe him, but all the gratitude of 4 which our souls are capable is his due. Who is so ignorant of the world around him, so absolutely careless of the public good as not to realize that if Marcus Antonius could have returned from Brundisium to Rome, as he threatened to do, with the forces that he expected to have under his command, he would have left no form of cruelty unemployed? Under his host's roof at Brundisium he ordered very brave men and most loyal citizens to be murdered;[4] it was commonly reported that their blood splashed into his wife's face as they lay dying at his feet. Stained by such cruelty, and far more angry with all of us than he had been

the defection of the two legions (§§6–7) by condemning a significant number of soldiers to death (cf. 3.10; 5.22; 13.18).

omnibus veniret iratior quam illis fuerat quos trucidarat,
cui tandem nostrum aut cui omnino bono pepercisset?
5 Qua peste rem publicam privato consilio—neque enim
fieri potuit aliter—Caesar liberavit: qui nisi in hac re publica natus esset, rem publicam scelere Antoni nullam haberemus. Sic enim perspicio, sic iudico, nisi unus adulescens
illius furentis impetus crudelissimosque conatus cohibuis-
set, rem publicam funditus interituram fuisse. Cui quidem
hodierno die, patres conscripti—nunc enim primum ita
convenimus ut illius beneficio possemus ea quae sentiremus libere dicere—tribuenda est auctoritas, ut rem publicam non modo a se susceptam sed etiam a nobis commen-
datam possit defendere.

6 [3] Nec vero de legione Martia, quoniam longo intervallo loqui nobis de re publica licet, sileri potest. Quis enim
unus fortior, quis amicior umquam rei publicae fuit quam
legio Martia universa? Quae cum hostem populi Romani
Antonium iudicasset, comes esse eius amentiae noluit: re-
liquit consulem; quod profecto non fecisset, si eum consulem iudicasset quem nihil aliud agere, nihil moliri nisi
caedem civium atque interitum civitatis videret. Atque ea
legio consedit Albae. Quam potuit urbem eligere aut op-
portuniorem ad res gerendas aut fideliorem aut fortiorum
7 virorum aut amic<i>orum[3] rei publicae civium? Huius legionis virtutem imitata quarta legio duce L. Egnatuleio
quaestore, civi optimo et fortissimo, C. Caesaris auctoritatem atque exercitum persecuta est. Faciendum est igitur
nobis, patres conscripti, ut ea quae sua sponte clarissimus

[3] *ed. Iuntina*: fortium (-tiorem *D*) . . . amicorum *codd.*

---

[5] The period of Caesar's dictatorship and Antony's consulship.

with the slaughtered victims, which of us or which single decent man would he have spared? From that scourge 5 Caesar by his private initiative—there was no other way for it to be accomplished—delivered the Republic: had he not been born in this Republic, through the crime of Antonius we should no longer have a Republic. For it is my perception and judgment, that if this one young man had not checked that madman's rushing attacks and most savage purposes, the Republic would have perished utterly. Today, Members of the Senate, since for the first time thanks to him we have met under conditions which make it possible for us to give free expression to our sentiments, we must grant him authority so that he can defend the Republic not only on his own initiative but with our blessing.

[3] And since after so long an interval[5] we are permitted 6 to speak on public affairs, one cannot keep silent about the Martian Legion. For what individual has ever proved a braver and better friend to the Republic than the entire Martian Legion? Judging Antonius to be an enemy of the Roman people, they refused to be party to his madness: they deserted the consul, which they would surely not have done if they had judged him to be a consul; but they saw that his only purpose and plan was to massacre citizens and destroy the community. And this legion encamped at Alba. It could have chosen no city more strategically suitable or more faithful, none with a braver population or more supportive of the community. Modeling itself upon the cour- 7 age of this legion, the Fourth Legion, under the command of quaestor Lucius Egnatuleius, a most loyal and courageous citizen, has followed the authority and army of Gaius Caesar. So it is for us, Members of the Senate, to see to it that what this illustrious and most eminent young man has

adulescens atque omnium praestantissimus gessit et gerit, haec auctoritate nostra comprobentur, veteranorumque, fortissimorum virorum, tum legionis Martiae quartaeque mirabilis consensus ad rem publicam recuperandam laude et testimonio nostro confirmetur, eorumque commoda, honores, praemia, cum consules designati magistratum inierint, curae nobis fore hodierno die spondeamus.

8   [4] Atque ea quidem quae dixi de Caesare deque eius exercitu iam diu nota sunt nobis. Virtute enim admirabili Caesaris constantiaque militum veteranorum legionumque earum quae optimo iudicio auctoritatem nostram, libertatem populi Romani, virtutem Caesaris secutae sunt a cervicibus nostris est depulsus Antonius. Sed haec, ut dixi, superiora: hoc vero recens edictum D. Bruti quod paulo ante propositum est certe silentio non potest praeteriri. Pollicetur enim se provinciam Galliam retenturum in senatus populique Romani potestate. O civem natum rei publicae, memorem sui nominis imitatoremque maiorum! Neque enim Tarquinio expulso maioribus nostris tam fuit optata libertas quam est depulso Antonio retinenda nobis.

9   Illi regibus parere iam a condita urbe didicerant: nos post reges exactos servitutis oblivio ceperat. Atque ille Tarquinius quem maiores nostri non tulerunt non crudelis, non impius, sed superbus est habitus et dictus: quod nos vitium in privatis saepe tulimus, id maiores nostri ne in rege quidem ferre potuerunt. L. Brutus regem superbum non tulit: D. Brutus sceleratum atque impium regnare patietur? Quid Tarquinius tale qualia innumerabilia et facit et fecit

---

[6] The Bruti of Cicero's time were widely thought to be related to L. Iunius Brutus, who overthrew the monarchy and founded the Republic.

done and is doing of his own accord is sanctioned by our authority; we must further confirm by our approving testimony the wonderful unanimity for the restoration of the Republic that is displayed by the veterans, most courageous men, and also by the Martian and Fourth Legions; and we must this day make our pledge that their interests, honors, and rewards shall be our care when the consuls-elect have come into office.

[4] What I have just said about Caesar and his army has 8 been known to us for some time past. By Caesar's admirable courage and by the resolution of the veteran soldiers and those legions who with excellent judgment have placed themselves behind our authority, the liberty of the Roman people, and the courage of Caesar, Antonius has been dislodged from our necks. But all this came earlier, as I have said: Decimus Brutus' dispatch is recent, it has just been published. Assuredly it cannot be passed over in silence. For he promises to keep the province of Gaul in the control of the senate and people of Rome. A citizen born for the Republic, mindful of his name, following in the footsteps of his ancestors![6] When Tarquin was driven out, our ancestors welcomed freedom; even more must we retain it, now that Antonius has been dislodged. *They* had 9 learned obedience to kings right from the foundation of the city, but after the expulsion of the kings *we* had forgotten what slavery was. And this Tarquin that our ancestors did not endure was reckoned and called not "the cruel" or "the impious," but "the proud": our ancestors could not bear even in a king a fault that we have often put up with in private persons. Lucius Brutus did not tolerate a proud king: shall Decimus Brutus suffer a criminal and impious person to reign? What did Tarquin ever do to compare

185

CICERO

Antonius? Senatum etiam reges habebant: nec tamen, ut
Antonio senatum habente, in consilio regis versabantur
barbari armati. Servabant auspicia reges; quae hic consul
augurque neglexit, neque solum legibus contra auspicia
ferendis sed etiam collega una ferente eo quem ipse emen-
10 titis auspiciis vitiosum fecerat. Quis autem rex umquam
fuit tam insignite impudens ut haberet omnia commoda,
beneficia, iura regni venalia? Quam hic immunitatem,
quam civitatem, quod praemium non vel singulis hominibus vel civitatibus vel universis provinciis vendidit? Nihil
humile de Tarquinio, nihil sordidum accepimus: at vero
huius domi inter quasilla pendebatur aurum, numerabatur
pecunia; una in domo omnes quorum intererat totum imperium populi Romani nundinabantur. Supplicia vero in
civis Romanos nulla Tarquini accepimus: at hic et Suessae
iugulavit eos quos in custodiam dederat et Brundisi ad
trecentos fortissimos viros civisque optimos trucidavit.
11 Postremo Tarquinius pro populo Romano bellum gerebat
tum cum est expulsus: Antonius contra populum Romanum exercitum adducebat tum cum a legionibus relictus
nomen Caesaris exercitumque pertimuit neglectisque sacrificiis sollemnibus ante lucem vota ea quae numquam
solveret nuncupavit, et hoc tempore in provinciam populi
Romani conatur invadere. Maius igitur a D. Bruto bene-

7 Antony had tried to obstruct Dolabella's election to the consulship by announcing (allegedly) unfavorable auspices (cf. 2.79–
84), but accepted him as his consular colleague after Caesar's
assassination (cf. 1.31; 2.84; 5.9).

8 Suggests that important political and financial business was
conducted in the domestic quarters and that Antony's wife Fulvia
was involved in the trafficking (cf. 2.95).

with countless deeds both past and present of Antonius? The kings too had a senate: but armed barbarians did not figure in the royal council chamber as they do when Antonius holds a senate. The kings observed the auspices, which this consul and augur has neglected, not only by putting through legislation in defiance of the auspices but by doing so in conjunction with a colleague whose election he himself had flawed by announcing false auspices.[7] And what king ever had the unmitigated impudence to put up all benefits, grants, and rights in his realm for sale? Exemptions, citizen rights, rewards—are there any that *he* has not sold to individuals or communities or whole provinces? Nothing base or sordid is told of Tarquin: but in *his* house gold was weighed and money counted among the women's wool baskets;[8] in a single dwelling all persons interested trafficked in the entire empire of the Roman people. We are not told that Tarquin ever executed Roman citizens: whereas *he* murdered those whom he had thrown into custody at Suessa, and at Brundisium he slaughtered some three hundred very brave men and most loyal citizens. Finally, at the time when Tarquin was driven out, he was waging war on behalf of the Roman people: Antonius was leading an army against the Roman people when he was deserted by the legions and, in terror of Caesar's name and army, neglecting the customary sacrifices, he took vows before daybreak which he shall never discharge;[9] and at this moment he is attempting to invade a province of the Roman people. So the Roman people has and expects a

10

11

[9] Typically, consuls took auspices on the Capitol after sunrise and made vows for success before they left Rome to go to war or into a province. Antony's vows are therefore invalid (cf. also 5.24).

ficium populus Romanus et habet et exspectat quam maiores nostri acceperunt a L. Bruto, principe huius maxime
12   conservandi generis et nominis. [5] Cum autem est omnis servitus misera, tum vero intolerabile est servire impuro, impudico, effeminato, numquam ne in metu quidem sobrio. Hunc igitur qui Gallia prohibet, privato praesertim consilio, iudicat verissimeque iudicat non esse consulem. Faciendum est igitur nobis, patres conscripti, ut D. Bruti privatum consilium auctoritate publica comprobemus. Nec vero M. Antonium consulem post Lupercalia debuistis putare: quo enim ille die, populo Romano inspectante, nudus, unctus, ebrius est contionatus et id egit ut collegae diadema imponeret, eo die se non modo consulatu sed etiam libertate abdicavit. Esset enim ipsi certe statim serviendum, si Caesar ab eo regni insigne accipere voluisset. Hunc igitur ego consulem, hunc civem Romanum, hunc liberum, hunc denique hominem putem qui foedo illo et flagitioso die et quid pati Caesare vivo posset et quid eo mortuo consequi ipse cuperet ostendit?

13   Nec vero de virtute, constantia, gravitate provinciae Galliae taceri potest. Est enim ille flos Italiae, illud firmamentum imperi populi Romani, illud ornamentum dignitatis. Tantus autem est consensus municipiorum coloniarumque provinciae Galliae ut omnes ad auctoritatem huius ordinis maiestatemque populi Romani defendendam conspirasse videantur.

Quam ob rem, tribuni plebis, quamquam vos nihil aliud nisi de praesidio, ut senatum tuto consules Kalendis Ia-

---

10 When Antony offered Caesar a diadem on 15 Feb. 44 (cf. 2.84–87).

greater benefit from Decimus Brutus than our ancestors received from Lucius Brutus, who founded this clan and name, to be cherished above all others. [5] And while all slavery is miserable, slavery to a vile, debauched effeminate, who is never sober even when he is terrified, is downright intolerable. In barring him from Gaul, and that by private initiative, Brutus judges that he is not consul, and he is entirely right. Accordingly, Members of the Senate, it is our duty to approve Decimus Brutus' initiative by public authority. Indeed, you ought not to have regarded Marcus Antonius as consul after the Feast of Lupercal:[10] on that day, when before the eyes of the Roman people he made a public speech naked, oiled, and drunk and tried to place a diadem on his colleague, on that day he not only abdicated the consulship but his personal freedom as well. For he himself would certainly have become a slave then and there if Caesar had chosen to accept the emblem of monarchy from his hands. Am I then to think of him as a consul, as a Roman citizen, as a free man, or even as a human being, when on that day of infamy and shame he showed what he was capable of enduring while Caesar lived and equally what he himself desired to achieve after Caesar's death?

A word must also be said about the valor, resolution, and responsibility of the province of Hither Gaul, as it is the flower of Italy, the bulwark of the empire of the Roman people, the ornament of its dignity. The municipalities and colonies of the province of Gaul are at one: they all seem to have banded together in unanimous defense of the authority of this body and the majesty of the Roman people.

Therefore, Tribunes of the Plebs, although your reference is confined to the matter of a guard so that the consuls may hold a senate in safety on the first of January, I think

189

nuariis habere possint, rettulistis, tamen mihi videmini
magno consilio atque optima mente potestatem nobis de
tota re publica fecisse dicendi. Cum autem[4] tuto haberi senatum sine praesidio non posse iudicavistis, tum statuistis
etiam intra muros Antoni scelus audaciamque versari. [6]

14 Quam ob rem omnia mea sententia complectar, vobis, ut
intellego, non invitis: ut et praestantissimis ducibus a nobis
detur auctoritas et fortissimis militibus spes ostendatur
praemiorum et iudicetur non verbo, sed re non modo non
consul sed etiam hostis Antonius. Nam si ille consul, fus-
tuarium meruerunt legiones quae consulem reliquerunt,
sceleratus Caesar, Brutus nefarius qui contra consulem
privato consilio exercitus comparaverunt. Si autem militibus exquirendi sunt honores novi propter eorum divinum
atque immortale meritum, ducibus autem ne referri quidem potest gratia, quis est qui eum hostem non existimet
quem qui armis persequuntur conservatores rei publicae
iudicantur?

15 At quam contumeliosus in edictis, quam barbarus,
quam rudis! Primum in Caesarem maledicta congessit de-
prompta ex recordatione impudicitiae et stuprorum suorum. Quis enim hoc adulescente castior, quis modestior,
quod in iuventute habemus illustrius exemplum veteris
sanctitatis? Quis autem illo qui male dicit impurior? Igno-
bilitatem obicit C. Caesaris filio, cuius etiam natura pater,
si vita suppeditasset, consul factus esset. "Aricina mater":

---

4 *SB*: cum enim *codd*.

---

11 Octavian's natural father C. Octavius was a candidate for
the consulship when he died in 59.　　　12 Octavian's mother
Atia was a daughter of M. Atius Balbus, whose family was from
Aricia, and of Iulia minor, a sister of Caesar.

you have shown great judgment and excellent intentions in thus giving us an opportunity to speak on public affairs in general. Moreover, your decision that a senate cannot be held in safety without a guard also implies that Antonius' crime and audacity is at large even within the walls. [6] Accordingly, I shall embrace it all in my proposal, as I believe will not be disagreeable to you: to provide that authority be given by us to the eminent commanders, hope of rewards held out to the very brave soldiers, and Antonius judged, not in word but in fact, to be not only not a consul but a public enemy. For if he *is* a consul, the legions that deserted a consul have deserved to be beaten to death, Caesar is a criminal and Brutus a villain for having raised armies against a consul by private initiative. If, on the contrary, unprecedented honors are to be devised for the soldiers in recognition of their divine and unforgettable service, if it is beyond our power to recompense their commanders, who cannot but consider Antonius a public enemy, when those who attack him in arms are judged saviors of the Republic? 14

But how insolent he is in his edicts, what ill-breeding, what ignorance! First, he heaped abuse on Caesar, taken straight from the recollection of his own vicious, debauched past. Yet is there anyone more pure and modest than this young man, is there a more conspicuous example of old-time morality in our younger generation? And what fouler person is there than he the traducer? He taunts Gaius Caesar's son with humble birth, though even his natural father would have been elected consul had he lived.[11] "A mother from Aricia":[12] you would think he was saying 15

Trallianam aut Ephesiam putes dicere. Videte quam de-
spiciamur omnes qui sumus e municipiis, id est omnes
plane: quotus enim quisque nostrum non est? Quod autem
municipium non contemnit is qui Aricinum tanto opere
despicit, vetustate antiquissimum, iure foederatum, pro-
pinquitate paene finitimum, splendore municipum hones-
16 tissimum? Hinc Voconiae, hinc Atiniae leges; hinc multae
sellae curules et patrum memoria et nostra; hinc equites
Romani lautissimi et plurimi. Sed si Aricinam uxorem non
probas, cur probas Tusculanam? Quamquam huius sanc-
tissimae feminae atque optimae pater, M. At[t]ius[5] Balbus,
in primis honestus, praetorius fuit: tuae coniugis, bonae feminae, locupletis quidem certe, Bambalio quidam pater,
homo nullo numero. Nihil illo contemptius, qui propter
haesitantiam linguae stuporemque cordis cognomen ex
contumelia traxerat.[6] "at avus nobilis." Tuditanus nempe
ille, qui cum palla et cothurnis nummos populo de rostris
spargere solebat. Vellem hanc contemptionem pecuniae
suis reliquisset! Habetis nobilitatem generis gloriosam!
17 Qui autem evenit ut tibi Iulia nata[7] ignobilis videatur, cum
tu eodem materno genere soleas gloriari? Quae porro
amentia est eum dicere aliquid de uxorum ignobilitate

---

[5] *corr. Ferrarius*   [6] *Halm*: traxit traxerat *V in ras.*
[7] *Muretus*: Iulia natus *V*

---

[13] One *Lex Voconia*, proposed by Q. Voconius Saxa, is known.
Three *Leges Atiniae* are attested.   [14] I.e. magistrates.

[15] The hometown of Antony's wife Fulvia.

[16] The *cognomen* of M. Fulvius Bambalio, Fulvia's father (cf.
2.90), is derived from a Greek verb meaning "to clatter with one's
teeth / stutter."

[17] Sempronius Tuditanus was Fulvia's maternal grandfather.

"from Tralles" or "from Ephesus." Notice how all of us who come from country towns are looked down upon—which is to say, just about all of us: for how many of us do not? And if he has such contempt for Aricia, an immemorially ancient community, in status a Roman ally under treaty, so close as almost to be our next-door neighbor, distinguished by the high standing of its members, what municipality does he not despise? From Aricia came the Voconian and the Atinian laws,[13] many curule chairs[14] in our fathers' time and in our own, great numbers of very wealthy Roman knights. But if you do not approve of a wife from Aricia, why do you approve of one from Tusculum[15]? Particularly as the father of this blameless and excellent lady from Aricia was Marcus Atius Balbus, a highly respected man of praetorian rank, whereas your wife, good lady that she is (rich, at all events), is the daughter of a certain Bambalio,[16] a person of no consequence, in fact a contemptible being who got his opprobrious name from his stammering tongue and dull wits. "But her grandfather was a nobleman." Of course, this Tuditanus,[17] who used to throw coins from the Rostra among the crowd, dressed in an actor's robe and buskins. I could wish that his family had inherited his contempt for money! Well, there you have a noble family to boast of! But how is it that Antonius thinks the daughter of a Julia a commoner when he constantly brags of coming from the same family on his mother's side?[18] What folly, again, this talk about low-born wives

16

17

In old age he was mentally disturbed: he threw coins among the crowd, dressed in an actor's costume.

18 Atia's mother, Octavian's grandmother, was Iulia minor, a sister of the dictator Caesar. Antony's mother was also related to the family of the Iulii Caesares on the paternal side.

cuius pater Numitoriam Fregellanam, proditoris filiam, habuerit uxorem, ipse ex libertini filia susceperit liberos? Sed hoc clarissimi viri viderint, L. Philippus qui habet Aricinam uxorem, C. Marcellus qui Aricinae filiam; quos certo scio dignitatis optimarum feminarum non paenitere.

[7] Idem etiam Q. Ciceronem, fratris mei filium, compellat edicto, nec sentit amens commendationem esse compellationem suam. Quid enim accidere huic adulescenti potuit optatius quam cognosci ab omnibus Caesaris consiliorum esse socium, Antoni furoris inimicum? At etiam gladiator ausus est scribere hunc de patris et patrui parricidio cogitasse. O admirabilem impudentiam, audaciam, temeritatem, in eum adulescentem hoc scribere audere quem ego et frater meus propter eius suavissimos atque optimos mores praestantissimumque ingenium certatim amamus omnibusque horis oculis, auribus, complexu tenemus! Nam me isdem edictis nescit laedat an laudet: cum idem supplicium minatur optimis civibus quod ego de sceleratissimis ac pessimis sumpserim, laudare videtur, quasi imitari velit; cum autem illam pulcherrimi facti memoriam refricat, tum a sui similibus invidiam aliquam in me commoveri putat.

18

---

19 The first wife of Antony's father, M. Antonius Creticus, was the daughter of Q. Numitorius Pullus, who betrayed the town of Fregellae to a besieging Roman army in 125.   20 Cf. 2.3.
21 After the death of her first husband C. Octavius, Octavian's mother, Atia from Aricia, married L. Marcius Philippus in *c.* 58/57. Atia's daughter Octavia was married to C. Claudius Marcellus; her second husband later was Mark Antony.   22 According to his letters, Cicero's opinion of young Quintus was not entirely favorable at the time, owing to Quintus' alignment with the cause

from a man whose father married Numitoria of Fregellae, the daughter of a traitor,[19] and who himself acknowledged children by the daughter of a freedman?[20] However, I leave this matter to two illustrious gentlemen, Lucius Philippus, who has the woman from Aricia as his wife, and Gaius Marcellus, who is married to the daughter of the lady from Aricia;[21] I am sure they are well satisfied with the social status of these excellent ladies.

[7] He further takes my brother's son, Quintus Cicero, to task in an edict, not having the sense to perceive that such treatment coming from him is a commendation. For what better could the young man hope for than to be generally recognized as associated in the counsels of Caesar and hostile to the madness of Antonius? But this gladiator 18 actually dared to write that Quintus had formed designs on the lives of his father and his uncle. Ah, amazing impudence, audacity, recklessness, to dare write such stuff about a young man for whom my brother and I vie in affection, which his personal charm, fine character, and outstanding talents so well deserve, who is constantly in our sight, in our hearing, in our arms![22] And in the same edicts he mentions me, without knowing whether he is praising or attacking me: when he threatens most loyal citizens with the punishment that I inflicted on the worst criminals and traitors, he seems to be praising me, as though he wished to imitate me; but when he refurbishes the memory of that glorious act,[23] he thinks that he is stirring up some odium against me on the part of persons like himself.

of Caesar and Antony; yet in the second half of 44 Quintus seems to have gradually parted company with Antony.

[23] The execution of Catilinarian conspirators in 63.

19   [8] Sed quid fecit ipse? Cum tot edicta ⟨pro⟩posuisset,[8]
edixit ut adesset senatus frequens a.d. VIII Kalendas Decembris:[9] eo die ipse non adfuit. At quo modo edixit? Haec
sunt, ut opinor, verba in extremo: "Si quis non adfuerit,
hunc existimare omnes poterunt et interitus mei et perditissimorum consiliorum auctorem fuisse." Quae sunt perdita consilia? An ea quae pertinent ad libertatem populi
Romani recuperandam? Quorum consiliorum Caesari me
auctorem et hortatorem et esse et fuisse fateor. Quamquam ille non eguit consilio cuiusquam; sed tamen curren-
tem, ut dicitur, incitavi. Nam interitus quidem tui quis
bonus non esset auctor, cum in eo salus et vita optimi
cuiusque, libertas populi Romani dignitasque consisteret?
20   Sed cum tam atroci edicto nos concitavisset, cur ipse non
adfuit? Num putatis aliqua re tristi ac severa? Vino atque
epulis retentus, si illae epulae potius quam popinae nomi-
nandae sunt, diem edicti obire neglexit: in a.d. IV Kalendas Decembris distulit. Adesse in Capitolio iussit; quod in
templum ipse nescio qua per Gallorum cuniculum ascen-
dit. Convenerunt corrogati et quidem ampli quidam homines sed immemores dignitatis suae. Is enim erat dies, ea
fama, is qui senatum vocarat ut turpe senatori esset nihil timere. Ad eos tamen ipsos qui convenerant ne verbum qui-

[8] *Naugerius*: posuisset *codd*.

[9] ⟨At⟩ cum tot edicta ⟨pro⟩posuisset, edixit ut adesset senatus
frequens a.d. VIII Kalendas Decembris. sed quid fecit ipse?
transpos. SB

---

[24] In fact, the reason for the postponement was probably that
Antony had received word of the defection of the Martian legion
(13.19).

196

coach,[29] turned from an orator into a farmer, occupies two thousand *iugera* of public land in the plain of Leontini tax-free, just to make a fool more fatuous still at the public expense!

These are trivialities perhaps. But I should like to ask 23 why he was so gentle in the senate after such ferocities in his edicts. For what purpose did it serve to threaten with death the tribune of the plebs, Lucius Cassius, a most courageous and resolute citizen, if he came to the senate; or to drive from the senate with violence and threats to his life Decimus Carfulenus, loyal to the community; or to bar from approaching the Capitol, let alone entering the temple, Tiberius Cannutius, whose most commendable speeches have often and rightly harassed Antonius? Was he afraid of their vetoing a senatorial decree? What decree? That for the illustrious Marcus Lepidus' public thanksgiving, I suppose. Not much danger that a normal honor would be obstructed when every day we were thinking out some extraordinary honor for him! And when he 24 was about to lay the state of the Republic before the senate, he lost his nerve when news arrived about the Fourth Legion, and so as not to appear to have summoned the meeting for nothing, being eager to run away, he had the decree for the public thanksgiving carried by a floor vote,[30] even though this was an unprecedented procedure. [10] And then his departure: the route he took in his general's cloak, avoiding men's eyes, the daylight, the city, and the Forum! What a miserable, unseemly, disgraceful fashion of running away! However, the senate passed some very fine decrees that same day in the evening:[31] a scrupu-

decrees could be passed before sunrise and after sunset (cf. Gell. *NA* 14.7.8).

giosa sortitio, divina vero opportunitas ut, quae cuique
apta esset, ea cuique obveniret.

25   Praeclare igitur facitis, tribuni plebis, qui de praesidio
consulum senatusque referatis, meritoque vestro maximas
vobis gratias omnes et agere et habere debemus. Qui enim
carere metu et periculo[12] possumus in tanta hominum
cupiditate et audacia? Ille autem homo adflictus et perdi-
tus quae de se exspectat iudicia graviora quam amicorum
suorum? Familiarissimus eius, mihi homo coniunctus, L.
Lentulus, et P. Naso, omni carens cupiditate, [nullam se
habere provinciam,][13] nullam Antoni sortitionem fuisse iudicaverunt. Quod idem fecit L. Philippus, vir patre, avo
maioribusque suis dignissimus; in eadem sententia fuit
homo summa integritate atque innocentia, C. Turranius;
idem fecit Sp. Oppius; ipsi etiam qui amicitiam M. Antoni
veriti plus ei tribuerunt quam fortasse vellent, M. Piso, ne-
cessarius meus, et vir et civis egregius, parique innocentia
M. Vehilius, senatus auctoritati se obtemperaturos esse
26 dixerunt. Quid ego de L. Cinna loquar, cuius spectata multis magnisque rebus singularis integritas minus admirabilem facit huius honestissimi facti gloriam? Qui omnino
provinciam neglexit; quam item magno animo et constanti
C. Cestius repudiavit. Qui sunt igitur reliqui quos sors

---

[12] *D*: metu et periculo carere *Fedeli, SB*: periculo carere *V*
[13] *om. V1*: nullam se habere provinciam *V2D, SB*

---

[32] The adopted reading of the Latin supports the interpretation that the first five men mentioned in Cicero's enumeration did
not take part in the lottery, but just voiced their opinions on the
procedure. The remaining names only would then refer to recipi-

lous lottery of provinces took place, in which it fell out most providentially that every man got just what suited him best.

So, Tribunes of the Plebs, you do very well to put up for 25 discussion the matter of a guard for the consuls and the senate, and your action deserves the warmest thanks and gratitude of us all. For amid so much unscrupulous self-seeking how can we not be in fear and danger? As for that ruined and desperate individual, what harsher verdict upon himself does he expect than that of his friends? A special intimate of his, and a friend of mine, Lucius Lentulus, and Publius Naso, who is devoid of all selfish ambition, declared that Antonius' lottery was null and void.[32] Lucius Philippus, a gentleman wholly worthy of his father, grandfather, and ancestors, did likewise; the same view was taken by Gaius Turranius, a man of stainless integrity and probity; Spurius Oppius did the same. Even my friend Marcus Piso, an exemplary man and citizen, and the equally upright Marcus Vehilius, who out of consideration for their friendship with Antonius went further in his direction than perhaps they would have wished to do, declared that they would defer to the authority of the senate. What shall I say of Lucius Cinna, whose outstanding 26 integrity, proved in many affairs of great consequence, makes his highly praised and honorable action on this occasion less surprising? He would have nothing to do with a province; and Gaius Cestius refused one in a similarly disinterested and resolute spirit. Who then are the others who find delight in the providentially guided lots? Titus

ents, and their number agrees with the number of provinces still available for allotment at the time.

CICERO

divina delectet? T. Annius, †M. Antonius†.[14] O felicem
utrumque! Nihil enim maluerunt. C. Antonius Macedo-
niam. Hunc quoque felicem! Hanc enim habebat semper
in ore provinciam. C. Calvisius Africam. Nihil felicius!
Modo enim ex Africa decesserat et quasi divinans se rediturum duos legatos Uticae reliquerat. Deinde M. Cusini
Sicilia, Q. Cassi Hispania. Non habeo quid suspicer: dua-
rum credo provinciarum sortis minus divinas fuisse.

27   [11] O C. Caesar—adulescentem appello—quam tu salutem rei publicae attulisti, quam improvisam, quam re-
pentinam! Qui enim haec fugiens fecit, quid faceret inse-
quens? Etenim in contione dixerat se custodem fore urbis,
seque usque ad Kalendas Maias ad urbem exercitum habiturum. O praeclarum custodem ovium, ut aiunt, lupum!
Custosne urbis an direptor et vexator esset Antonius? Et
quidem se introiturum in urbem dixit exiturumque cum
vellet. Quid illud? Nonne audiente populo sedens pro
aede Castoris dixit, nisi qui vicisset, victurum neminem?

28   Hodierno die primum, patres conscripti, longo intervallo in possessionem[15] libertatis pedem ponimus: cuius

14 l. annius m. antonius V: t. (om. t, l. n²) antonius m. (a. s¹)
antonius D: T. Annius, M. Gallius *Clark*

15 *codd.*: possessione *Ferrarius, SB*

33 The transmitted text is corrupt and obviously hides two
names, most likely *T. Annius* (perhaps T. Annius Cimber, cf. 11.14;
13.26, 28) and *M. Gallius* (cf. 13.26; *Att.* 11.20.2; *Fam.* 8.4.1). Possibly, the passage also contained the names of the provinces these
men received.

34 Africa Vetus had been allotted to Q. Cornificius for his
provincial governorship in 44. On 28 Nov. 44 this province was

Annius, * * *.³³ A lucky pair! Exactly what they both wanted. Gaius Antonius draws Macedonia. Another lucky man! For he always had his eye on that province. Gaius Calvisius gets Africa. Nothing could be luckier! He had just left Africa, and as though warned by a prophetic instinct that he would return he had left two legates behind in Utica.³⁴ Then we have Marcus Cusinius with Sicily and Quintus Cassius with Spain. Nothing suspicious there: I suppose Providence was less active in the draws for those two provinces.

[11] Gaius Caesar—the young man I mean—what salvation have you brought to the Republic, how unexpected, how sudden! For he who did things like this as he ran away, what would he be doing if he were on our heels? He had stated at a public meeting that he would be the guardian of the city and would keep an army near the city until the first of May. Ah, a fine guardian, the proverbial wolf to guard the sheep!³⁵ Would Antonius be the city's guardian or her plunderer and oppressor? He further said that he would enter the city and leave it when he chose.³⁶ To cap all, did he not say in the hearing of the people as he sat in front of the Temple of Castor that none but victors would be left alive?

Today for the first time, Members of the Senate, after a long interval we plant our feet on the soil of freedom, the

27

28

given to his predecessor C. Calvisius Sabinus, which allotment was again annulled by the senate decree initiated by the present speech.

³⁵ Cf. Ter. *Eun.* 832: *scelesta, ovem lupo commisisti.*

³⁶ As imperator, Antony could not legally cross the city boundary without special dispensation from the senate.

quidem ego quoad potui non modo defensor sed etiam conservator fui. Cum autem id facere non possem, quievi, nec abiecte nec sine aliqua dignitate casum illum temporum et dolorem tuli. Hanc vero taeterrimam beluam quis ferre potest aut quo modo? Quid est in Antonio praeter libidinem, crudelitatem, petulantiam, audaciam? Ex his totus vitiis conglutinatus est. Nihil apparet in eo ingenuum,

29 nihil moderatum, nihil pudens, nihil pudicum. Quapropter, quoniam res in id discrimen adducta est utrum ille poenas rei publicae luat an nos serviamus, aliquando, per deos immortalis, patres conscripti, patrium animum virtutemque capiamus, ut aut libertatem propriam Romani generis et nominis recuperemus aut mortem servituti anteponamus! Multa quae in libera civitate ferenda non essent tulimus et perpessi sumus, alii spe forsitan recuperandae libertatis, alii vivendi nimia cupiditate: sed si illa tulimus quae nos necessitas ferre coegit, quae vis quaedam paene fatalis—quae tamen ipsa non tulimus—etiamne huius impuri latronis feremus taeterrimum crudelissimumque do-

30 minatum? [12] Quid hic faciet, si poterit, iratus qui, cum suscensere nemini posset, omnibus bonis fuerit inimicus? Quid hic victor non audebit qui nullam adeptus victoriam tanta scelera post Caesaris interitum fecerit, refertam eius domum exhauserit, hortos compilaverit, ad se ex eis omnia ornamenta transtulerit, caedis et incendiorum causam quaesierit ex funere, duobus aut tribus senatus consultis bene et e re publica factis reliquas res ad lucrum praedamque revocaverit, vendiderit immunitates, civitates li-

freedom which, while I could, I not only defended but preserved. When I could play that role no longer, I held my peace and endured those disastrous and grievous times, not abjectly nor quite without dignity. But this hideous monster—who can endure him or how? What is there in Antonius save lust, cruelty, insolence, audacity? He is wholly compacted of these vices. No trace in him of gentlemanly feeling, none of moderation, none of self-respect, none of modesty. Therefore, since there is now the critical   29
question before us whether he pays his penalty to the Republic or we become slaves, by the immortal gods, Members of the Senate, let us at last take our fathers' spirit and courage, resolving to regain the freedom that belongs to the Roman race and name, or else to prefer death to slavery! Much that should be intolerable in a free community we steeled ourselves to tolerate, some of us maybe in the hope of regaining freedom, others from too much love of living. But if we bore what necessity and a force that seemed like destiny compelled us to bear (and yet we did *not* bear it), shall we bear the most cruel and horrible despotism of this foul cutthroat? [12] What will he do, given   30
the power, when he is angry, seeing that he was the enemy of all decent men when he had no grievance against anyone? What lengths will he not go to as a victor when without gaining any victory he committed such heinous crimes after Caesar's death? He emptied Caesar's well-stocked house, plundered his gardens, transferred all their ornaments to his own; he sought to make the funeral a pretext for massacre and arson; having passed two or three good senatorial decrees in the public interest, in all else he thought only of profit and plunder; he sold exemptions, granted freedom to communities, removed entire prov-

CICERO

beraverit, provincias universas ex imperi populi Romani
iure sustulerit, exsules reduxerit, falsas leges C. Caesaris
nomine et falsa decreta in aes incidenda et in Capitolio
figenda curaverit, earumque rerum omnium domesticum
mercatum instituerit, populo Romano leges imposuerit,
armis et praesidiis populum et magistratus foro excluserit,
senatum stiparit armis, armatos in cella Concordiae, cum
senatum haberet, incluserit, ad legiones Brundisium cu-
currerit, ex eis optime sentientis centuriones iugulaverit,
cum exercitu Romam sit ad interitum nostrum et ad †dis-
31 persionem†[16] urbis venire conatus? Atque is ab hoc impetu
abstractus consilio et copiis Caesaris, consensu veteranorum, virtute legionum, ne fortuna quidem fractus minuit
audaciam nec ruere demens nec furere desinit. In Galliam
mutilatum ducit exercitum; cum una legione et ea vacil-
lante Lucium fratrem exspectat, quo neminem reperire
potest sui similiorem. Ille autem ex myrmillone dux [ex
gladiatore imperator][17] quas effecit strages, ubicumque
posuit vestigium! ⟨Fundit apothecas,⟩[18] caedit greges
armentorum reliquique pecoris quodcumque nactus est;
epulantur milites; ipse autem se, ut fratrem imitetur,
obruit vino; vastantur agri, diripiuntur villae, matres familiae, virgines, pueri ingenui abripiuntur, militibus tra-

16 dispersionem *Vtv*: disperditionem *bcns*: dispertitionem
Klotz   17 *del. SB*
18 *add. Ernesti ex Serv. ad Verg. Ecl. 6.55*

37 Antony seems to have led to Gaul the *legio V Alaudae* and
one of the four legions from Macedonia (*legio secunda* or *legio
tricesima quinta*). Of the remaining three, two (*legio Martia* and

inces from the imperial jurisdiction of the Roman people,
brought back exiles, caused false laws and false decrees in
Gaius Caesar's name to be inscribed on bronze and posted
up on the Capitol, and set up a market for all these items in
his house; he imposed laws on the Roman people, exclud-
ing people and magistrates from the Forum with armed
soldiers; he surrounded the senate with armed men, put
armed men inside the sanctuary of Concord while holding
a senate; he hurried to Brundisium to the legions there,
slaughtered their most loyal-minded centurions, tried to return to Rome with an army to destroy us and sack the city.
And when diverted from this headlong career by the initia-   31
tive and forces of Caesar, the consensus of the veterans,
and the valor of the legions, undismayed even by the
change of fortune, he lessens none of his audacity nor does
he desist from his mad, furious plunge. He is leading his
truncated army into Gaul; he waits for his brother
Lucius—no one more like himself could he find—coming
with a single legion, and that a wavering one.[37] As for that
myrmillo[38] turned general, what havoc he has made wherever he set his foot! He empties barns, slaughters herds of
cattle and other animals, whatever comes his way. The soldiers feast; and he himself, in imitation of his brother,
drowns himself in wine. Fields are laid waste, farmhouses
ransacked, mothers of families, unmarried girls, and boys
of free birth torn away and handed over to the soldiery.

legio quarta) defected to Octavian, while the fourth presumably
was the one that Lucius Antonius commanded.
    [38] A type of gladiator, referring to Lucius Antonius, who
fought a combat in this guise at Mylasa in Asia (5.20), probably in
50–49 when quaestor/proquaestor in this province (cf. 7.17).

duntur. Haec eadem, quacumque exercitum duxit, fecit
M. Antonius.

32   [13] His vos taeterrimis fratribus portas aperietis, hos
umquam in urbem recipietis? Non tempore oblato, ducibus paratis, animis militum incitatis, populo Romano con-
spirante, Italia tota ad libertatem recuperandam excitata,
deorum immortalium beneficio utemini? Nullum erit
tempus hoc amisso. A tergo, fronte, lateribus tenebitur, si
in Galliam venerit. Nec ille armis solum sed etiam decretis nostris urgendus est. Magna vis est, magnum numen
unum et idem sentientis senatus. Videtisne refertum forum, populumque Romanum ad spem recuperandae libertatis erectum? Qui longo intervallo cum frequentis hic
33   videt nos, tum sperat etiam liberos convenisse. Hunc ego
diem exspectans M. Antoni scelerata arma vitavi, tum cum
ille in me absentem invehens non intellegebat quod ad
tempus me et meas viris reservarem. Si enim tum illi caedis a me initium quaerenti respondere voluissem, nunc rei
publicae consulere non possem. Hanc vero nactus facultatem, nullum tempus, patres conscripti, dimittam neque
diurnum neque nocturnum quin de libertate populi Romani et dignitate vestra quod cogitandum sit cogitem,
quod agendum atque faciendum, id non modo non recu-
sem sed etiam appetam atque deposcam. Hoc feci dum licuit; intermisi quoad non licuit. Iam non solum licet sed
etiam necesse est, nisi servire malumus quam ne servia-
34   mus armis animisque decernere. Di immortales nobis

39 By his invective in the senate on 19 Sept. 44, which provoked the *Second Philippic*.

210

Marcus Antonius has done just the same, wherever he has led his army.

[13] Will you open the gates to these hideous brothers   32
or ever admit them into the city? Will you not rather use
this heaven-sent boon: the proffered opportunity, the generals available, the spirit of the troops aroused, the Roman
people united, all Italy stirred up to recover freedom? If
we miss this moment, there will not come another. If he
enters Gaul, he will be caught in a trap—rear, front, and
flanks. And he must be pressed not only with arms but also
with our decrees. Mighty is the force, mighty the control-
ling power of the senate united in a single purpose. Do you
see the crowd in the Forum, the Roman people excited by
the prospect of liberty regained? After a long interval they
see us meeting here in full numbers, and they also hope we
have met as free men. In expectation of this day I avoided   33
Marcus Antonius' criminal violence, when he assailed me
in my absence;[39] little did he realize that I was reserving
myself and my strength for a particular juncture. If I had
elected to answer him then, just when he was looking for
an excuse to start a massacre with me, I should be in no position to support the Republic now. But the opportunity
has arrived: Members of the Senate, I shall employ every
moment of the day and of the night in thinking, insofar as
thought is required, of the freedom of the Roman people
and of your dignity; I shall not only not recoil from action
and activity, where that is called for, but I shall even seek
and demand it. This I did while it was permitted; I ceased
to do it temporarily, so long as it was not permitted. Now
not only is it permitted, it is even necessary, unless we prefer to be slaves rather than fight to determine with our
courage and our weapons that slaves we shall not be. The   34

211

haec praesidia dederunt: urbi Caesarem, Brutum Galliae.
Si enim ille urbem opprimere potuisset, statim, si Galliam
tenere, paulo post optimo cuique pereundum, reliquis
serviendum. [14] Hanc igitur occasionem oblatam tenete,
per deos immortalis, patres conscripti, et amplissimi orbis
terrae consili principes vos esse aliquando recordamini!
Signum date populo Romano consilium vestrum non
deesse rei publicae, quoniam ille virtutem suam non defu-
turam esse profitetur. Nihil est quod moncam vos. Nemo
est tam stultus qui non intellegat, si indormierimus huic
tempori, non modo crudelem superbamque dominatio-
nem nobis sed ignominiosam etiam et flagitiosam feren-
35 dam. Nostis insolentiam Antoni, nostis amicos, nostis
totam domum. Libidinosis, petulantibus, impuris, impu-
dicis, aleatoribus, ebriis servire, ea summa miseria est
summo dedecore coniuncta. Quod si iam—quod di omen
avertant!—fatum extremum rei publicae venit, quod gla-
diatores nobiles faciunt, ut honeste decumbant, faciamus
nos, principes orbis terrarum gentiumque omnium, ut
cum dignitate potius cadamus quam cum ignominia ser-
36 viamus. Nihil est detestabilius dedecore, nihil foedius servitute. Ad decus et ad libertatem nati sumus: aut haec te-
neamus aut cum dignitate moriamur. Nimium diu teximus
quid sentiremus; nunc iam apertum est. Omnes patefa-
ciunt in utramque partem quid sentiant, quid velint. Sunt
impii cives—pro caritate rei publicae nimium multi, sed
contra multitudinem bene sentientium admodum pauci—
quorum opprimendorum di immortales incredibilem rei
publicae potestatem et fortunam dederunt. Ad ea enim

immortal gods have given us two bulwarks: Caesar for the
city, Brutus for Gaul. For if Antonius had been able to
crush the city or to lay hold of Gaul, it would have meant
death for all the best men and slavery for the rest, immediate in the first case, a little later in the second. [14] Therefore, Members of the Senate, by the immortal gods, seize
this proffered opportunity and at long last remember that
you are leaders of the most august council in the world!
Give a signal to the Roman people that your wisdom will
not fail the Republic, since they declare that their courage
will not be wanting. You do not need me to advise you. No
man is so dull as not to realize that if we doze over this
point in time, we shall have to endure a despotism not only
cruel and arrogant but also ignominious and disgraceful.
You know Antonius' insolence, you know his friends, you   35
know his whole household. To be slaves to libertines, bul-
lies, foul profligates, gamblers, and drunkards, that is the
ultimate in misery joined with the ultimate in dishonor.
If—may the gods avert the omen!—the final episode in
the history of the Republic has arrived, let us behave like
champion gladiators: they meet death honorably; let us,
who stand foremost in the world and all its nations, see to it
that we fall with dignity rather than serve with ignomy.
Nothing is more abominable than disgrace, nothing is ug-   36
lier than servitude. We were born for honor and freedom:
let us either retain them or die with dignity. Too long we
have kept our feelings hidden. Now they are in the open.
All are making plain on one side or the other what they feel
and wish for. There are traitors: too many, given the precious worth of the Republic, but quite few compared with
the multitude of loyal-minded citizens; the immortal gods
have given the Republic incredible power and good for-

praesidia quae habemus iam accedent consules summa prudentia, virtute, concordia, multos mensis de populi Romani libertate commentati atque meditati. His auctoribus et ducibus, dis iuvantibus, nobis vigilantibus et multum in posterum providentibus, populo Romano consentiente, erimus profecto liberi brevi tempore. Iucundiorem autem faciet libertatem servitutis recordatio.

37   [15] Quas ob res, quod tribuni plebis verba fecerunt uti senatus Kalendis Ianuariis tuto haberi sententiaeque de summa re publica libere dici possint, de ea re ita censeo: "Uti C. Pansa A. Hirtius, consules designati, dent operam uti senatus Kalendis Ianuariis tuto haberi possit. Quodque edictum D. Bruti, imperatoris, consulis designati, propositum sit, senatum existimare D. Brutum, imperatorem, consulem designatum, optime de re publica mereri, cum senatus auctoritatem populique Romani libertatem impe-

38 riumque defendat; quodque provinciam Galliam citeriorem, optimorum et fortissimorum virorum[19] amicissimorumque rei publicae civium, exercitumque in senatus potestate retineat, id eum exercitumque eius, municipia, colonias provinciae Galliae recte atque ordine exque re publica fecisse et facere. Senatum ad summam rem publicam pertinere arbitrari ab D. Bruto et L. Planco imperatoribus, consulibus designatis itemque a ceteris qui provin-

---

[19] *bnstv*: optimorum et fortissimorum *V, SB*: optimorum virorum et fortissimorum *c*

---

[40] Both men were designated as consuls for 42 by Caesar and had won the title of imperator as a result of military campaigns in 44.

tune by which to crush them. To the forces already at our disposal will shortly be added consuls of outstanding wisdom, courage, like-mindedness, who for many months have been pondering deeply on the freedom of the Roman people. With their advice and leadership, with the gods' help, with our vigilance and farsighted provision, and with the Roman people united, we shall without doubt be free in no long time. And freedom will be made sweeter by the memory of servitude.

[15] Accordingly, whereas the tribunes of the plebs 37 have spoken to the intent that a meeting of the senate may be held in safety on the first of January and that views on the state of the Republic may be freely expressed, I propose as follows: "That Gaius Pansa and Aulus Hirtius, consuls-elect, take measures to ensure that a meeting of the senate can be held in safety on the first of January. Further that, whereas a dispatch has been issued by Decimus Brutus, imperator and consul-elect, the senate judges Decimus Brutus, imperator and consul-elect, to deserve excellently well of the Republic in that he defends the authority of the senate and the liberty and empire of the Roman people; and, whereas he retains the province of 38 Hither Gaul, with its excellent and most courageous inhabitants and citizens most supportive of the Republic, and his army under control of the senate, the senate judges that he and his army and the municipalities and colonies of the province of Gaul have acted and are acting rightly, properly, and in the public interest. That the senate considers it of the highest public importance that Decimus Brutus and Lucius Plancus, imperators and consuls-elect,[40] along with other holders of provinces, should continue to hold them

cias obtinent obtineri ex lege Iulia, quoad ex senatus consulto cuique eorum successum sit, eosque dare operam ut eae provinciae eique exercitus in senati populique Romani potestate praesidioque rei publicae sint. Cumque opera, virtute, consilio C. Caesaris summoque consensu militum veteranorum, qui eius auctoritatem secuti rei publicae praesidio sunt et fuerunt, a gravissimis periculis populus Romanus defensus sit et hoc tempore defendatur;

39 cumque legio Martia Albae constiterit, in municipio fidelissimo et fortissimo, seseque ad senatus auctoritatem populique Romani libertatem contulerit; et quod pari consilio eademque virtute legio quarta usa, L. Egnatuleio duce, quaestore optimo, civi egregio,[20] senatus auctoritatem populique Romani libertatem defendat ac defenderit, senatui magnae curae esse ac fore ut pro tantis eorum in rem publicam meritis honores eis habeantur gratiaeque referantur. Senatui placere uti C. Pansa A. Hirtius, consules designati, cum magistratum inissent, si eis videretur, primo quoque tempore de his rebus ad hunc ordinem referrent, ita uti e re publica fideque sua videretur."

[20] *Muretus*: l. egn. que opti egregio mo V: l. egn. duce civi egregio D: duce L. Egnatuleio quaestore, civi egregio *Orelli, SB*

under the Julian Law[41] until such time as a successor be appointed to each by decree of the senate, and that they see to it that those provinces and those armies be in the control of the senate and Roman people, ready to defend the Republic. Further, since by the agency, courage, and judgment of Gaius Caesar and the united action of the veteran soldiers, who following his lead are and have been defending the Republic, the Roman people has been protected from very grave dangers and is protected at this present time; and since the Martian Legion has stationed itself in Alba, a most loyal and brave township, and placed itself in support of the authority of the senate and the liberty of the Roman people; and whereas the Fourth Legion, with equal judgment and the same courage, under the leadership of Lucius Egnatuleius, an excellent quaestor and outstanding citizen, is defending and has defended the authority of the senate and the liberty of the Roman people: that it is and will be of great concern to the senate that in return for their eminent services to the Republic, honors be accorded and gratitude shown to them. That it pleases the senate that Gaius Pansa and Aulus Hirtius, consuls-elect, if they see fit, should as soon as possible after taking office consult this body concerning these matters in whatever manner may appear consonant with the public interest and their own duty."

39

41 The *Lex Iulia de provinciis* of 46 was a Caesarian law that limited the length of provincial governorships to one year for ex-praetors and to two years for ex-consuls (cf. 1.19). Here Cicero must have in mind exceptions for special cases outlined by this law or refer to the original distribution of provinces according to this law.

PHILIPPIC 4

INTRODUCTION

After the proceedings in the senate on 20 December 44, at which Cicero delivered his *Third Philippic*, he addressed the *Fourth Philippic* to a public meeting (4.1–2; 7.22) convened in the Forum by a tribune of the plebs, M. Servilius (4.16). Cicero informed the people about the decisions of the senate, yet did not present an unbiased report of the debate. Rather, he placed his own interpretation on the decree that the senate had just passed and that he himself had initiated (cf. 3.37–39). He claimed that the force of the recently adopted decree, which commended private initiatives taken against Mark Antony by Decimus Brutus, Octavian, and two legions that had defected to him, was in effect to declare Antony a "public enemy" (*hostis*), though not yet explicitly in a formal decree (4.1–2). This reading of the senate's action became the basis for Cicero's subsequent argumentation in the course of the struggle with Antony.

The speech before the people builds on the recent decree passed in the senate: after Cicero had been successful in persuading the senators to adopt his motion (4.4), he tried to influence the people to support the situation established thereby. This oration, therefore, presents arguments similar to those used previously in the senate and develops them further in the light of Cicero's interpretation of the decree. Hence the speech forms an integral element in the development and dissemination of Cicero's conception of the threat posed by Antony and the best ways to meet that threat. The oration itself and Cicero's characterization of the audience's reaction to it as highly enthusiastic seek to show that the individuals and groups opposed to Antony (Cicero, the senate, and the Roman people) all shared the same opinion of Antony and of the measures appropriate to be taken against him (e.g. 4.2, 5, 6–7, 8, 9, 12, 15). Cicero's aim is to demonstrate that the overall consensus proves this view to be correct and leaves potential opponents no room for dissent.

INTRODUCTION TO PHILIPPIC 4

STRUCTURE

Exordium

(1–2a) Present situation and importance of the recent senate decree

Narratio

(2b–10) Report on activities on behalf of the Republic, acknowledged by senate
  (2b–5a) By Octavian
  (5b–7a) By the *legio Martia* and the *legio quarta*
  (7b–8) By D. Iunius Brutus
  (9a) By the province of Gaul
  (9b–10) Conclusions and expectations for the future

Propositio

(11–16a) Exhortation to war, like a general's speech
  (11–12a) Impossibility of peace with Antony
  (12b–13) Consensus of senate and people, bravery of the Romans
  (14–15) Lawlessness and weakness of opponent
  (16a) Cicero's contribution to regaining liberty

Peroratio

(16b) Importance of present day as a first step toward recovery of liberty

M. TULLI CICERONIS
IN M. ANTONIUM
ORATIO PHILIPPICA QUARTA

1   [1] Frequentia vestrum incredibilis, Quirites, contioque tanta quantam meminisse non videor et alacritatem mihi summam defendendae rei publicae adfert et spem recuperandae.[1] Quamquam animus mihi quidem numquam defuit: tempora defuerunt, quae simul ac primum aliquid lucis ostendere visa sunt, princeps vestrae libertatis defendendae fui. Quod si id ante facere conatus essem, nunc facere non possem. Hodierno enim die, Quirites, ne mediocrem rem actam arbitremini, fundamenta iacta sunt reliquarum actionum. Nam est hostis a senatu nondum

2   verbo appellatus, sed re iam iudicatus Antonius. Nunc vero multo sum erectior quod vos quoque illum hostem esse tanto consensu tantoque clamore approbavistis. Neque enim, Quirites, fieri potest ut non aut ei sint impii qui contra consulem exercitus comparaverunt aut ille hostis contra quem iure arma sumpta sunt. Hanc igitur dubitationem, quamquam nulla erat, tamen ne qua posset esse senatus hodierno die sustulit.

    C. Caesar, qui rem publicam libertatemque vestram

---

[1] *V*: spem recuperandae libertatis *D*: spem ⟨libertatis⟩ recuperandae *SB*

MARCUS TULLIUS CICERO'S
FOURTH PHILIPPIC ORATION
AGAINST MARCUS ANTONIUS

[1] Your extraordinary numbers, Men of Rome, and the 1
size of this meeting, larger than any I can remember, fills
me with a lively eagerness to defend the Republic and with
hope of regaining it. True, my courage has never failed me;
it was the times that failed. As soon as they seemed to show
a glimmer of light, I took the lead in defending your freedom. Had I attempted to do this earlier, I would not be
able to do it now. For today, Men of Rome, in case you
think we have been transacting some business of minor importance, the groundwork has been laid for future operations. For Antonius has been pronounced a public enemy by the senate—in actuality, though not yet in words.
Now it much emboldens me, this loud and unanimous 2
agreement from you that he *is* a public enemy. And after
all, Men of Rome, there is no way out of it: either those
who have raised armies against a consul are traitors, or he
against whom arms have rightfully been taken up is an enemy. This doubt, therefore, the senate has today eliminated—not that any doubt existed, but in case there could
be any.

Gaius Caesar, who has protected and is protecting the

suo studio, consilio, patrimonio denique tutatus est et tuta-
3 tur, maximis senatus laudibus ornatus est. Laudo, laudo
vos, Quirites, quod gratissimis animis prosequimini nomen clarissimi adulescentis vel pueri potius; sunt enim
facta eius immortalitatis, nomen aetatis. Multa memini,
multa audivi, multa legi, Quirites: nihil ex omnium saeculorum memoria tale cognovi: qui cum servitute premere-
mur, in dies malum cresceret, praesidi nihil haberemus,
capitalem et pestiferum a Brundisio M. Antoni reditum timeremus, hoc insperatum omnibus consilium, incognitum
certe ceperit, ut exercitum invictum ex paternis militibus
conficeret Antonique furorem crudelissimis consiliis inci-
4 tatum a pernicie rei publicae averteret. [2] Quis est enim
qui hoc non intellegat, nisi Caesar exercitum paravisset,
non sine exitio nostro futurum Antoni reditum fuisse? Ita
enim se recipiebat ardens odio vestri, cruentus sanguine
civium Romanorum quos Suessae, quos Brundisi occide-
rat ut nihil nisi de pernicie populi Romani cogitaret. Quod
autem praesidium erat salutis libertatisque vestrae, si C.
Caesaris fortissimorum sui patris militum exercitus non
fuisset? Cuius de laudibus et honoribus, qui ei pro divinis
et immortalibus meritis divini immortalesque debentur,
mihi senatus adsensus paulo ante decrevit ut primo quo-
5 que tempore referretur. Quo decreto quis non perspicit
hostem esse Antonium iudicatum? Quem enim possumus
appellare eum contra quem qui exercitus ducunt, eis senatus arbitratur singularis exquirendos honores?

---

[1] Cf. 3.3, n. 3.

Republic and your freedom with his zeal, judgment, even his patrimony, has been honored by the senate's highest commendations. I commend, I commend you, Men of Rome, for saluting in heartfelt gratitude the name of an illustrious young man, or rather boy; for his deeds belong to immortality, the name is a matter of age.[1] I remember many things, Men of Rome, have been told of many, read of many: the like of this I have never met with in the history of all ages. When we were under the yoke of slavery, with the evil gaining day by day and none to defend us, dreading the return of Marcus Antonius from Brundisium and the death and ruin it would bring, Caesar took a decision which none of us hoped for and certainly none of us knew of in advance: to raise from his father's soldiers an army which had never known defeat and turn Antonius' fury and the cruel designs which inspired it, away from the destruction of the Republic. [2] For who does not realize that if Caesar had not raised an army, Antonius' return would have entailed our destruction? He was coming back in a fever of hatred against you, stained with the blood of the Roman citizens he had killed in Suessa and Brundisium, his only thought being the ruin of the Roman people. What was there to defend your lives and liberty, if it had not been for Gaius Caesar's army composed of his father's very brave soldiers? The senate has just accepted my motion that a discussion be opened at the earliest possible time concerning the commendations and honors due to him, godlike and immortal to match his godlike and immortal services. Who fails to see that Antonius has been pronounced an enemy by this decree? What else can we call him, when the senate decides that exceptional honors must be devised for those who lead armies against him?

Quid? Legio Martia, quae mihi videtur divinitus ab eo
deo traxisse nomen a quo populum Romanum generatum
accepimus, non ipsa suis decretis prius quam senatus hostem iudicavit Antonium? Nam si ille non hostis, hos qui
consulem reliquerunt hostis necesse est iudicemus. Praeclare et loco, Quirites, reclamatione vestra factum pul-
cherrimum Martialium comprobavistis: qui se ad senatus
auctoritatem, ad libertatem vestram, ad universam rem
publicam contulerunt, hostem illum et latronem et parrici-
6 dam patriae reliquerunt. Nec solum id animose et fortiter
sed considerate etiam sapienterque fecerunt: Albae con-
stiterunt, in urbe opportuna, munita, propinqua, fortissimorum virorum, fidelissimorum civium atque optimorum.
Huius [Martiae][2] legionis legio quarta imitata virtutem,
duce L. Egnatuleio, quem senatus merito paulo ante lau-
davit, C. Caesaris exercitum persecuta est. [3] Quae exspectas, M. Antoni, iudicia graviora? Caesar fertur in
caelum qui contra te exercitum comparavit; laudantur ex-
quisitissimis verbis legiones quae te reliquerunt, quae a te
arcessitae sunt, quae essent, si te consulem quam hostem
maluisses, tuae: quarum legionum fortissimum verissi-
mumque iudicium confirmat senatus, comprobat univer-
sus populus Romanus; nisi forte vos, Quirites, consulem,
7 non hostem iudicatis Antonium. Sic arbitrabar, Quirites,
vos iudicare ut ostenditis. Quid? Municipia, colonias,
praefecturas num aliter iudicare censetis? Omnes morta-

[2] *del. Manutius*

So who but brigands think him a consul? And even they do not believe what they say; and villainous traitors as they may be, as they in fact are, they cannot dissent from the judgment of all mankind. But the hope of loot and plunder makes blind the minds of those who have not been satisfied by the gift of goods, the allocation of lands, the limitless auctioning.[3] They have marked the city, the goods and fortunes of its citizens for plunder. While there is something here for them to loot and rob, they reckon they will not go short of anything. And Marcus Antonius—I call upon the immortal gods to avert and ward off this omen!—has promised to divide the city up among them. May it so befall him, Men of Rome, as you pray, and may the retribution for this madness recoil upon himself and his family! I am confident it will be so. For it seems to me that now not only men but also the immortal gods have united to save the Republic. If the immortal gods predict the future for us by prodigies and portents, these have been set forth so openly that retribution is coming to him and liberty to us; or if such a universal consensus could not exist without an impulse from the gods, how can we doubt the will of the heavenly divinities? 10

[5] It only remains, Men of Rome, that you stand fast in the sentiments you proclaim. So I shall do as generals are accustomed to do when the army is drawn up for battle: though they see that the soldiers are fully ready for the fray, they exhort them all the same; in the same way, I shall urge you, eager and ready though you are, to recover freedom. Men of Rome, you are not fighting the kind of enemy 11

[3] Refers to the distribution of property confiscated from the Pompeians by the dictator Caesar. A lance (*hasta*) was a characteristic sign of such auctions; cf. 2.64, n. 72.

quo aliqua pacis condicio esse possit. Neque enim ille servitutem vestram, ut antea, sed iam iratus sanguinem concupiscit. Nullus ei ludus videtur esse iucundior quam cruor, quam caedes, quam ante oculos trucidatio civium.

12 Non est vobis res, Quirites, cum scelerato homine ac nefario, sed cum immani taetraque belua quae, quoniam in foveam incidit, obruatur. Si enim illim emerserit, nullius supplici crudelitas erit recusanda. Sed tenetur, premitur, urgetur nunc eis copiis quas iam habemus, mox eis quas paucis diebus novi consules comparabunt.

Incumbite in causam, Quirites, ut facitis. Numquam maior consensus vester in ulla causa fuit; numquam tam vehementer cum senatu consociati fuistis. Nec mirum: agitur enim non qua condicione victuri, sed victurine si-

13 mus an cum supplicio ignominiaque perituri. Quamquam mortem quidem natura omnibus proposuit, crudelitatem mortis et dedecus virtus propulsare solet, quae propria est Romani generis et seminis. Hanc retinete, quaeso, Quirites, quam vobis tamquam hereditatem maiores vestri reliquerunt! Nam cum alia omnia falsa, incerta sint,[6] caduca, mobilia, virtus est una altissimis defixa radicibus, quae numquam vi ulla labefactari potest, numquam demoveri loco. Hac [virtute][7] maiores vestri primum universam Italiam devicerunt, deinde Carthaginem exciderunt, Numantiam everterunt, potentissimos reges, bellicosissimas gentis in dicionem huius imperi redegerunt.

[6] nam cum . . . sint *P. R. Müller*: quamquam . . . . sint *V* (sunt *D*): [quamquam] . . . sunt *Madvig, SB*
[7] *del. ed. Aldina*

[4] I.e. expansion of the Roman empire over Italy up to the Second Punic War; sack of Carthage in 146; victory over Numantia

with whom any terms of peace are possible. For he does not, as formerly, desire to make slaves of you; he is angry now and thirsts for your blood. No sport appears more pleasing to him than gore, than carnage, than the slaughter of countrymen before his eyes. You are not dealing, Men of Rome, with a wicked villain but with a cruel, hideous monster, who must be overwhelmed inasmuch as he has fallen into a trap. For if he gets out of it, there is no torment however cruel that we shall not have to face. But he is being held, he is being pushed and pressed, now with the forces we already have and soon with others that the new consuls will raise in a few days' time. 12

Put your shoulders to the wheel, Men of Rome, as you are doing. You have never been more united in any cause, never so strongly linked with the senate. Little wonder! It is not *how* we are going to live that is at stake, but whether we are to live or to perish in agony and shame. Though death is indeed ordained by nature for all, a cruel and dishonorable death is generally warded off by courage, and courage is the badge of the Roman race and breed. Cling fast to it, I beg you, Men of Rome, as a heritage bequeathed to you by your ancestors! While all else is false and doubtful, ephemeral and inconstant, only courage stands firmly fixed with its very deep roots, which no violence can ever shake or ever shift from its place. Thereby your ancestors conquered all Italy first, then razed Carthage, overthrew Numantia, brought the most powerful kings and the most warlike nations under the sway of this empire.[4] 13

in Spain in 133; further countries and peoples defeated by the Romans and attached to their empire.

14   [6] Ac maioribus quidem vestris, Quirites, cum eo
hoste res erat qui haberet rem publicam, curiam, aerarium, consensum et concordiam civium, rationem aliquam, si ita res tulisset, pacis et foederis: hic vester hostis
vestram rem publicam oppugnat, ipse habet nullam; senatum, id est orbis terrae consilium, delere gestit, ipse consilium publicum nullum habet; aerarium vestrum exhausit,
suum non habet. Nam concordiam civium qui habere potest, nullam cum habet civitatem? Pacis vero quae potest
esse cum eo ratio in quo est incredibilis crudelitas, fides
15   nulla? Est igitur, Quirites, populo Romano, victori omnium gentium, omne certamen cum percussore, cum latrone, cum Spartaco. Nam quod se similem esse Catilinae
gloriari solet, scelere par est illi, industria inferior. Ille cum
exercitum nullum habuisset, repente conflavit: hic eum
exercitum quem accepit amisit. Ut igitur Catilinam dili-
gentia mea, senatus auctoritate, vestro studio et virtute
fregistis, sic Antoni nefarium latrocinium vestra cum senatu concordia tanta quanta numquam fuit, felicitate et
virtute exercituum ducumque vestrorum brevi tempore
oppressum audietis.

16   Equidem quantum cura, labore, vigiliis, auctoritate,
consilio eniti atque efficere potero, nihil praetermittam
quod ad libertatem vestram pertinere arbitrabor; neque
enim id pro vestris amplissimis in me beneficiis sine scelere facere possum.

Hodierno autem die primum referente viro fortissimo
vobisque amicissimo, hoc M. Servilio, collegisque eius, or-
natissimis viris, optimis civibus, longo intervallo me auctore et principe ad spem libertatis exarsimus.

---

⁵ One of the tribunes of the plebs who convened the senate
prior to this public meeting at which he invited Cicero to speak.

[6] Your ancestors, Men of Rome, had to deal with the   14
kind of enemy who possessed a state, a senate, a public
treasury, a consensus of like-minded citizens, and a consideration for a treaty of peace, if events had developed that
way: this enemy of yours is attacking your state, but he
himself has none; he is eager to destroy the senate, the
council of the world, but he himself has no public council;
he has emptied your treasury, but has none of his own. As
for a united citizenry, how can he have that when he has no
community? What basis for peace can there be with a person whose cruelty taxes belief and whose good faith is non-
existent? So, Men of Rome, the whole conflict lies be-   15
tween the Roman people, the conqueror of all nations, and
an assassin, a bandit, a Spartacus. He likes to boast of his
resemblance to Catilina, but though he is his equal in criminality, he is his inferior in energy. Catilina, when he lacked
an army, suddenly threw one together: Antonius received
an army and lost it. Just as by my exertions, by the senate's
authority, and by your zeal and courage you broke Catilina,
even so you will soon be hearing that Antonius' villainous
band of robbers has been crushed through your enormous,
unprecedented cooperation with the senate, as well as the
good fortune and valor of the armies and generals.

For my part, whatever I can achieve and effect by   16
means of care, toil, wakefulness, influence, and counsel, I
shall neglect nothing that in my view concerns your freedom. I should be a criminal if I did, after the signal favors
you have lavished upon me.

And today, at the initiative of Marcus Servilius[5] here, a
very courageous gentleman who loves you well, and his
colleagues, distinguished men and most patriotic citizens,
after a long interval, with me to prompt and lead, our
hearts have been kindled to hope for liberty.

PHILIPPIC 5

INTRODUCTION

On 1 January 43, the new consuls A. Hirtius and C. Vibius Pansa took office and chaired a meeting of the senate that was convened in the Temple of Jupiter Capitolinus and launched a discussion extending over four successive days. The first meeting of the year, as was customary, was dedicated to the general political situation (5.34; 6.1); this included the question of how to deal with Mark Antony, who was now besieging Decimus Brutus in the town of Mutina in Cisalpine Gaul. Beyond that, there was the specific issue of how the senate should carry out the decree of 20 December 44 (cf. 3.37–39), which called for honors to be conferred on various private initiatives that had been taken against Antony, since the selection of honors had been referred to this meeting (5.4, 28, 35; 6.1).

The opening speech of the new consuls was to Cicero's satisfaction (5.1), but the first consular to be called upon, Q. Fufius Calenus (Pansa's father-in-law), advised that an embassy be sent to Antony (5.1–5, 25; 10.3). In the *Fifth Philippic*, delivered on 1 January 43, Cicero spoke in opposition, proposing instead the declaration of a public emergency (*tumultus*) and active prosecution of the war (5.31–34; 6.2). Cicero pressed for this plan of action in reaction to Antony's recent lawless and tyrannical conduct and in keeping with the decisions already taken by the senate in its previous decree of 20 December 44.

Cicero, however, failed to persuade the senate to vote for an immediate declaration of war. During the four-day debate, the mood fluctuated, and it occasionally seemed likely that Cicero's position would prevail (6.2–3; 7.14). But on 4 January, according to Cicero, the hope that peace might be achieved by negotiating with Antony prevailed, and the senate adopted Calenus' proposal. So an embassy was decreed (5.4; 6.3; 7.14), composed of three senior consulars (Ser. Sulpicius Rufus, L. Marcius Philippus, L. Calpurnius Piso Caesoninus, cf. 9.1). These envoys were commissioned to convey to Antony the senate's instructions that he raise the siege of Mutina, evacuate Cisalpine Gaul but not bring his army within 200 miles of Rome, and submit to the authority of the senate and the people of Rome. If he did not comply, war was to be declared (6.4–6, 9, 16; 7.26).

The outcome of the vote on honors for Antony's opponents was more satisfying for Cicero: the senate adopted motions, largely in line with Cicero's recommendations, to honor and commend Decimus Brutus, Octavian, L. Egnatuleius and their troops as well as M. Lepidus, whose loyalty to the senate's cause Cicero hoped to ensure thereby (5.35–53a).

STRUCTURE

Exordium

(1–2) Resolute and prompt action is needed from 1 January forward

INTRODUCTION TO PHILIPPIC 5

Argumentatio

(3–34) Characterization of the present political situation
  (3–6a) Decree of 20 Dec. 44 and change of opinion within the senate
  (6b–25a) Antony's lawless and tyrannical conduct
    (7b–10) Flawed legislation
    (11–12a) Embezzlement of public money and sale of forged privileges
    (12b–16) Judiciary law
    (17–18) Employment of armed guards
    (19–20a) Mistreatment of Cicero
    (20b–21a) Threats against Roman citizens
    (21b–25a) Military activities over the past few months
  (25b–31a) The embassy and its potential consequences
    (25b–26) Blunting of readiness for war
    (27–31a) Inevitable failure because of circumstances and character of recipient
  (31b–34) Counterproposal: no negotiations, but war to be declared

Propositio

(35–53a) Honors for initiatives taken against Antony (including *sententiae*)
  (35–37) For D. Iunius Brutus
  (38–41) For M. Aemilius Lepidus
  (42–52a) For Octavian
  (52b) For L. Egnatuleius
  (53a) For the troops

Peroratio

(53b) Call for swift approval of the proposed measures

M. TULLI CICERONIS
IN M. ANTONIUM
ORATIO PHILIPPICA QUINTA

1 [1] Nihil umquam longius his Kalendis Ianuariis mihi
visum est, patres conscripti: quod idem intellegebam per
hos dies uni cuique vestrum videri. Qui enim bellum cum
re publica gerunt, hunc diem non exspectabant; nos autem, tum cum maxime consilio nostro subvenire communi
saluti oporteret, in senatum non vocabamur. Sed querelam
praeteritorum dierum sustulit oratio consulum, qui ita lo-
cuti sunt ut magis exoptatae Kalendae quam serae esse videantur. Atque ut oratio consulum animum meum erexit
spemque attulit non modo salutis conservandae verum
etiam dignitatis pristinae recuperandae, sic me perturbas-
set eius sententia qui primus rogatus est, nisi vestrae virtuti

2 constantiaeque confiderem. Hic enim dies vobis, patres
conscripti, illuxit, haec potestas data est ut quantum virtutis, quantum constantiae, quantum gravitatis in huius ordinis consilio esset, populo Romano declarare possetis. Recordamini qui dies nudius tertius decimus fuerit, quantus
consensus vestrum, quanta virtus, quanta constantia;

---

¹ Q. Fufius Calenus (cf. 10.3, 6).   ² I.e., to 20 Dec. 44,
when Cicero delivered the *Third* and the *Fourth Philippics*, and
his motion (3.37–39) was carried by the senate.

MARCUS TULLIUS CICERO'S
FIFTH PHILIPPIC ORATION
AGAINST MARCUS ANTONIUS

[1] Nothing has ever seemed to me longer in the coming, Members of the Senate, than this first of January, a view that I saw each one of you share during the past few days. Those who are making war upon the Republic were not waiting for this day; while we, just when it was most incumbent on us to come to the aid of the common safety with our counsel, were not summoned to the senate. But all complaint of days past has been set aside by the speech of the consuls, who have spoken in such a manner as to make the first day of the month seem eagerly awaited rather than too long delayed. Yet even as the speech of the consuls raised my spirits and gave me hope not only for preserving safety but also for recovering former dignity, the proposal of the gentleman first called[1] would have perturbed me, if I did not have confidence in your courage and resolution. For the day has dawned, Members of the Senate, the opportunity has been offered to you to show the Roman people how much courage, constancy, and resolution lie in the deliberations of this body. Cast your minds back twelve days:[2] what a day that was, what unity, what courage, what constancy you displayed! What

1

2

quantam sitis a populo Romano laudem, quantam gloriam, quantam gratiam consecuti. Atque illo die, patres conscripti, ea constituistis ut vobis iam nihil sit integrum nisi aut honesta pax aut bellum necessarium.

3   Pacem vult M. Antonius? Arma deponat, roget, deprecetur. Neminem aequiorem reperiet quam me, cui, dum se civibus impiis commendat, inimicus quam amicus esse maluit. Nihil est profecto quod possit dari bellum gerenti; erit fortasse aliquid quod concedi possit roganti. Legatos vero ad eum mittere de quo gravissimum et severissimum iudicium nudius tertius decimus feceritis, non iam levitatis est, sed, ut quod sentio dicam, dementiae. [2] Primum duces eos laudavistis qui contra illum bellum privato consilio suscepissent; deinde milites veteranos qui, cum ab Antonio in colonias essent deducti, illius beneficio libertatem

4   populi Romani anteposuerunt. Quid, legio Martia? Quid, quarta? Cur laudantur? Si enim consulem suum reliquerunt, vituperandae sunt; si inimicum rei publicae, iure laudantur. Atqui cum consules nondum haberetis, decrevistis ut et de praemiis militum et de honoribus imperatorum primo quoque tempore referretur. Placet eodem tempore praemia constituere eis qui contra Antonium arma ceperint et legatos ad Antonium mittere, ut iam pudendum sit honestiora decreta esse legionum quam senatus? Si quidem legiones decreverunt senatum defendere contra Antonium, senatus decernit legatos ad Antonium. Utrum

---

3 The consuls-elect for 43, A. Hirtius and C. Vibius Pansa, did not attend the meeting of the senate on 20 Dec. 44 (cf. §30). And the consuls of 44, Mark Antony and P. Cornelius Dolabella, were not in Rome either, on top of which Cicero did not regard them as proper consuls in any case. – For the decree cf. 3.37–39.

praise, glory, and gratitude you won from the Roman people! And your decisions on that day, Members of the Senate, mean that you now have no choice except an honorable peace or a necessary war.

Does Marcus Antonius want peace? Let him lay down 3 his arms, make his petition, ask our pardon. Nobody will give him a fairer hearing than I, though in recommending himself to treacherous citizens he has preferred my enmity to my friendship. Obviously no concessions are possible while he is making war; if he petitions us, perhaps there will be something we can concede. But to send envoys to a man on whom twelve days ago you passed a judgment of the weightiest and sternest character is—not levity but, to speak my mind, stark lunacy. [2] First you commended those commanders who had started a war against him on their private initiative, then the veteran soldiers who, after having been settled in colonies by Antonius, preferred the freedom of the Roman people to his benefaction. What of 4 the Martian Legion and the Fourth? Why are they commended? For if it was their consul whom they abandoned, they are blameworthy; if it was an enemy of the Republic, they are rightly commended. But when you did not yet have any consuls,[3] you passed a decree providing that discussion be opened at the first opportunity concerning both rewards for the soldiers and honors for their commanders. Are you in favor of determining rewards for those who took up arms against Antonius and at the same time of sending envoys to Antonius? In that case we will have cause to be ashamed that the decrees of the legions are more honorable than those of the senate, if actually the legions decreed to defend the senate against Antonius, while the senate decrees to send envoys to Antonius. Is that fortify-

hoc est confirmare militum animos an debilitare virtutem?
5 Hoc dies duodecim profecerunt ut, quem nemo praeter
Cotylam[1] inventus sit qui defenderet, is habeat iam patronos etiam consularis?

Qui utinam omnes ante me sententiam rogarentur—
quamquam suspicor quid dicturi sint quidam eorum qui
post me rogabuntur—; facilius contra dicerem si quid videretur. Est enim opinio decreturum aliquem M. Antonio
illam ultimam Galliam quam Plancus obtinet. Quid est
aliud omnia ad bellum civile hosti arma largiri, primum
nervos belli, pecuniam infinitam, qua nunc eget, deinde
equitatum quantum velit? Equitatum dico? Dubitabit,
credo, gentis barbaras secum adducere. Hoc qui non videt,
6 excors, qui cum videt decernit, impius ⟨est⟩.[2] Tu civem
sceleratum et perditum Gallorum et Germanorum pecunia, peditatu, equitatu, copiis instrues? Nullae istae excu-
sationes sunt: "Meus amicus est." Sit patriae prius. "Meus
cognatus." An potest cognatio propior ulla esse quam
patriae, in qua parentes etiam continentur? "Mihi pecuniam tribuit." Cupio videre qui id audeat dicere.

Quid autem agatur cum aperuero, facile erit statuere
quam sententiam dicatis aut quam sequamini. [3] Agitur
utrum M. Antonio facultas detur opprimendae rei publicae, caedis faciendae bonorum, urbis dividendae, agrorum[3] suis latronibus condonandi, populi Romani[4] servitute opprimendi, an horum ei facere nihil liceat. Dubitate

[1] *corr. Poggius*

[2] *add. Lambinus*

[3] *Halm*: urbis eruendorum agrorum V[2] *in ras.*: eripiendorum
urbis agrorum *bntv*: diripiendorum urbis agrorum *s*

[4] *Manutius*: populum Romanum V*t*: rem publicam *bnsv*

ing the soldiers' morale or sapping their courage? Have 5
twelve days passed to such effect that a man who found nobody to defend him except Cotyla now has even consulars
as his patrons?

I wish that all of them were asked for their views ahead
of me—not that I do not have an inkling of what some of
those who will be asked after me are going to say—; it
would be easier to speak in opposition, if anything seemed
appropriate. For there is a notion that somebody will propose for Marcus Antonius the assignment of that Outer
Gaul, which is now being governed by Plancus. That would
simply be presenting the enemy with all the weapons required for civil war: first, the sinews of war, a limitless sup-
ply of money, of which he now stands in need; then, cavalry, all he wants. I say "cavalry," but will he hesitate to
bring up barbarous nations? Anyone who does not see this
is a fool; anyone who does and makes the proposal all the
same is a traitor. Are you going to furnish an abandoned 6
criminal with Gallic and German money, infantry, cavalry,
resources generally? Those excuses of yours amount to
nothing: "He is my friend." Let him be a friend to his native land first. "He is my relative." Can any relationship be
closer than that to your native land, in which parents also
are comprised? "He has given me money." I am eager to
see who has the boldness to say that.

Moreover, when I make plain what is at issue, it will be
easy then for you to decide what proposal to put forward or
what to support. [3] The issue is whether Marcus Antonius
is to be given the means of crushing the Republic, massa-
cring decent men, parceling out the city, bestowing lands
on his fellow robbers, enslaving the Roman people, or
whether none of this is to be placed within his power. Ex-

7 quid agatis! "At non cadunt haec in Antonium." Hoc ne
Cotyla quidem dicere auderet.

Quid enim in eum non cadit qui, cuius acta se defendere dicit, eius eas leges pervertit quas maxime laudare po-
teramus? Ille paludes siccare voluit: hic omnem Italiam
moderato homini, L. Antonio, dividendam dedit. Quid?
Hanc legem populus Romanus accepit? Quid? Per auspicia ferri potuit? Sed augur verecundus sine collegis de auspiciis.[5] Quamquam illa auspicia non egent interpretatione
augurum:[6] Iove enim tonante cum populo agi non esse fas
quis ignorat? Tribuni plebis tulerunt de provinciis contra
acta C. Caesaris: ille biennium, hi sexennium. Etiam hanc
legem populus Romanus accepit? Quid? Promulgata fuit?
Quid? Non ante lata quam scripta est? Quid? Non ante fac-
8 tum vidimus quam futurum quisquam est suspicatus? Ubi
lex Caecilia et Didia, ubi promulgatio trinum nundinum,
ubi poena recenti lege Iunia et Licinia? Possuntne hae leges esse ratae sine interitu legum reliquarum? Eccui potestas in forum insinuandi fuit? Quae porro illa tonitrua,
quae tempestas! Ut, si auspicia M. Antonium non move-

[5] *codd.*: de auspiciis ⟨silet⟩ *SB, praeeunte Madvig*
[6] augurum *om.* V

[4] Caesar had planned to drain the Pontine Marshes (cf. Suet.
Iul. 44.3; Plut. *Caes.* 58.9; Cass. Dio 44.5.1). – Lucius Antonius
was chair of the Board of Seven (*septemviri*), set up to implement
the *Lex Antonia agraria* of June 44, i.e., to arrange for the distribution of land.
[5] For Caesar's law cf. 1.19. A plebiscite of summer 44 extended the proconsulships for Antony and Dolabella to five years
(cf. 8.27–28; *Att.* 15.11.4). Here their term is inflated to six years,

press your uncertainty over what you are to do! "But all this does not apply to Antonius." Not even Cotyla would dare 7 to say that.

For what does not apply to a man who subverts the laws of the very person whose acts he claims to be defending, those laws that we could most approve of? Caesar wanted to drain marshes: Antonius gave all Italy over to that man of moderation, Lucius Antonius, to be parceled out.[4] Did the Roman people accept this law? Could it be carried according to the auspices? But this augur is diffident concerning auspices without his colleagues. Not that those auspices have any need for augurs to interpret them. Who does not know that it is contrary to the dictates of religion to transact business with the people when Jupiter thunders? The tribunes of the plebs proposed a law concerning provinces which ran contrary to the acts of Gaius Caesar: he fixed a two-year term, they a six-year.[5] Did the Roman people accept this law too? Was it promulgated? And was it not carried before it was drafted? Again, did we not see an accomplished fact before anyone suspected it was coming? What has become of the Caecilian and Didian Law, of the 8 three-market-day promulgation, of the penalty under the recent Junian and Licinian Law?[6] Can these laws[7] be valid without the dissolution of all the other laws? Was anyone given a chance to slip into the Forum? And the thunder, the storm! If the auspices had no effect on Marcus

probably in view of Antony already trying to take possession of the provinces during the latter part of his year in office in 44.

[6] The two laws, of 98 and 62 respectively, provided against the introduction of legislation without proper notice. On the *Lex Caecilia Didia*, see 2.6, n. 7.   [7] I.e. those of Antony.

CICERO

rent, sustinere tamen eum ac ferre posse tantam vim tempestatis, imbris, [ac][7] turbinum mirum videretur. Quam legem igitur se augur dicit tulisse non modo tonante Iove sed prope caelesti clamore prohibente, hanc dubitabit
9 contra auspicia latam confiteri? Quid? Quod cum eo collega tulit quem ipse fecit sua nuntiatione vitiosum, nihilne ad auspicia bonus augur pertinere arbitratus est? [4] Sed auspiciorum nos fortasse erimus interpretes qui sumus eius collegae: num ergo etiam armorum interpretes quaerimus? Primum omnes fori aditus ita saepti ut, etiam si nemo obstaret armatus, tamen nisi saeptis revulsis introiri in forum nullo modo posset; sic vero erant disposita praesidia ut quo modo hostium aditus urbe prohibentur castellis et operibus, ita ab ingressione fori populum tribunosque
10 plebis propulsari videres. Quibus de causis eas leges quas M. Antonius tulisse dicitur omnis censeo per vim et contra auspicia latas eisque legibus populum non teneri. Si quam legem de actis Caesaris confirmandis deve dictatura in perpetuum tollenda deve coloniis in agros deducendis tulisse M. Antonius dicitur, easdem leges de integro ut populum teneant salvis auspiciis ferri placet. Quamvis enim res bonas vitiose per vimque tulerit, tamen eae leges non sunt habendae, omnisque audacia gladiatoris amentis auctoritate nostra repudianda est.
11 Illa vero dissipatio pecuniae publicae ferenda nullo modo est per quam sestertium septiens miliens falsis per-

7 *del. Wesenberg*

8 Cf. 3.9 and n. 7.
9 These three Antonian laws go back to senatorial decrees passed soon after Caesar's assassination, during a period in which Antony still followed a moderate course.

252

Antonius, it still seemed astonishing that he could manage
to endure and bear such a fury of tempest, rain, and whirlwinds. So will he hesitate to admit that a law that he, an augur, says he carried not only while Jupiter was thundering
but almost with the heavens clamoring to forbid it, was carried in violation of the auspices? Add the fact that he 9
carried it jointly with a colleague whose status he caused to
be flawed by his own announcement:[8] did the adept augur
not think that relevant to the auspices? [4] However, perhaps we who are his colleagues will interpret the auspices:
do we require interpreters for the weapons too? Firstly, all
approaches to the Forum were barricaded, so that even if
no armed guard blocked entry, it was in no way possible to
get into the Forum without tearing down the barricades.
But furthermore, guards were posted, and the people and
the tribunes of the plebs might be seen being thrust back
from the entrances to the Forum, just as an approaching
enemy is denied access to a town by outposts and fortifica-
tions. For these reasons it is my judgment that the laws 10
which Marcus Antonius is said to have carried were all carried by violence and in contravention of the auspices, and
that the people are not bound by those laws. If Marcus
Antonius is said to have carried a law confirming Caesar's
acts or abolishing the dictatorship in perpetuity or found-
ing colonies on lands,[9] I think it proper that the same laws
be carried afresh with due observance of auspices so that
they may bind the people. For however good in themselves
may be the measures he carried improperly and by violence, they are still not to be considered laws. And the
crazy gladiator's insolence is to be repudiated in its entirety
by our authority.

Then there is this totally intolerable squandering of 11
public money through which he has embezzled seven hun-

scriptionibus donationibusque avertit, ut portenti simile
videatur tantam pecuniam populi Romani tam brevi tempore perire potuisse. Quid? Illi immanes quaestus feren-
dine quos M. Antoni †tota† exhausit[8] domus? Decreta falsa vendebat, regna, civitates, immunitates in aes accepta
pecunia iubebat incidi. Haec se ex commentariis C. Caesaris, quorum ipse auctor erat, agere dicebat. Calebant in in-
teriore aedium parte totius rei publicae nundinae; mulier
sibi felicior quam viris auctionem provinciarum regno-
rumque faciebat; restituebantur exsules quasi lege sine
lege; quae nisi auctoritate senatus rescinduntur, quoniam
ingressi in spem rei publicae recuperandae sumus, imago
nulla liberae civitatis relinquetur. Neque solum commentariis commenticiis chirographisque venalibus innumerabilis pecunia congesta in illam domum est, cum, quae vendebat Antonius, ea se ex actis Caesaris agere diceret, sed
senatus etiam consulta pecunia accepta falsa referebat,
syngraphae obsignabantur, senatus consulta numquam
facta ad aerarium deferebantur. Huius turpitudinis testes
erant etiam exterae nationes. Foedera interea facta, regna
data, populi provinciaeque liberatae, illarumque[9] rerum
falsae tabulae gemente populo Romano toto Capitolio
figebantur. Quibus rebus tanta pecunia una in domo coa-
cervata est ut, si hoc genus †pene in unum†[10] redigatur,
non sit pecunia rei publicae defutura.

12

[8] tota exhausit *codd.*, *Fedeli*: illi tot immanes . . . exhausit *Clark*
[9] *SB*: ipsarumque V: earumque D   [10] pene V (*om. D*) in
unum *Vbsnv* (unus *t*): pecuniae iure *Clark*: pecuniae *Ursinus*:
praedae *Clark dub. in app.*: in aerarium *Orelli*: *alii alia*

[10] These public funds were kept in the Temple of Ops (cf.
2.93a; 5.15).   [11] Cf. 2.11, n. 12.

dred million sesterces[10] in forged assignments and dona-
tions. It seems contrary to nature that so vast a sum belonging to the Roman people could have vanished in so
short a time. Well, can we tolerate the monstrous profits
that M. Antonius' house as a whole has absorbed? He sold
false decrees, caused kingdoms, grants of citizenship, exemptions from taxation to be inscribed on bronze tablets in
return for bribes. These things he claimed to do in execution of Gaius Caesar's memoranda, which were vouched
for by himself. A roaring trade involving the whole Republic was carried on in the inner part of the dwelling; a
woman who has brought more luck to herself than to her
husbands[11] put up provinces and kingdoms for auction; exiles were restored illegally under the pretense of law. If
these proceedings are not rescinded by authority of the
senate, since we are now in hopes of reestablishing the Republic, no semblance of a free community will be left. And 12
besides the money piled up beyond counting in that house
from forged memoranda and handwritten notes put up for
sale—Antonius all the while claiming these transactions to
be in execution of Caesar's acts—he even used to place on
record false senatorial decrees in return for bribes; bonds
were sealed; senatorial decrees which the senate never
made were deposited in the treasury. Even foreign nations
were witnesses of this scandal. Meanwhile, treaties were
made, kingdoms granted, freedom conferred on peoples
and provinces, and lying notices of those proceedings were
posted up all over the Capitol amid the groans of the Roman people. So much money from these activities was
heaped up in a single house that, if this sort of profit were
to be collected at the treasury, the Republic would not be
short of funds in days to come.

[5] Legem etiam iudiciariam tulit, homo castus atque
integer, iudiciorum et iuris auctor. In quo nos fefellit: ante-
signanos et manipularis et Alaudas iudices se constituisse
dicebat; at ille legit aleatores, legit exsules, legit Graecos.
O consessum iudicum praeclarum! O dignitatem consili
admirandam! Avet animus apud consilium illud pro reo dicere, ⟨en⟩[11] Cydam Cretensem, portentum insulae, hominem audacissimum et perditissimum. Sed facite non esse:
num Latine scit? Num est ex iudicum genere et forma?
Num, quod maximum est, leges nostras moresve novit?
Num denique homines? Est enim Creta vobis notior quam
Roma Cydae. Dilectus autem et notatio iudicum etiam in
nostris civibus haberi solet: Gortynium vero iudicem quis
novit aut quis nosse potuit? Nam Lysiaden Atheniensem
plerique novimus; est enim Phaedri, philosophi nobilis,
filius; homo praeterea festivus, ut ei cum Curio[12] conses-
sore eodemque collusore facillime possit convenire. Quaero igitur, si Lysiades citatus iudex non responderit excuse-
turque Areopagites esse nec debere eodem tempore
Romae et Athenis res iudicare, accipietne excusationem is
qui quaestioni praeerit Graeculi iudicis, modo palliati,
modo togati? An Atheniensium antiquissimas leges negle-
get? Qui porro ille consessus, di boni! Cretensis iudex
isque nequissimus. Quem[13] ad hunc reus adleget, quo

13

14

[11] *SB in app.*: dicere cydam *VD*: dicere, ⟨sedentem videre⟩ *SB*
[12] curio *V*: m. curio *D*: M'. Curio *Lambinus*
[13] *nsv*: que *bt*: quem ad modum *V*

[12] On Antony's judiciary law cf. 1.19–20 (and n.); 8.27; 13.3;
13.37.

[5] He also carried a judiciary law, this blameless and upright character, a supporter of law and law courts.[12] But he took us in: he used to say that he had made jurors of elite fighters, privates, and the Larks; in fact he chose gamblers, exiles, and Greeks. A fine assemblage of jurors! A wonderfully dignified court! I cannot wait to speak for the defense before that tribunal. There is Cydas of Crete, the island monster,[13] a most unscrupulous and desperate character. But suppose he isn't that: does he know Latin? Is he of the type and cut for a juror? Most important, does he know our laws and customs? In a word, does he know our folk? For Crete is better known to you than Rome is to Cydas. Even among our own countrymen it is customary for there to be exercised a selection and choice of jurymen; but who knows or could know a juryman from Gortyn? As for Lysiades of Athens, most of us know him; for he is the son of the eminent philosopher Phaedrus. Besides he is a cheerful person, who will have no difficulty in getting along with his fellow juror and also fellow gambler, Curius. So I put this question: suppose Lysiades does not respond to a summons for jury service and pleads as an excuse that he is a member of the Areopagus and cannot properly try cases in Rome and Athens at the same time, will the president of the court accept the excuse of a little Greek juryman, who wears Greek garb one day and the garb of a Roman citizen the next? Or will he take no account of the immemorially ancient laws of Athens? And what an assemblage, good gods! A Cretan juror and a complete rogue at that! Whom is a defendant to send to him as an intermedi-

13

14

---

[13] Probably an allusion to the Minotaur, a mythical Cretan monster.

modo accedat? Dura natio est. At Athenienses misericordes. Puto ne Curium quidem esse crudelem, qui periculum fortunae cotidie facit. Sunt item lecti iudices qui fortasse excusabuntur; habent enim legitimam excusationem,
15 exsili causa solum vertisse nec esse postea restitutos. Hos ille demens iudices legisset, horum nomina ad aerarium detulisset, his magnam partem rei publicae credidisset, si ullam speciem rei publicae cogitavisset?[14] [6] Atque ego de notis iudicibus dixi; quos minus nostis nolui nominare: saltatores, citharistas, totum denique comissationis Antonianae chorum in tertiam decuriam iudicum scitote esse coniectum. Em causam cur lex tam egregia tamque praeclara maximo imbri, tempestate, ventis, procellis, turbinibus, inter fulmina et tonitrua ferretur, ut eos iudices haberemus quos hospites habere nemo velit. Scelerum magnitudo, conscientia maleficiorum, direptio eius pecuniae cuius ratio in aede Opis confecta est hanc tertiam decuriam excogitavit. Nec ante turpes iudices quaesiti quam honestis iudicibus nocentium salus desperata est.
16 Sed illud os, illam impuritatem caeni fuisse ut hos iudices legere auderet quorum lectione duplex imprimeretur rei publicae dedecus: unum, quod tam turpes iudices essent; alterum, quod patefactum cognitumque esset quam multos in civitate turpis haberemus! Hanc ergo et reliquas eius modi leges, etiam si sine vi salvis auspiciis essent rogatae,

---

[14] ⟨relinquere⟩ cogitavisset *add. SB*

ary, how is he to approach him? They are a hard people. Well, but Athenians are merciful; and I don't suppose even Curius, who tries his luck every day, is a cruel man. There are likewise select jurors who perhaps will be excused: they have a legitimate excuse, that they have changed their country of residence by reason of banishment and have not subsequently been reinstated. Would that madman have 15 selected jurors such as these, given their names in to the treasury, entrusted them with an important component of our Republic, if he had considered any semblance of the Republic? [6] And I have been speaking of jurors who are known to you. I did not want to name persons whom you know less well, but take it from me that dancers, harpists, the whole Antonian troupe of carousers have been flung into the third panel of jurors. Here we have the reason why so excellent, so admirable a law was put through in violent rain, tempest, winds, gales, whirlwinds, amid lightning and thunder: it was to give us jurors whom nobody would want as guests. Crimes on a large scale, consciousness of wrongdoings, the plunder of the money the account of which was kept in the Temple of Ops have come up with this third panel. Disreputable jurors were sought out only when the guilty despaired of survival with respectable ones. But to think that such was his impudence, such his 16 utter loathsome filthiness that he dared to select these jurors, by whose selection a double disgrace was stamped upon the Republic, first because the jurors were such scoundrels and, second, because it thus stood revealed and ascertained how many scoundrels we had in our community! Therefore, even if this law and all the others of a like character had been passed without violence and with due observance of auspices, I would still hold that they ought to

censerem tamen abrogandas: nunc vero cur abrogandas
censeam, quas iudico non rogatas?

17   An illa non gravissimis ignominiis monumentisque huius
ordinis ad posteritatis memoriam sunt notanda, quod unus
M. Antonius in hac urbe post conditam urbem palam secum habuerit armatos? Quod neque reges nostri fecerunt
neque ei qui regibus exactis regnum occupare voluerunt.
Cinnam memini, vidi Sullam, modo Caesarem: hi enim
tres post civitatem a L. Bruto liberatam plus potuerunt
quam universa res publica. Non possum adfirmare nullis
18   telis eos stipatos fuisse; hoc dico: nec multis et occultis. At
hanc pestem agmen armatorum sequebatur; Crassicius,
Mustela, Tiro, gladios ostentantes, sui similis greges duce-
bant per forum; certum agminis locum tenebant barbari
sagittarii. Cum autem erat ventum ad aedem Concordiae,
gradus complebantur, lecticae collocabantur, non quo ille
scuta occulta esse vellet, sed ne familiares, si scuta ipsi fer-
rent, laborarent. [7] Illud vero taeterrimum non modo as-
pectu sed etiam auditu, in cella Concordiae collocari armatos, latrones, sicarios; de templo carcerem fieri; opertis
valvis Concordiae, cum inter subsellia senatus versarentur
latrones, patres conscriptos sententias dicere.

19   Huc nisi venirem [etiam]15 Kalendis Septembribus, fa-
bros se missurum et domum meam disturbaturum esse
dixit. Magna res, credo, agebatur: de supplicatione referebat. Veni postridie: ipse non venit. Locutus sum de re pu-

15 del. Kayser, Lutz

be repealed. As it is, however, why should I ask for the repeal of laws which in my judgment were never passed?

And is not this something to be censured by this body in the most severe and scathing terms as a record for posterity to remember? Marcus Antonius is the only man since the foundation of the city who has publicly kept armed men at his side in this city! Our kings did not do this, neither did those who after the expulsion of the kings have tried to usurp the kingship. I remember Cinna, I saw Sulla, recently Caesar, the three who since Lucius Brutus liberated the community have possessed more power than the entire Republic. I cannot say that no weapons surrounded them, but this I do say: there were not many, and they were hidden. But this noxious creature was attended by an armed column. Crassicius, Mustela, Tiro, brandishing their swords, used to lead squads of fellows like themselves through the Forum. Barbarian archers had their assured place in the column. When they reached the Temple of Concord, the steps would be filled up, the litters set down—not that he wanted the shields kept out of sight, but to spare his friends the trouble of carrying them. [7] Most horrible of all, even to tell of, let alone to see, armed men, bandits, cutthroats, were stationed in the sanctuary of Concord. The temple was turned into a jail. The doors of Concord were closed, and members of the senate gave their opinions with bandits moving among the senatorial benches.

If I did not come here on the first of September he said he would send workmen to wreck my house. The business in hand was of great importance, no doubt: he had a public thanksgiving discussed. I came the day following: he himself did not attend. I spoke on the Republic with some

blica, minus equidem libere quam mea consuetudo, liberius tamen quam periculi minae postulabant. At ille homo vehemens et violentus, qui hanc consuetudinem libere dicendi excluderet—fecerat enim hoc idem maxima cum laude L. Piso triginta diebus ante—inimicitias mihi denuntiavit; adesse in senatum iussit a.d. XIII Kalendas Octobris. Ipse interea septemdecim dies de me in Tiburtino Scipionis declamitavit, sitim quaerens; haec enim ei
20 causa esse declamandi solet. Cum is dies quo me adesse iusserat venisset, tum vero agmine quadrato in aedem Concordiae venit atque in me absentem orationem ex ore impurissimo evomuit. Quo die, si per amicos mihi cupienti in senatum venire licuisset, caedis initium fecisset a me; sic enim statuerat; cum autem semel gladium scelere imbuisset, nulla res ei finem caedendi nisi defetigatio et satietas attulisset.

Etenim aderat Lucius frater, gladiator Asiaticus, qui myrmillo Mylasis depugnarat: sanguinem nostrum sitiebat, suum in illa gladiatoria pugna multum profuderat. Hic pecunias vestras aestimabat; possessiones notabat et urbanas et rusticas; huius mendicitas aviditate coniuncta in fortunas nostras imminebat; dividebat agros quibus et quos volebat; nullus aditus erat privato, nulla aequitatis deprecatio. Tantum quisque habebat possessor quantum reli-
21 querat divisor Antonius. Quae quamquam, si leges irritas feceritis, rata esse non possunt, tamen separatim suo

---

14 In the *First Philippic*, delivered on 2 Sept. 44.
15 Piso gave a courageous speech in the senate on 1 Aug. 44 (cf. 1.10), approximately "thirty days" before Cicero's *First Philippic*.
16 To which Cicero's *Second Philippic* is the written rejoinder.
17 Cf. 3.31, n. 38.

freedom[14]—my custom called for more, the threats of danger for less. Then this man of vehemence and violence, wishing to ban this habit of free speech—for Lucius Piso had done the same with the utmost credit thirty days previously[15]—, declared himself my enemy; he demanded my presence in the senate on the nineteenth of September. Meanwhile he spent seventeen days declaiming about me on Scipio's estate at Tibur, working up a thirst—his usual reason for declaiming. When the day on which he had commanded my presence arrived, he entered the Temple of Concord with his bodyguard in proper battle array and vomited from his utterly foul mouth a speech against me in my absence.[16] If my friends had permitted me to come to the senate that day as I wanted to do, he would have launched a massacre beginning with me; so he had determined. And when once he had dipped his blade in crime, nothing but weariness and satiety would have made him stop the slaughter.

For his brother Lucius was with him, the Asiatic gladiator, who once fought in single combat as a myrmillo at Mylasa:[17] he was thirsting for our blood, having shed a good deal of his own in that gladiatorial combat. There he was, estimating your money, recording your properties both in town and in the country, his poverty joined with his greed threatening our possessions. He was assigning lands, whichever he pleased and to whom he pleased. There was no access for any individual, no appeal on grounds of equity. Every landowner possessed just so much as allocator Antonius had left him. Even though these proceedings cannot be valid if you have invalidated the laws, all the same, they should, in my judgment, be separately and specifically branded; there should be a rul-

nomine notanda censeo, iudicandumque nullos septem-
viros fuisse, nihil placere ratum esse quod ab eis actum
diceretur.

[8] M. vero Antonium quis est qui civem possit iudicare
potius quam taeterrimum et crudelissimum hostem, qui
pro aede Castoris sedens audiente populo Romano dixerit
nisi victorem victurum neminem? Num putatis, patres
conscripti, dixisse eum minacius quam facturum fuisse?
Quid vero quod in contione dicere ausus est, se, cum ma-
gistratu abisset, ad urbem futurum cum exercitu, introiturum quotienscumque vellet? Quid erat aliud nisi denun-
22 tiare populo Romano servitutem? Quod autem eius iter
Brundisium, quae festinatio, quae spes, nisi ad urbem vel
in urbem potius exercitum maximum adduceret? Qui autem dilectus centurionum, quae effrenatio impotentis animi! Cum eius promissis legiones fortissimae reclamassent,
domum ad se venire iussit centuriones quos bene sentire de re publica cognoverat eosque ante pedes suos uxo-
risque suae, quam secum gravis imperator ad exercitum
duxerat, iugulari coegit. Quo animo hunc futurum fuisse
censetis in nos quos oderat, cum in eos quos numquam
viderat tam crudelis fuisset, et quam avidum in pecuniis
locupletium qui pauperum sanguinem concupisset? Quorum ipsorum bona, quantacumque erant, statim suis comi-
23 tibus compotoribusque discripsit. Atque ille furens infesta
iam patriae signa a Brundisio inferebat, cum C. Caesar
deorum immortalium beneficio, divina animi, ingeni, con-

---

18 On the Board of Seven cf. §7, n. 4.
19 Cf. 3.27.
20 On the events in Brundisium cf. 3.4, 10.

ing that the Board of Seven had no legal existence and that it is the senate's pleasure that no alleged action of that board be valid.[18]

[8] As for Marcus Antonius, who can consider him as a citizen and not as a most dire and savage public enemy? Sitting in front of the Temple of Castor, in the hearing of the Roman people, he said that only victors would be left alive. Do you suppose, Members of the Senate, that he spoke more menacingly than he would have acted? And when he dared to say at a public meeting that after leaving office he would stay near the city with an army and enter as often as he pleased,[19] what was that but pronouncing slavery upon the Roman people? And what about his journey 22 to Brundisium: why the hurry, what did he have in view if he was not bringing up a great army close to the city or rather into the city? And the singling out of centurions, what an ungovernable outburst of fury![20] When the very brave legions shouted their rejection of his promises, he ordered those centurions whom he had ascertained to be loyal to the Republic to come to his house and had them slaughtered at his feet and those of his wife, whom this solemn general had brought with him to the army. What do you think his feelings would have been towards us whom he hated, when he had treated persons whom he had never seen with such cruelty? How greedily would he have dealt with the fortunes of the wealthy, when he had been so eager for poor men's blood? And these same men's belongings, such as they were, he distributed on the spot among his comrades and drinking companions. And now in his 23 rage he was bringing hostile standards from Brundisium against his native land, when Gaius Caesar intervened: by grace of the immortal gods and by godlike greatness of

sili magnitudine, quamquam sua sponte eximiaque virtute,
tamen approbatione auctoritatis meae colonias patrias
adiit, veteranos milites convocavit, paucis diebus exercitum fecit, incitatos latronum impetus retardavit. Postea
vero quam legio Martia ducem praestantissimum vidit, nihil egit aliud nisi ut aliquando liberi essemus; quam est
imitata quarta legio. [9] Quo ille nuntio audito cum senatum vocasset adhibuissetque consularem qui sua sententia
24 C. Caesarem hostem iudicaret, repente concidit. Post autem neque sacrificiis sollemnibus factis neque votis nuncu-
patis non profectus est, sed profugit paludatus. At quo? In
provinciam firmissimorum et fortissimorum civium qui illum, ne si ita quidem venisset ut nullum bellum inferret,
ferre potuissent, impotentem, iracundum, contumeliosum, superbum, semper poscentem, semper rapientem,
semper ebrium. At ille cuius ne pacatam quidem nequitiam quisquam ferre posset bellum intulit provinciae
Galliae: circumsedet Mutinam, firmissimam et splendidis-
simam populi Romani coloniam; oppugnat D. Brutum,
imperatorem, consulem designatum, civem non sibi, sed
25 nobis et rei publicae natum. Ergo Hannibal hostis, civis
Antonius? Quid ille fecit hostiliter quod hic non aut fecerit
aut faciat aut moliatur et cogitet? Totum iter Antoniorum
quid habuit nisi depopulationes, vastationes, caedis, rapinas? Quas non faciebat Hannibal, quia multa ad usum
suum reservabat: at hi, qui in horam viverent, non modo de

21 On 28 Nov. 44 (cf. 3.24).

heart, mind, and judgment, of his own volition and noble impulse though not without the approval of my authority, he visited his father's colonies, called the veteran soldiers together, created an army in a matter of days, and put a brake on the rapid rush of the bandits. When the Martian Legion saw this peerless leader, it became their only purpose that we should at last be free; the Fourth Legion followed this example. [9] On receipt of this news,[21] after he had previously summoned the senate and brought along a consular who was to propose a motion that Gaius Caesar be judged a public enemy, he suddenly collapsed. Afterwards, without making the customary sacrifices or taking vows, he did not set out but rather ran away in his general's cloak. Where did he run? Into a province of very loyal and very brave citizens, who, even if he had come without any warlike intent, could not have put up with him: immoderate, irascible, abusive, arrogant, always demanding, always grabbing, always drunk. Nobody could put up with his villainy, even if non-belligerent, but Antonius made war on the province of Gaul: he is besieging Mutina, one of the most loyal and distinguished colonies of the Roman people; he is attacking Decimus Brutus, imperator, consulelect, a citizen born not for himself but for us and the Republic. Therefore: was Hannibal an enemy and is Antonius a citizen? What hostile act did Hannibal commit which Antonius has not committed or is not committing or is not putting in hand and planning? Was not the entire march of the Antonii a series of acts of depopulation, devastation, massacre, and pillaging? Hannibal did not behave so because he reserved much for his own use; but these men, living from one hour to the next, had no thought for the

24

25

fortunis et de bonis civium, sed ne de utilitate quidem sua cogitaverunt.

Ad hunc, di boni, legatos mitti placet? Norunt isti homines formam rei publicae, iura belli, exempla maiorum, cogitant quid populi Romani maiestas, quid senatus severitas postulet? Legatos decernis? Si ut deprecere, contemnet; si ut imperes, non audiet; denique quamvis severa legatis mandata dederimus, nomen ipsum legatorum hunc quem videmus populi Romani restinguet ardorem, municipiorum atque Italiae franget animos. Ut omittam haec, quae magna sunt, certe ista legatio moram et tarditatem

26 adferet bello. Quamvis dicant quod quosdam audio dicturos, "legati proficiscantur: bellum nihilo minus paretur," tamen legatorum nomen ipsum et animos hominum molliet[16] et belli celeritatem morabitur. [10] Minimis momentis, patres conscripti, maximae inclinationes temporum fiunt, cum in omni casu rei publicae tum in bello et maxime civili, quod opinione plerumque et fama gubernatur. Nemo quaeret quibus cum mandatis legatos miserimus: nomen ipsum legationis ultro missae timoris esse signum videbitur. Recedat a Mutina, desinat oppugnare Brutum, decedat ex Gallia; non est verbis rogandus, cogendus est armis.

27 Non enim ad Hannibalem mittimus ut a Sagunto recedat, ad quem miserat olim senatus P. Valerium Flaccum et

[16] *Graevius*: animos hominum *V*: animos molliet *D*

---

[22] Addressed mainly to Q. Fufius Calenus (cf. 7.5; 14.18).

fortunes and property of their countrymen and not even
for their own advantage.

And, good gods, is this the man to whom it is decided to
send envoys? Do those fellows know the structure of the
Republic, the laws of war, the precedents set by our ancestors? Have they any thought for what the majesty of the
Roman people and the gravity of the senate require? You[22]
propose envoys? If your purpose is to plead with him, he
will despise you; if it is to give him orders, he will not listen.
Finally, however stern a commission we give the envoys,
the very term "envoys" will quench the ardor of the Roman people, of which we see the evidence around us, will
break the spirit of the townships and Italy. To leave aside
these considerations, important as they are, such an embassy will at least mean delay and retardation for the war.
Though people may say, as I hear some are going to say: 26
"Let the envoys set out, and let preparations for war go
on just the same," nevertheless, the very term "envoys"
will both soften men's minds and slow the pace of the war.
[10] Very small impulses, Members of the Senate, sometimes change situations dramatically: it happens not only
in every crisis of the Republic, but particularly in war, and
above all in civil war, which is apt to be ruled by public
opinion and report. Nobody will ask what commission we
have given the envoys to deliver: the very notion of an embassy dispatched of our own volition will be taken as a sign
of fear. Let Antonius retire from Mutina, let him cease attacking Brutus, let him withdraw from Gaul; he is not to be
asked in words, he is to be compelled by force of arms.

We are not sending to Hannibal to demand that he   27
retire from Saguntum, Hannibal, to whom once upon a
time the senate sent Publius Valerius Flaccus and Quintus

Q. Baebium Tamphilum—qui, si Hannibal non pareret,
Carthaginem ire iussi erant:[17] nostros quo iubemus ire, si
non paruerit Antonius?—ad nostrum civem mittimus, ne
imperatorem, ne coloniam populi Romani oppugnet.
Itane vero? Hoc per legatos rogandum est? Quid interest,
per deos immortalis, utrum hanc urbem oppugnet an
huius urbis propugnaculum, coloniam populi Romani
praesidi causa collocatam? Belli Punici secundi quod contra maiores nostros Hannibal gessit causa fuit Sagunti op-
pugnatio. Recte ad eum legati missi: mittebantur ad Poe-
num; mittebantur pro Hannibalis hostibus, nostris sociis.
Quid simile tandem? Nos ad civem mittimus ne imperatorem populi Romani, ne exercitum, ne coloniam circumsedeat, ne oppugnet, ne agros depopuletur, ne sit hostis.

28   [11] Age, si paruerit, hoc civi uti aut volumus aut possumus? Ante diem XIII Kalendas Ianuarias decretis vestris
eum concidistis; constituistis ut haec ad vos Kalendis Ianuariis referrentur quae referri videtis, de honoribus et
praemiis bene de re publica meritorum et merentium:
quorum principem iudicastis eum qui fuit, C. Caesarem,
qui M. Antoni impetus nefarios ab urbe in Galliam avertit,
deinde milites veteranos qui primi Caesarem secuti sunt,
tum illas caelestis divinasque legiones, Martiam et quartam, comproba⟨s⟩tis, quibus, cum consulem suum non
modo reliquissent sed bello etiam persequerentur, honores et praemia spopondistis; eodemque die D. Bruti,

---

[17] *Halm*: iussi sunt V², *SB*: iusserunt V¹

---

[23] The senatorial decrees passed on the motion proposed in
the *Third Philippic* (3.37–39).

Baebius Tamphilus—they had been instructed to go on to Carthage if Hannibal refused compliance: where do we instruct our men to go if Antonius refuses?—we are sending to a fellow countryman, to ask him not to attack an imperator and a colony of the Roman people. Is this to happen indeed? Is this a request that ought to be made through envoys? What, by the immortal gods, is the difference between attacking this city and attacking an outpost of this city, a colony of the Roman people founded to provide protection? The cause of the Second Punic War, waged by Hannibal against our ancestors, was the attack on Saguntum. It was right to send envoys to *him*: they were sent to a Carthaginian; they were sent on behalf of Hannibal's enemies, our allies. What is at all similar? We are sending to a countryman to ask him not to blockade an imperator and an army and a colony of the Roman people, not to attack, not to devastate lands, not to be an enemy.

[11] Now then, supposing he complies, do we wish or   28
are we able to have him in our community? On the twentieth of December you cut him to pieces by your decrees:[23] you determined that on the first of January a discussion be initiated (as you see, it is) concerning honors and rewards for those who have deserved and are deserving well of the Republic, first among whom you judged to be (and first he was) Gaius Caesar, who turned Marcus Antonius' wicked onset away from the city to Gaul; next you gave your approval to the veteran soldiers who were the first to follow Caesar and after them to those wonderful and divine legions, the Martian and the Fourth, to whom you pledged honors and rewards after they had not only abandoned their consul but were actually making war on him. On the same day, the dispatch of our very distinguished country-

praestantissimi civis, edicto adlato atque proposito factum
eius collaudastis, quodque ille bellum privato consilio sus-
29 ceperat, id vos auctoritate publica comprobastis. Quid
igitur illo die aliud egistis nisi ut hostem iudicaretis Antonium? His vestris decretis aut ille vos aequo animo aspicere poterit aut vos illum sine dolore summo videbitis?
Exclusit illum a re publica, distraxit, segregavit non solum
scelus ipsius sed etiam, ut mihi videtur, fortuna quaedam
rei publicae. Qui si legatis paruerit Romamque redierit,
num ‹um›quam[18] perditis civibus vexillum quo concur-
rant defuturum putatis? Sed hoc minus vereor: sunt alia
quae magis timeam et cogitem. Numquam parebit ille legatis. Novi hominis insaniam, adrogantiam; novi perdita
30 consilia amicorum, quibus ille est deditus. Lucius quidem
frater eius, utpote qui peregre depugnarit, familiam ducit.
Sit per se ipse sanus, quod numquam erit: per hos esse ei
tamen non licebit.

Teretur interea tempus; belli apparatus refrigescent.
Unde est adhuc bellum tractum nisi ex retardatione et
mora? Ut primum post discessum latronis vel potius des-
peratam fugam libere senatus haberi potuit, semper flagi-
tavi ut convocaremur. Quo die primum convocati sumus,
cum designati consules non adessent, ieci sententia mea
maximo vestro consensu fundamenta rei publicae, serius
omnino quam decuit—nec enim ante potui—sed tamen, si
ex eo tempore dies nullus intermissus esset, bellum pro-
31 fecto nullum haberemus. Omne malum nascens facile op-

___

[18] *corr. Garatoni*

[24] Cf. §20 and n. 17. [25] On 20 Dec. 44, when Cicero's
motion was carried (3.37–39; cf. also §4).

man Decimus Brutus arrived and was published; you
praised what he had done and endorsed by public authority his action in starting war on his private initiative. What,   29
then, was your purpose that day but to declare Antonius a
public enemy? After those decrees of yours will he be able
to look at you calmly, or will you see him without fierce indignation? His own crime and also, as it seems to me, a
stroke of good fortune for the Republic has shut him out,
separated, segregated from the Republic. If he obeys the
envoys and returns to Rome, do you imagine that abandoned citizens will ever lack a banner to rally behind? This,
however, is not my main apprehension: there are other
dangers I fear more, have more in mind. He will never
obey the envoys. I know this man's madness, his arrogance;
I know the desperate counsels of the friends to whom he
has surrendered himself. His brother Lucius leads this   30
troop, with his experience of combat in foreign parts.[24]
Suppose Antonius is sane in himself, which he will never
be: he will still not be allowed to be so by these fellows.

Meanwhile, time will be wasted; military preparations
will cool off. Is not the protraction of the war till now due
solely to hesitation and waiting? From the moment when
the senate could be convened without intimidation, after
the departure of the bandit, or rather after his desperate
flight, I continually demanded that we be convoked. As
soon as we were convoked, in the absence of the consuls-
elect, I put forward a proposal by which I laid the foundations of the Republic, with your greatest assent.[25] It is true
that it was later than it should have been—for I had no earlier opportunity—; but if no day had been lost from that
time forward, it is pretty clear that we should not have a
war on our hands. Every evil is easily nipped in the bud;   31

primitur; inveteratum fit plerumque robustius. Sed tum
exspectabantur Kalendae Ianuariae, fortasse non recte.
[12] Verum praeterita omittamus: etiamne hanc moram,
dum proficiscantur legati, dum revertantur? Quorum exspectatio dubitationem belli adfer⟨e⟩t:[19] bello autem du-
bio quod potest studium esse dilectus?

Quam ob rem, patres conscripti, legatorum mentionem
nullam censeo faciendam; rem administrandam arbitror
sine ulla mora et confestim gerendam [censeo];[20] tumultum decerni, iustitium edici, saga sumi dico oportere, di-
lectum haberi sublatis vacationibus in urbe et in Italia
32 praeter Galliam tota. Quae si erunt facta, opinio ipsa et
fama nostrae severitatis obruet scelerati gladiatoris amen-
tiam. Sentiet ⟨s⟩ibi bellum cum re publica esse susceptum; experietur consentientis senatus nervos atque viris;
nam nunc quidem partium contentionem esse dictitat.
Quarum partium? Alteri victi sunt, alteri sunt e mediis C.
Caesari⟨s⟩ partibus; nisi forte Caesaris partis a Pansa et
Hirtio consulibus et a filio C. Caesaris oppugnari putamus.
Hoc vero bellum non ⟨est⟩[21] ex dissensione partium, sed
ex nefaria spe perditissimorum civium ex[er]citatum,[22]
quibus bona fortunaeque nostrae notatae sunt et iam ad
33 cuiusque optionem[23] distributae. Legi epistulam Antoni
quam ad quendam septemvirum, capitalem hominem,

---

[19] SB: adfert codd. [20] del. Lambinus
[21] add. ed. Gryph. [22] corr. Poggius
[23] Manutius: opinionem V

---

[26] Cicero probably refers to the two groups comprising the
former Pompeians and Caesarians. In contrast to Antony (cf.
13.38–39, 42, 45–47), he believed that the present struggle was a

with age it usually gets stronger. But then we were waiting for the first of January; perhaps that was a mistake. [12] But let bygones be bygones: is there now to be yet further delay while the envoys set out and return? To wait for them will raise doubts about the war; and if the war is in doubt, how can there be an enthusiastic response to a levy of troops?

Therefore, Members of the Senate, in my judgment no mention should be made of envoys. I think the business should be put in hand without any delay and prosecuted at once. I say that a state of public emergency should be decreed, suspension of business proclaimed, military cloaks donned, and a levy held with no exemptions in the city and in the whole of Italy, Gaul excepted. If these measures are 32 adopted, the mere opinion and report of our sternness will crush the madness of a felonious gladiator. He will realize that he has taken up arms against the Republic; he will feel the sinews and strength of a united senate, while at present he talks of a conflict between parties. What parties? One group has been defeated; the other comes from the midst of Gaius Caesar's partisans. Or do we suppose that Caesar's partisans are under attack from the consuls Pansa and Hirtius and from Gaius Caesar's son?[26] But this war is not due to a quarrel involving parties: instead, it has been stirred up from the wicked hopes of totally desperate citizens, for whom our goods and fortunes have been marked down and already distributed to suit each individual's preference. I have read a letter that Antonius had sent to one 33 member of the Board of Seven, a right dangerous charac-

war of the united citizenry against one public enemy and his followers.

collegam suum, miserat. "Quid concupiscas tu videris: quod concupiveris certe habebis." Em ad quem legatos mittamus, cui bellum moremur inferre: qui ne sorti quidem fortunas nostras destin⟨a⟩vit, sed libidini cuiusque nos ita addixit ut ne sibi quidem quicquam integrum quod non alicui promissum iam sit reliquerit. Cum hoc, patres conscripti, bello, ⟨bello⟩[24] inquam, decertandum est, idque confestim: legatorum tarditas repudianda est.

34   Quapropter ne multa nobis cotidie decernenda sint, consulibus totam rem publicam commendandam censeo eisque permittendum ut rem publicam defendant provide⟨a⟩ntque ne quid res publica detrimenti accipiat, censeoque ut eis qui in exercitu M. Antoni sunt ne sit ea res fraudi, si ante Kalendas Februarias ab eo discesserint. Haec si censuerit⟨is⟩, patres conscripti, brevi tempore libertatem populi Romani auctoritatemque vestram recuperabitis. Si autem lenius agetis, tamen eadem, sed fortasse serius decernetis. De re publica quod ret⟨t⟩ulistis satis decrevisse videor.

35   [13] Altera res est de honoribus; de quibus deinceps intellego esse dicendum. Sed qui ordo in sententiis rogandis servari solet, eundem tenebo in viris fortibus honorandis. A Bruto igitur, consule designato, more maiorum capiamus exordium. Cuius ut superiora omittam, quae sunt

---

[24] *add. Naugerius*

---

[27] Cicero proposes a *senatus consultum ultimum*, using one of the traditional formulae (cf. 2.51, n. 56).
[28] I.e. the consuls.   [29] Senators were called on to speak according to rank (in descending order). Cf. 1.15, n. 30.
[30] I.e. Caesar's assassination.

ter, his colleague: "You must make up your mind what you want; what you want you will certainly get." Look, this is the man to whom we are to send envoys, against whom we are to delay launching a war! He who has not even put our fortunes into a lottery, but has given us over to every individual's desires, so as not even to leave something uncommitted for himself, since everything has already been promised to somebody. With this man, Members of the Senate, we must fight it out. It must be war, I repeat, war, and that right away: no drawn-out business of envoys!

Therefore, to spare ourselves the necessity of many decrees day after day, I propose that the whole Republic be committed to the consuls and that they be given full discretion to defend the Republic and take measures to ensure that the Republic suffer no harm.[27] I further propose that men now in the army of Marcus Antonius be subject to no penalty on that account provided that they leave him before the first of February. If you so decide, Members of the Senate, you will soon recover the liberty of the Roman people and your own authority. If, on the other hand, you take a milder course, you will nonetheless eventually pass the same decrees, but perhaps too late. So far as the question you[28] wished to be discussed concerns the state of the Republic, I think it is sufficiently covered by my motion. 34

[13] The other matter concerns honors; this must evidently be my next theme. Well, I shall observe the same order of precedence in honoring brave men as is customarily used in calling on senators to speak.[29] Therefore, following traditional practice, let us begin with Brutus, consul-elect. Even leaving aside his earlier achievements,[30] which, how- 35

maxima illa quidem sed adhuc hominum magis iudiciis quam publice laudata, quibusnam verbis eius laudes huius ipsius temporis consequi possumus? Neque enim ullam mercedem tanta virtus praeter hanc laudis gloriaeque desiderat, qua etiam si careat, tamen sit se ipsa contenta; quamquam in memoria gratorum civium tamquam in luce posita laetatur.[25] Laus igitur iudici testimonique nostri tribuenda Bruto est.

36 Quam ob rem his verbis, patres conscripti, senatus consultum faciendum censeo: "Cum D. Brutus, imperator, consul designatus, provinciam Galliam in senatus populique Romani potestate teneat, cumque exercitum tantum tam brevi tempore summo studio municipiorum coloniarumque provinciae Galliae, optime de re publica meritae merentisque, conscripserit, compararit, id eum recte et ordine exque re publica fecisse, idque D. Bruti praestantissimum meritum in rem publicam senatui populoque Romano gratum esse et fore: itaque senatum populumque Romanum existimare, D. Bruti imperatoris, consulis designati, opera, consilio, virtute incredibilique studio et consensu provinciae Galliae rei publicae difficillimo tempore esse subventum."

37 Huic tanto merito Bruti, patres conscripti, tantoque in rem publicam beneficio quis est tantus honos qui non debeatur? Nam si M. Antonio patuisset Gallia, si oppressis municipiis et coloni⟨i⟩s imparatis in illam ultimam Galliam penetrare potuisset, quantus rei publicae terror im-

---

[25] *SB*: laetentur V: laete[n]tur *Poggius*

ever great, have hitherto received general approval rather than official acknowledgment, how can we find words to praise his exemplary conduct at this very time? And indeed such virtue asks for no reward save this of praise and glory, and even if that were not forthcoming, it would be content with itself; not but what it rejoices, placed in the memory of grateful countrymen as in a pool of light. So Brutus must be given the praise of our judgment and testimony.

Accordingly, Members of the Senate, I propose that 36 a decree of the senate be passed in the following terms: "Whereas Decimus Brutus, imperator, consul-elect, is holding the province of Gaul in the control of the senate and people of Rome, and whereas he has enrolled and mustered so large an army in so short a time with the enthusiastic support of the municipalities and colonies of the province of Gaul, a province which has deserved and is deserving excellently well of the Republic: that he has acted rightly and properly and in the public interest; and that this outstanding service to the Republic on the part of Decimus Brutus is and will be pleasing to the senate and people of Rome; therefore the senate and people of Rome consider that by the activity, judgment, and courage of Decimus Brutus, imperator, consul-elect, and by the extraordinary zeal and unanimity of the province of Gaul, aid has been rendered to the Republic at a most difficult time."

For this sovereign service of Brutus, Members of the 37 Senate, and such a great benefaction conferred upon the Republic, what honor could be too great? If Gaul had lain wide open to Marcus Antonius, if, after crushing its unprepared municipalities and colonies, he had been able to penetrate into that Outer Gaul, what a cloud of terror

CICERO

penderet! Dubitaret, credo, homo amentissimus atque in
omnibus consiliis praeceps et devius non solum cum exercitu suo sed etiam cum omni immanitate barbariae bellum
inferre nobis, ut eius furorem ne Alpium quidem muro co-
hibere possemus. Haec igitur habenda gratia est D. Bruto
qui illum, nondum interposita auctoritate vestra, suo consilio atque iudicio, non ut consulem recepit, sed ut hostem
arcuit Gallia seque obsideri quam hanc urbem maluit. Habeat ergo huius tanti facti tamque praeclari decreto nostro
testimonium sempiternum; Galliaque, quae semper prae-
sidet atque praesedit huic imperio libertatique communi,
merito vereque laudetur, quod se suasque viris non tradidit, sed opposuit Antonio.

38   [14] Atque etiam M. Lepido pro eius egregiis in rem
publicam meritis decernendos honores quam amplissimos
censeo. Semper ille populum Romanum liberum voluit
maximumque signum illo die dedit voluntatis et iudici sui,
cum Antonio diadema Caesari imponente se avertit gemi-
tuque et maestitia declaravit quantum haberet odium servitutis, quam populum Romanum liberum cuperet, quam
illa quae tulerat temporum magis necessitate quam iudicio
tulisset. Quanta vero is moderatione usus sit in illo tempore civitatis quod post mortem Caesaris consecutum est,
quis nostrum oblivisci potest? Magna haec, sed ad maiora
39   properat oratio. Quid enim, o di immortales, admirabilius
omnibus gentibus, quid optatius populo Romano accidere

---

[31] At the festival of the Lupercalia on 15 Feb. 44 (cf. 2.84–87).

would be hanging over the Republic! He would hesitate, I am sure, this absolute madman, whose every move is an erratic plunge, to bring war upon us not only with his army but with all the savagery of a barbarous land. Even with the rampart of the Alps we would be powerless to contain his fury. For this, then, we have Decimus Brutus to thank, who, prior to the confirmation by your authority, exercising his own initiative and judgment, did not admit Antonius as a consul but barred him from Gaul as an enemy and preferred to have himself, rather than this city, besieged. So let him by our decree have everlasting testimony to this great and noble action; and let Gaul, which protects and always has protected this empire and the common freedom, be deservedly and truly commended in that instead of surrendering herself and her strength to Antonius she placed them in his path.

[14] I further propose that the most ample honors possible be decreed to Marcus Lepidus for his outstanding services to the Republic. Lepidus has ever wished the Roman people to be free; and he gave an unmistakable indication of his wishes and judgment that day when Antonius tried to place a diadem on Caesar's head:[31] Lepidus turned away and declared by a groan and a sad countenance how much he hated slavery and desired the Roman people to be free, how his tolerance of what he had tolerated had been due to the necessity of the times rather than his own choice. Which of us can forget his great moderation in the national crisis that followed Caesar's death? These are great merits, but my words hasten on to others greater still. What event, by the immortal gods, could have created greater admiration among all nations and what could the Roman people more earnestly have desired to happen 38

39

potuit quam, cum bellum civile maximum esset, cuius belli
exitum omnes timeremus, sapientia et misericordia[26] id
potius exstingui quam armis et ferro rem in discrimen adduci?[27] Quod si eadem ratio Caesaris[i] fuisset in illo taetro
miseroque bello, ut omittam patrem, duos Cn. Pompei,
summi et singularis viri, filios incolumis haberemus: quibus certe pietas fraudi esse non debuit. Utinam omnis M.
Lepidus servare potuisset! Facturum fuisse declaravit in
eo quod potuit, cum Sex. Pompeium restituit civitati,
maximum ornamentum rei publicae, clarissimum monu-
mentum clementiae suae. Gravis illa fortuna populi Romani, grave fatum! Pompeio enim patre, quod imperi[o]
populi Romani lumen fuit, exstincto interfectus est patris
40 simillimus filius. Sed omnia mihi videntur deorum immortalium iudicio expiata Sex. Pompeio rei publicae con-
servato.

[15] Quam ob causam iustam atque magnam et quod
periculosissimum civile bellum maximumque humanitate
et sapientia sua M. Lepidus ad pacem concordiamque
convertit, senatus consultum his verbis censeo perscriben-
dum: "Cum a M. Lepido imperatore, pontifice maximo,
saepe numero res ‹publica›[28] et bene et feliciter gesta sit,
populusque Romanus intellexerit ei dominatum regium
maxime displicere, cumque eius opera, virtute, consilio
singularique clementia et mansuetudine bellum acerbissi-
41 mum civile ‹s›it restinctum, Sextusque Pompeius Cn. f.

26 *Clark*: et iam V   27 *Lambinus*: addecere V: adducere
Poggius   28 *add. Poggius*

---

32 Probably in the autumn of 44, Lepidus negotiated a settlement with Pompey's sole surviving son Sextus, who commanded a
sizeable rebel force in Spain.

than the extinction of a civil war by wisdom and compassion, instead of provoking a crisis by weapons and the sword, just when that war was at its most threatening and we all dreaded its outcome?[32] If Caesar had taken the same course in that other hideous, miserable struggle, we should have the two sons of Gnaeus Pompeius, a most noble and distinguishcd gentleman, safe in our midst (to say nothing of their father). Assuredly they ought not to have suffered for being good sons. If only Marcus Lepidus could have saved all of them! That he would have done so he made plain by doing what he could, in restoring Sextus Pompeius to the community, a shining ornament of the Republic and a most notable memorial of his own clemency. Grievous was that stroke of fortune to the Roman people, a grievous destiny! In Pompeius the father the light of the Roman people's empire was put out; and then his son, who resembled him so closely, was slain. But by the judgment of the 40 gods, the preservation of Sextus Pompeius to the Republic, has, as I see it, made amends for all.

[15] For this great and just reason and because Marcus Lepidus by his humanity and wisdom has transformed a very big and dangerous civil war into peace and concord, I propose that a decree of the senate be entered in the following terms: "Whereas Marcus Lepidus, imperator, pontifex maximus, has on many occasions well and successfully conducted the affairs of the Republic, and the Roman people has perceived that monarchical rule is strongly repugnant to him; and whereas by his activity, courage, judgment, outstanding clemency, and gentle dealing a most bitter civil war has been extinguished, and Sextus Pom- 41 peius Magnus, son of Gnaeus, has laid down his arms by

Magnus huius ordinis auctoritate ab armis discesserit et a
M. Lepido imperatore, pontifice maximo, summa senatus
populique Romani voluntate civitati restitutus sit, senatum
populumque Romanum pro maximis plurimisque in rem
publicam M. Lepidi meritis magnam spem in eius virtute,
auctoritate, felicitate re⟨ponere⟩[29] oti, pacis, concordiae,
libertatis, eiusque in rem publicam meritorum senatum
populumque Romanum memorem fore, eique statuam
equestrem inauratam in rostris aut quo alio loco in foro
vellet ex huius ordinis sententia statui placere." Qui honos,
patres conscripti, mihi maximus videtur, primum qu⟨i⟩a
iustus est; non enim solum datur propter spem temporum
reliquorum sed pro amplissimis meritis redditur; nec vero
cuiquam possumus commemorare hunc honorem a senatu
tributum iudicio senatus soluto et libero.

42   [16] Venio ad C. Caesarem, patres conscripti; qui nisi
fuisset, quis nostrum esse potuisset? Advolabat ad urbem a
Brundisio homo impotentissimus, ardens odio, animo hos-
tili in omnis bonos cum exercitu Antonius. Quid huius audaciae et sceleri poterat opponi? Nondum ullos duces ha-
bebamus, non copias; nullum erat consilium publicum,
nulla libertas; dandae cervices erant crudelitati nefariae;
fugam quaerebamus omnes, quae ipsa exitum non habe-
43   bat. Quis tum nobis, quis populo Romano obtulit hunc divinum adulescentem deus? Qui, cum omnia ad perniciem
nostram pestifero illi civi paterent, subito praeter spem
omnium exortus prius confecit exercitum quem furori M.
Antoni opponeret quam quisquam hoc eum cogitare suspi-

---

[29] *add. Poggius*

the authority of this body and been restored to the community by Marcus Lepidus, imperator, pontifex maximus, with the wholehearted endorsement of the senate and people of Rome: that the senate and people of Rome, conscious of Marcus Lepidus' very great and very numerous services to the Republic, place high hope for peace, tranquillity, concord, and liberty in his courage, authority, and good fortune; and that the senate and people of Rome will be mindful of his outstanding services to the Republic; and that it pleases the senate that by the decision of this body a gilt equestrian statue to him be placed on the Rostra or in any other position in the Forum which he may choose." This honor, Members of the Senate, I consider to be very great, first and foremost, because it is rightful; for it is not granted simply in the hope of things to come but rendered in recognition of very important services. Nor can we name any other person to whom this honor has been granted by the senate acting freely and without constraint.

[16] I come to Gaius Caesar, Members of the Senate. Had it not been for him, what chance would there have been for any of us to survive? Hastening up from Brundisium to the city was a man of violent temper, burning with hatred, hostile to all decent men, with an army at his back: Antonius. What could we oppose to his audacity, his criminal intent? At that time we had no leaders, no forces; there was no public council, no freedom; we were forced to submit our necks to the villain's cruelty; we all sought flight, which itself offered no escape. What god then presented to us and to the Roman people this godlike young man? When every road to our destruction lay open to that baneful citizen, suddenly, to the surprise of all, *he* arose: he got together an army to oppose Marcus Antonius' madness be-

42

43

caretur. Magni honores habiti Cn. Pompeio cum esset adulescens, et quidem iure. Subvenit enim rei publicae, sed aetate multo robustior et militum ducem quaerentium studio par⟨a⟩tior et in alio genere belli. Non enim omnibus Sullae causa grata: declarat multitudo proscriptorum, tot
44 municipiorum maximae calamitates. Caesar autem annis multis minor veteranos cupientis iam requiescere armavit; eam complexus est causam quae esset senatui, quae populo, quae cunctae Italiae, quae dis hominibusque gratissima. Et Pompeius ad L. Sullae maximum imperium victoremque exercitum accessit: Caesar se ad neminem adiunxit, ipse princeps exercitus faciendi et praesidi comparandi fuit. Ille [in] adversariorum partibus agrum Picenum habuit inimicum: hic ex Antoni amicis sed amicioribus libertati[s][30] contra Antonium confecit exercitum. Illius opibus Sulla regnavit: huius praesidi⟨o⟩ Antoni dominatus oppressus est. Demus igitur imperium Caesari
45 s⟨i⟩ne quo res militaris administrari, teneri exercitus, bellum geri non potest: sit pro praetore eo iure quo qui optimo. Qui honos quamquam est magnus illi aetati, tamen ad necessitatem rerum gerendarum, non solum ad dignitatem valet. [17] Itaque[31] illa quaeramus quae vix hodierno die consequemur. Sed saepe spero fore huius adulescenti⟨s⟩ [hortandi][32] honorandi et nobis et populo Romano potestatem.

[30] del. ed. Romana
[31] ⟨ne⟩ add. SB post itaque
[32] del. Halm: hortandi honorandi V¹ (-que add. V²): ornandi C. F. W. Müller

fore anyone suspected him of such a thought. Great honors were accorded to Gnaeus Pompeius when he was a young man, and rightly so; for he came to the aid of the Republic, but he was much stronger in years, had a better basis in the soldiers' zeal in looking for a leader, and it was a different sort of war.[33] Sulla's cause was not universally favored: witness the multitude of the proscribed and the terrible disasters that befell so many townships. Caesar, many years 44 younger, armed veterans who now wanted peace and quiet; and he embraced a cause most highly favored by the senate, by the people, by all Italy, by gods and men. Also Pompeius joined Lucius Sulla's mighty command and victorious army: Caesar attached himself to nobody, was himself the first to form an army and to create a defense. Pompeius held the territory of Picenum, hostile to the opposing party: Caesar raised an army against Antonius from Antonius' friends—but better friends of freedom. With Pompeius' help Sulla reigned: by Caesar's intervention Antonius' despotism has been crushed. Therefore, let 45 us give Caesar that authority without which no military business can be conducted, no army held, no war waged: let him be propraetor in full status. While it is a great honor at his age, it is yet relevant to the necessity of military operations, not just to prestige. [17] So let us ask for what we shall obtain just as of today; but I expect that both we and the Roman people will have many opportunities in times to come of conferring honors on this young man.

[33] The twenty-three-year-old Cn. Pompeius Magnus raised troops comprised chiefly of veterans of his father's army in the region of Picenum, to support Sulla upon the latter's return to Italy from the war against Mithridates in Asia Minor (89–84 B.C.).

46   Hoc autem tempore ita censeo decernendum: "Quod C. Caesar C. f. pontifex pro praetore[33] summo rei publicae tempore milites veteranos ad libertatem populi Romani cohortatus sit eosque conscripserit, quodque legio Martia ⟨legio⟩que quarta[34] summo studio optimoque in rem publicam consensu C. Caesare duce et auctore rem publicam, libertatem populi Romani defendant defe⟨nde⟩rint, et quod C. Caesar pro praetore[35] Galliae provinciae cum exercitu subsidio profectus sit, equites, sagitt⟨ar⟩ios, elephantos in suam populique Romani potestatem redegerit, difficillimoque rei publicae tempore saluti dignitatique populi Romani subvenerit, ob eas causas senatui placere C. Caesarem C. f. pontificem, pro praetore,[36] senatorem esse sententiamque loco praetorio dicere, eiusque rationem, quemcumque magistratum petet, ita haberi ut haberi per leges liceret si anno superiore quaestor fuisset."

47   Quid est enim, patres conscripti, cur eum non quam primum amplissimos honores capere cupiamus? Legibus enim annalibus cum grandiorem aetatem ad consulatum constituebant, adulescentiae temeritatem verebantur: C. Caesar ineunte aetate docuit ab excellenti eximiaque virtute progressum aetatis exspectari non oportere. Itaque

---

[33] pro praetore *del. SB*
[34] *add. SB*: q. quarta V: quartaque *Poggius*
[35] pro praetore *del. SB*
[36] pro praetore ⟨eo iure quo qui optimo et⟩ *add. SB*

---

[34] Octavian was made a pontifex by his adoptive father Caesar in 47. Although Cicero has only just demanded that the title "propraetor" be awarded to Octavian (§45), Cicero already accepts this status for Octavian here and below (§53), and also in as-

At present, however, I move a decree as follows:
"Whereas Gaius Caesar, son of Gaius, pontifex, proprae-   46
tor,[34] at a grave crisis of the Republic urged veteran soldiers to defend the freedom of the Roman people and enrolled them; and whereas the Martian Legion and the
Fourth Legion with the greatest enthusiasm, in unanimous loyalty to the Republic, under the leadership and at
the instigation of Gaius Caesar, are defending and have
defended the Republic and the freedom of the Roman
people; and whereas Gaius Caesar, propraetor, has set out
with his army to the assistance of the province of Gaul, has
brought cavalry, archers, and elephants under his own control and that of the Roman people, and at a most difficult
crisis of the Republic has come to the aid of the safety and
dignity of the Roman people: for these reasons that the
senate decree that Gaius Caesar, son of Gaius, pontifex,
propraetor, become a member of the senate, that he give
his opinion among the ex-praetors, and that his candidature for whatever magistracy he shall be a candidate be
accepted as it would legally be accepted if he had been
quaestor in the year previous to this one."

For why, Members of the Senate, should we not wish   47
him to gain the highest offices as soon as possible? For
when people fixed a later age for the consulship by means
of laws regulating age requirements, they were afraid of
the rashness of youth. But Gaius Caesar has shown immediately upon achieving manhood that outstanding and exceptional abilities need not await advancing years. And so

signing him his position in the sequence of people whose honors
are being discussed (cf. §35).

CICERO

maiores nostri veteres illi admodum antiqui leges annalis
non habebant, quas multis post annis attulit ambitio, ut
gradus essent petitionis inter aequalis. Ita saepe magna in-
doles virtutis, prius quam rei publicae prodesse potuisset,
48   exstincta est. At vero apud antiquos Rulli, Decii, Corvini
multique alii, recentiore autem memoria superior Africanus, T. Flamini⟨n⟩us admodum adulescentes consules facti tantas res gesserunt ut populi Romani imperium auxe-
rint, nomen ornarint. Quid? Macedo Alexander, cum ab
ineunte aetate res maximas gerere coepisset, nonne tertio
et tricesimo anno mortem obiit? Quae est aetas nostris legibus decem annis minor quam consularis.[37] Ex quo iudi-
cari potest virtu⟨ti⟩s esse quam aetatis cursum celeriorem.

[18] Nam quod ei qui Caesari invident simulant se timere, ne verendum quidem est ut tenere se possit, ut mo-
derari, ne honoribus nostris elatus intemperantius suis
49   opibus utatur. Ea natura rerum est, patres conscripti, ut
qui sensum verae gloriae ceperit quique se ab senatu, ab
equitibus Romanis populoque Romano universo senserit
civem c[l]arum haberi salutaremque rei publicae, nihil
cum hac gloria comparandum putet. Utinam C. Caesari,
pa⟨t⟩ri dico, contigisset adulescenti ut esset senatui atque
optimo cuique carissimus! Quod cum consequi neglexis-
set, omnem vim ingeni, quae summa fuit in illo, in populari
levitate consumpsit. Itaque cum respectum ad senatum et
ad bonos non haberet, eam sibi viam ipse patefecit ad opes

[37] V: quae . . . consularis del. Fedeli in app.

290

our early ancestors, the men of old, did not have any laws regulating age requirements. These laws came in many years later as a result of the struggle for offices, to create stages at which men of the same age should compete. The consequence often was that great natural abilities were extinguished before they could be of service to the Republic. But in ancient times men like Rullus, Decius, Corvinus, and many others, and in more recent memory the elder Africanus and Titus Flamininus were elected consuls quite young, and by their great achievements they enlarged the empire of the Roman people and added luster to its name. To take another example, did not Alexander of Macedon begin his career of glorious achievement directly upon achieving manhood and die in his thirty-third year? This age is ten years below the consular qualification under our laws. Hence we may conclude that ability outruns age. 48

[18] Persons jealous of Caesar pretend to dread that he may be unable to keep himself within the bounds of moderation, may be puffed up by our honors and use his power intemperately: not even an apprehension on this account is justified. It is a law of nature, Members of the Senate, that once a man has come to a perception of true glory and perceived that in the eyes of the senate, the Roman knights, and the entire Roman people he is a valued citizen and a benefit to the Republic, he will think nothing comparable to this glory. I only wish it had been Gaius Caesar's fortune in early life (I am speaking of the father) to be highly valued by the senate and all the best of our community! Neglecting to win that esteem, he squandered all his powers of mind, which were of the highest order, on the fickleness of the people. And so, paying no consideration to the senate and to decent men, he opened a path to his own aggran- 49

suas amplificandas quam virtus liberi populi ferre non posset. Eius autem fili longissime diversa ratio est: qui cum omnibus ⟨carus⟩[38] est, tum optimo cuique carissimus. In hoc spes libertatis posita est; ab hoc accepta iam salus; huic
50 summi honores et exquiruntur et parati sunt. Cuius igitur singularem prudentiam admiramur, eius stultitiam timemus? Quid enim stultius quam inutilem potentiam, invidiosas opes, cupiditatem dominandi praecipitem et lubricam anteferre verae, gravi, solidae gloriae? An hoc vidit puer: si aetate processerit, non videbit? "At est quibusdam inimicus clarissimis atque optimis civibus." Nullus iste timor esse debet. Omnis Caesar inimicitias rei publicae condonavit; hanc sibi iudicem constituit, hanc moderatricem omnium ⟨consiliorum⟩[39] atque factorum. Ita enim [ut enim][40] ad rem publicam accessit ut eam confirmaret, non ut everteret. Omnis habeo cognitos sensus adulescentis. Nihil est illi re publica carius, nihil vestra auctoritate gravius, nihil bonorum virorum iudicio optatius, nihil vera gloria dulcius.
51   Quam ob rem ab eo non modo nihil timere sed maiora et meliora exspectare debetis, neque in eo qui ad D. Brutum obsidione liberandum profectus sit timere ne memoria maneat domestici doloris quae plus apud eum possit quam salus civitatis. Audeo etiam obligare fidem meam, patres conscripti, vobis populoque Romano reique publicae; quod profecto ⟨pro alio⟩,[41] cum me nulla vis cogeret, facere non auderem pertimesceremque in maxima re

[38] add. Muretus
[39] om. V: post omnium add. Halm: ante omnium add. Faërnus
[40] del. Poggius
[41] add. Sternkopf: profecto cum V, SB

dizement such as the spirit of a free people could not tolerate. Far different is the course chosen by his son: he is
valued by all, but is particularly dear to the best of the community. In him resides the hope of freedom; to him we
already owe our lives; for him the highest honors are
being sought out and are in readiness. In a man whose   50
exceptional good sense we admire, do we fear folly? For
what would be greater folly than to prefer unprofitable
power, invidious riches, the hazardous, treacherous desire
for domination, to true, stable, solid glory. He has seen this
while yet a lad: will he not see it once he has grown older?
"But he has a vendetta against certain excellent and illustrious citizens."[35] There is nothing to fear on that score.
Caesar has sacrificed all personal grudges to the Republic,
which he has made his arbiter and guide in all his decisions and actions. He has entered public life to strengthen
the Republic, not to overthrow it. I know the young man's
mind inside out. He values nothing more than the Republic, respects nothing more than your authority, desires
nothing more than the good opinion of decent men, rel-
ishes nothing more than true glory.

For this reason, so far from being in any way afraid of   51
him, you should expect greater and better things of him.
And as he has set out to liberate Decimus Brutus from
siege, you should have no fear that the memory of a private
grief may stay with him so as to outweigh the safety of the
community. I even dare to pledge my word, Members of
the Senate, to you and to the Roman people and to the Republic—and that is something that I obviously should not
dare to do in the case of someone else, since no force com-

35 I.e. Caesar's assassins.

periculosam opinionem[42] temeritatis. Promitto, recipio, spondeo, patres conscripti, C. Caesarem talem semper fore civem qualis hodie sit qualemque eum maxime velle esse et optare debemus. [19] Quae cum ita sint, de Caesare satis hoc tempore dictum habebo.

52

Nec vero de L. Egnatuleio, fortissimo et constantissimo civi amicissimoque rei publicae, silendum arbitror; sed tribuendum testimonium virtutis egregiae, quod is legionem quartam ad Caesarem adduxerit, quae praesidio consulibus, senatui populoque Romano reique publicae esset: ob eam causam placere uti L. Egnatuleio triennio[43] ante legitimum tempus magistratus petere, capere, gerere liceat. In quo, patres conscripti, non tantum commodum tribuitur L. Egnatuleio quantus honos: in tali enim re satis est nominari.

53

De exercitu autem C. C⟨aes⟩aris[44] ita censeo decernendum: "Senatui placere militibus veteranis qui ⟨C.⟩[45] Caesaris pontificis, ⟨pro praetore, auctoritatem secuti libertatem populi Romani⟩[46] auctoritatemque huius ordinis defenderint atque defendant i⟨ps⟩is[47] liberisque eorum militiae vacationem esse, utique C. Pansa A. Hirtius consules, alter ambove, si eis videretur, cognoscerent qui ager eis coloniis esset quo milites veterani deducti essent qui contra legem Iuliam possideretur, ut is militibus veteranis

[42] V: in maxima re ⟨et⟩ periculosa opinionem *SB*

[43] *Lambinus*: triennium V

[44] *corr. Poggius*

[45] *add. SB*

[46] pro praetore *add. Lambinus* | auctoritatem . . . populi Romani *add. Garatoni*

[47] *corr. C. F. W. Müller*

pels me; I would be afraid of earning the dangerous reputation of rashness in so great a business. I give you my promise, my guarantee, my pledge, Members of the Senate, that Gaius Caesar will always be such a citizen as he is today and such as we ought most to wish and pray for him to be. [19] Accordingly, I shall take it that enough has been said about Caesar at this time. 52

Nor do I think it fitting that Lucius Egnatuleius, a very brave, most resolute, and patriotic citizen, receive no mention. Instead, his conspicuous merit in bringing over the Fourth Legion to Caesar for the protection of the consuls, the senate and the people of Rome, and the Republic, deserves a testimonial: for that reason I move that it please the senate that Lucius Egnatuleius be permitted to stand for, enter upon, and administer public offices three years before the time by law prescribed. This proposal, Members of the Senate, is more to Lucius Egnatuleius' honor than to his practical advantage: in such a case to be named is enough.

Now concerning Gaius Caesar's army I move the following decree: "That it please the senate that the veteran soldiers who, following the authority of Gaius Caesar, pontifex, propraetor, have defended and are defending the freedom of the Roman people and the authority of this body, be granted exemption from military service for themselves and their children; further, that the consuls Gaius Pansa and Aulus Hirtius, either or both, if they see fit, make inquiry concerning land occupied in contravention of the Julian Law[36] appertaining to those colonies in 53

---

[36] Caesar's *lex agraria* of 59. For Antony's settlements in violation of it cf. 2.100–102.

divideretur; de agro Campano separatim cognoscerent ini-
rentque rationem de commodis militum veteranorum au-
gendis, legionique Martiae et legioni quartae et eis militibus qui de legione secunda, tricesima quinta ad C. Pansam
A. Hirtium consules venissent suaque nomina edidissent,
quod eis auctoritas senatus populique Romani libertas ca-
rissima sit et fuerit, vacationem militiae ipsis liberisque eorum esse placere extra tumultum Gallicum Italicumque:
easque legiones bello confecto missas fieri placere; quan-
tamque pecuniam militibus earum legionum in singulos C.
Caesar pontifex, pro praetore pollicitus sit, tantam dari
placere; utique C. Pansa A. Hirtius consules, alter ambove,
si eis videretur, rationem agri habe<re>nt qui sine iniuria
privatorum dividi posset, eisque militibus, legioni Martiae
et legioni quartae ita darent, adsignarent ut quibus militibus amplissime dati, adsignati essent."

Dixi ad ea omnia, consules, de quibus rettulistis: quae si
erunt sine mora matureque decreta, facilius apparabitis ea
quae tempus et necessitas flagitat. Celeritate autem opus
est: qua si essemus usi, bellum, ut saepe dixi, nullum haberemus.

which veteran soldiers have been settled, with a view to the division of such land among the veteran soldiers; that they make separate inquiry concerning the Campanian land and investigate means of increasing the benefits of the veteran soldiers; and that it please the senate that the Martian Legion, the Fourth Legion, and those soldiers of the Second and Thirty-fifth Legions who shall have presented themselves before the consuls Gaius Pansa and Aulus Hirtius, and given in their names, in that by doing so they show and have shown their high regard for the authority of the senate and the freedom of the Roman people, be granted exemption from military service for themselves and their children, except in case of a public emergency in Gaul or Italy; and that it please the senate that those legions be discharged at the end of the war; and that it please the senate that money to the amount promised by Gaius Caesar, pontifex, propraetor, to the soldiers of those legions individually be given them; further, that the consuls Gaius Pansa and Aulus Hirtius, either or both, if they see fit, take cognizance of land available for division without prejudice to individuals and do grant and assign such land to the said soldiers, the Martian Legion, and the Fourth Legion in terms no less liberal than any hitherto used in such grants and assignments."

I have spoken to all those matters, Consuls, concerning which you have opened discussion. If the decrees are passed promptly and without delay, you will find it easier to make such preparations as the necessity of the situation urgently demands. But speed is essential: had we used it, we would, as I have often said, have no war on our hands.

PHILIPPIC 6

INTRODUCTION

Soon after the four-day debate in the senate came to a conclusion on 4 January 43, on that same day, a tribune of the plebs, P. Apuleius, convened a meeting of the people in the Forum (6.1, 3; 7.22). Cicero delivered the *Sixth Philippic* on that occasion and spoke to the Roman people about the debate in the senate and its result. Yet, apart from a brief reference to the abolition of the *Lex Antonia agraria* (6.14), Cicero only discusses the senate's decision to send an embassy to Mark Antony, while he omits entirely other aspects of the debate such as the decrees honoring Octavian and D. Brutus and the soldiers who went over to them.

Cicero's account is obviously not objective or neutral but is rather aimed at putting a good face on an outcome that was unfavorable from his point of view. Clearly any negotiations with Antony ran counter to Cicero's demand for an immediate declaration of war, but in the *Sixth Philippic* he chose to portray the decision to send envoys as, in essence, an indirect declaration of war and thus in line with his strategy (esp. 6.4, 7). He did so by arguing that war would inevitably result since Antony was certain not to comply with the demands of the senate that the envoys were to convey. Thus the embassy would lead to what Cicero had been demanding; there would just be some delay, but that delay would provide the advantage of making the front against Antony firmer and more comprehensive (6.15–16). This assessment of sending an embassy differs markedly from the line of argument in the *Fifth Philippic* of 1 January. But since decisions already taken could not be altered at that stage, it had become more practical for Cicero to gloss over his defeat and instead to co-opt the altered conditions into his strategy. In that way, he could maintain his standing as a successful politician and continue his war policy from a new perspective. Cicero exploits the opportunity to influence public opinion by attacking Antony and his followers (6.3, 4, 10–15) and by emphasizing the unanimity of the people and the senate (esp. 6.18).

STRUCTURE

Exordium

(1–3a) Information on debate in the senate and decision for an embassy

Narratio

(3b–15a) Significance of the embassy
  (3b–9a) Decree of an embassy to be regarded as a declaration of war
  (9b–15a) Impossibility of success because of character of Antony and his men

Peroratio

(15b–19) Appeal to wait for return of envoys; fight for liberty

M. TULLI CICERONIS
IN M. ANTONIUM
ORATIO PHILIPPICA SEXTA

1   [1] Audita vobis esse arbitror, Quirites, quae sint acta in
senatu, quae fuerit cuiusque sententia. Res enim ex Kalendis Ianuariis agitata paulo ante confecta est, minus quidem
illa severe quam decuit, non tamen omnino dissolute.
Mora est adlata bello, non causa sublata. Quam ob rem,
quod quaesivit ex me P. Apuleius, homo et multis officiis
mihi et summa familiaritate coniunctus et vobis amicissi-
mus, ita respondebo ut ea quibus non interfuistis nosse
possitis. Causa fortissimis optimisque consulibus Kalendis
Ianuariis de re publica primum referendi fuit ex eo quod
‹a.d.›[1] XIII Kalendas Ianuarias senatus me auctore decre-
2   vit. Eo die primum, Quirites, fundamenta sunt iacta
[sunt][2] rei publicae: fuit enim longo intervallo ita liber senatus ut vos aliquando liberi essetis. Quo quidem tempore,
etiam si ille dies vitae finem mihi adlaturus esset, satis
magnum ceperam f‹r›uctum, cum vos universi una mente

[1] *add. Orelli*
[2] *del. Garatoni*

MARCUS TULLIUS CICERO'S
SIXTH PHILIPPIC ORATION
AGAINST MARCUS ANTONIUS

[1] I think you have heard, Men of Rome, what has taken place in the senate and the views expressed by the several speakers. The question that has been at issue since the first of January has just been settled, in a fashion less stringent than befitted, but still not altogether lax. War has been delayed, but the ground for it has not been removed. So I will reply to the inquiry put to me by Publius Apuleius, to whom I am bound by many good offices and closest friendship and who loves you well, so as to make you acquainted with proceedings at which you were not present. On the first of January our most courageous and excellent consuls first opened discussion concerning the Republic, an action arising from the decrees passed by the senate on my motion on the twentieth of December.[1] On that day, Men of Rome, the foundations of the Republic were first laid: for after a long interval the senate was free, so free that at long last *you* were free. Even if that day were to have been the last of my life, it would have been fulfillment enough when with one heart and voice you all cried out

1

2

---

[1] When Cicero delivered the *Third Philippic* (cf. 3.37–39).

atque voce iterum a me conservatam esse rem publicam
conclamastis. Hoc vestro iudicio tanto tamque praeclaro
excitatus ita Kalendis Ianuariis veni in senatum ut memi-
nissem quam personam impositam a vobis sustinerem.
Itaque bellum nefarium illatum rei publicae cum viderem,
nullam moram interponendam insequendi M. Antonium
putavi, hominemque audacissimum, qui multis nefariis
rebus ante commissis hoc tempore imperatorem populi
Romani oppugnaret, coloniam vestram fidissimam fortissi-
mamque obsideret, bello censui persequendum. Tumultum esse decrevi; iustitium edici, saga sumi dixi placere,
quo omnes acrius graviusque incumberent ad ulciscendas
rei publicae iniurias, si omnia gravissimi belli insignia sus-
3 cepta a senatu viderent. Itaque haec sententia, Quirites,
sic per triduum valuit ut, quamquam discessio facta non
est,[3] tamen praeter paucos [homines][4] omnes mihi adsen-
suri videren⟨tur⟩.[5] Hodierno autem die spe nescio qua
⟨pa⟩cis obiecta remissior[6] senatus fuit. Nam plures eam
sententiam secuti sunt ut, quantum senatus auctoritas
vesterque consensus apud Antonium valiturus esset, per
legatos experiremur. [2] Intellego, Quirites, a vobis hanc
sententiam repudiari, neque iniuria.

Ad quem enim legatos? Ad eumne qui pecunia publica
dissipata atque effusa, per vim et contra auspicia impositis
rei publicae legibus, fugata contione, obsesso senatu, ad

---

[3] *Clark dub. in app.*: esset V   [4] *del.* V[2]
[5] *corr.* V[2]   [6] *corr. Garatoni / Rau*

---

[2] Allegedly at the public meeting to which Cicero addressed
the *Fourth Philippic* on 20 Dec. 44.

[3] Antony was besieging D. Iunius Brutus in Mutina.

that I had saved the Republic a second time.[2] Aroused by so weighty and unambiguous a verdict, I entered the senate on the first of January mindful of the role for which you had cast me and which I was sustaining. And seeing that a wicked war had been launched against the Republic, I considered that no delay should be allowed to hold up going after Marcus Antonius; I gave it as my judgment that war should be waged against this most audacious man, who after many other acts of villainy was at this time attacking an imperator of the Roman people and laying siege to one of your bravest and most loyal colonies.[3] I proposed a decree recognizing a state of public emergency, I presented a resolution calling for a proclamation to be issued suspending business and for the donning of military cloaks in order that all might press to avenge the injuries of the Republic more intensely and energetically if they saw the senate authorizing all the outward signs of a most serious war. Accordingly, this proposal of mine, Men of Rome, was so strongly favored for a period of three days that, although no vote was taken, all but a few seemed likely to support me. Today, however, the senate's determination relaxed a bit after some sort of hope for peace had been held out; and a majority backed the proposal calling for us to test through envoys how much the senate's authority and your unanimous sentiment would count with Antonius. [2] I realize, Men of Rome, that you repudiate this proposal, and you are not wrong to do so.

To whom are we sending envoys? To the man who, after dissipating and pouring out public money, foisting laws on the Republic by violence and against the auspices, putting a meeting of the people to flight, and laying siege to the

3

opprimendam rem publicam Brundisio legiones arcessie-
rit, ab eis relictus cum latronum manu in Galliam irruperit,
Brutum oppugnet, Mutinam circumsedeat? Quae vobis
potest cum hoc gladiatore condicionis, aequitatis, legatio-
4 nis esse communitas? Quamquam, Quirites, non est illa legatio, sed denuntiatio belli, nisi paruerit: ita enim est decretum ut si legati ad Hannibalem mitterentur. Mittuntur
enim qui nuntient ne oppugnet consulem designatum, ne
Mutinam obsideat, ne provinciam depopuletur, ne dilectus habeat, sit in senatus populique Romani potestate. Facile vero huic denuntiationi parebit, ut in patrum conscrip-
torum atque in vestra potestate sit qui in sua numquam
fuerit! Quid enim ille umquam arbitrio suo fecit? Semper
eo tractus est quo libido rapuit, quo levitas, quo furor, quo
vinolentia; semper eum duo dissimilia genera ⟨ten⟩ue-
runt, lenonum et latronum. Ita domesticis stupris, forensi-
bus parricidiis delectatur[7] ut mulieri citius avarissimae pa-
5 ruerit quam senatui populoque Romano. [3] Itaque, quod
paulo ante feci in senatu, faciam apud vos: testificor, denuntio, ante praedico nihil M. Antonium eorum quae sunt
legatis mandata facturum: vastaturum agros, Mutinam ob-
sessurum, dilectus qua possit habiturum. Is est enim ille
qui semper senatus iudicium et auctoritatem, semper voluntatem vestram potestatemque contempserit. An ille id
faciat quod paulo ante decretum est, ut exercitum citra
⟨flu⟩men ⟨Rubiconem⟩,[8] qui finis est Galliae, educeret,
dum ne propius urbem Romam ducenta milia admove-

[7] *post* delectatur *aliqua excidisse suspicatur SB*
[8] *add.* V[2]

[4] His wife Fulvia.

senate, summoned legions from Brundisium to crush the
Republic and, when those abandoned him, burst into Gaul
with a band of cutthroats and is now attacking Brutus, besieging Mutina? What common ground can there be between you and this gladiator to form the basis of an understanding, of fair play, of an embassy? And yet, Men of   4
Rome, that is not an embassy but rather a declaration of
war if he does not obey: the decree reads as though envoys were being dispatched to Hannibal. For they are sent
to order him not to attack a consul-elect, not to besiege
Mutina, not to lay waste the province, not to levy troops,
and to submit to the control of the senate and people of
Rome. Doubtless he will find it an easy matter to obey this
order to submit to your control and that of the senators—
a man who was never in control of himself! What did he
ever do by his own free will? Always he has been dragged in
the wake of lust, frivolity, madness, drunkenness; always
two quite different types of men have had him in their
grip: pimps and robbers. Such pleasure does he take in private debauchery and public murders that he preferred to
obey a thoroughly rapacious female[4] rather than the senate
and people of Rome. [3] And so I shall do before you what I   5
have just done in the senate: I testify, I warn, I predict in
advance that Marcus Antonius will not carry out a single
item in the envoys' commission: he *will* ravage the country,
he *will* besiege Mutina, he *will* levy troops where he can.
For he is a man who has always flouted the judgment and
authority of the senate, as he has your will and power. Or is
he likely to do what has just been decreed and withdraw his
army to this side of the river Rubicon, the boundary of
Gaul, but not bring it within less than two hundred miles of

ret? Huic denuntiationi ille pareat, ille se fluvio Rubicone, ‹ille›[9] ducentis milibus circumscriptum esse patiatur?

6   Non is est Antonius. Nam si esset, non commisisset ut ei senatus tamquam Hannibali initio belli Punici denuntiaret ne oppugnaret Saguntum. Quod vero ita avocatur a Mutina ut ab urbe tamquam pestifera flamma arceatur, quam habet ignominiam, quod iudicium senatus! Quid quod a senatu dantur mandata legatis ut D. Brutum ‹exercitum›que[10] eius adeant eisque demonstrent summa in rem publicam merita beneficiaque eorum grata esse senatui populoque Romano eisque eam rem magnae laudi magnoque honori fore? Passurumne censetis Antonium introire Mutinam legatos, exire inde tuto? Numquam patietur, mihi credite. Novi vi[n]olentiam, novi impuden-

7   tiam, novi audaciam. Nec vero de illo sicut de homine aliquo debemus, sed ut de importunissima belua cogitare. Quae cum ita sint, non omnino dissolutum est quod decrevit senatus: habet atrocitatis aliquid legatio: utinam nihil haberet morae! Nam cum plerisque in rebus gerendis tarditas et procrastinatio odiosa est, tum hoc bellum indiget celeritatis. Succurrendum est D. Bruto, omnes undique copiae colligendae; operam exhibere nullam[11] in tali cive

8   liberando sine scelere non possumus. An ille non potuit, si Antonium consulem, si Galliam Antoni provinciam iudicasset, legiones Antonio et provinciam tradere, domum redire, triumphare, primus in hoc ordine, quoad magistra-

---

[9] add. Schöll

[10] add. Hasebroek

[11] *Sternkopf*: horam eximere unam *Budaeus / Lutz*, *SB*: horam exhibere nullam V

the city of Rome? Is he likely to obey such an order, to let himself be circumscribed by the river Rubicon and by a two-hundred-mile limit?

No, this is not like Antonius. If it were, he would never 6 have so acted as to receive such a message, like Hannibal at the beginning of the Punic War, warned by the senate not to attack Saguntum. Now he is ordered off from Mutina in such a fashion that he is barred from the city like a destructive conflagration: what a disgrace, what a censure by the senate does that entail! Add to this the fact that the envoys are also commissioned by the senate to proceed to Decimus Brutus and his troops and make clear to them that their fine services and benefactions to the Republic are appreciated by the senate and people of Rome and that their conduct will be to their great credit and honor. Do you suppose Antonius will allow the envoys to enter Mutina or to leave the place in safety? He never will, take my word. I know his violence, his shamelessness, his au- 7 dacity. And truly we should not think of him as a human being, but as the most relentless sort of beast. Given these facts, what the senate decreed is not altogether remiss: the embassy carries a certain amount of bite. I only wish it involved no delay! While tardiness and procrastination are annoying in warfare generally, this war particularly calls for speed. We have to come to Decimus Brutus' aid; all forces must be assembled from every quarter; taking no action for the liberation of such a fellow countryman will necessarily mean that we are committing a crime. Yet, if 8 Brutus had thought of Antonius as consul and of Gaul as Antonius' province, could he not have handed over the legions and the province to Antonius and returned home, celebrated a triumph, spoken first in this body until he

9   tum iniret, sententiam dicere? Quid negoti fuit? Sed cum
se Brutum esse meminisset vestraeque libertati natum,
non otio suo, quid egit aliud nisi ut paene corpore suo Gallia prohiberet Antonium? Ad hunc utrum legatos an legiones ire oportebat? Sed praeterita omittamus: properent
legati, quod video esse facturos; vos saga parate. Est enim
ita decretum ut, si ille auctoritati senatus non paruisset, ad
saga iretur. Ibitur; non parebit: nos amissos tot dies rei
ge‹re›ndae queremur.

[4] Non metuo, Quirites, ne, cum audierit Antonius,
me hoc et in senatu et in contione confirmasse, numquam
illum futurum in senatus potestate, refellendi mei causa,
ut ego nihil vidisse videar, vertat se et senatui pareat. Numquam faciet; non invidebit huic meae gloriae; malet me sa-
10   pientem a vobis quam se modestum existimari. Quid? Ipse
si velit, num etiam Lucium fratrem passurum arbitramur?
Nuper quidem dicitur ad Tibur, ut opinor, cum ei labare
M. Antonius videretur, mortem fratri esse minitatus.
Etiamne ab hoc myrmillone Asiatico senatus mandata,
legatorum verba audientur? Nec enim secerni a fratre
poterit, tanta praesertim auctoritate. Nam hic inter illos
Africanus[12] est: pluris habetur quam L. Trebellius, pluris

---

[12] illos ‹Laelius, ille› Africanus *add. SB*

---

5 As consul-elect for 42 Brutus would have been the first to be
called on to speak in the senate (cf. 1.15, n. 30).

6 As an alleged descendant of L. Iunius Brutus (cf. 3.8 and n. 6).

7 On L. Antonius' alleged gladiatorial past cf. 3.31, n. 38.

8 Cicero compares L. Antonius' position to the key advisory
role played by P. Cornelius Scipio Africanus (maior) as legate of

came into office?[5] What was the matter? But since he re-   9
membered that he is a Brutus, born for your freedom,[6] not
his own comfort, what else did he do but block Antonius'
entry into Gaul almost with his own body? Which should
we have sent to this man, envoys or legions? But let us not
dwell on what is past: let the envoys make haste, as I see
they will; you, on your side, get your military cloaks ready.
For it is so decreed: if he does not obey the authority of the
senate, all shall put on military cloaks. That is what will
happen; he will not obey. But we shall lament that so many
days for action have been lost.

[4] I am not afraid, Men of Rome, that when Antonius
hears I have asserted both in the senate and before a meeting of the people that he will never submit to the control of
the senate, he will turn around and obey the senate in order to refute me, so that I seem to have been blind. He will
never do that; he will not begrudge me this credit. He will
prefer you to think me shrewd than to think him well-be-
haved. Again, even if he himself were to be willing, do we   10
suppose that his brother Lucius will allow it? Not long ago,
near Tibur I think, Lucius is said to have threatened his
brother with death, when he thought Marcus Antonius was
wavering. Will the senate's commission, the words of the
envoys, be listened to even by this myrmillo from Asia?[7]
For it will be impossible to separate him from his brother,
especially as he enjoys such great authority. For in
that company he is the Africanus:[8] he stands in higher regard than Lucius Trebellius, higher than Titus Plancus.

his brother L. Cornelius Scipio Asiagenus in the war against
Antiochus.

CICERO

quam T. Plancus. Videte quantum exsiluerit adulescens
nobilis! Plancum, qui[13] omnibus sententiis maximo vestro
plausu condemnatus nescio quo modo se coniecit in tur-
bam atque ita maestus redi‹i›t ut retractus, non reversus
videretur, sic contemnit tamquam si illi aqua et igni inter-
dictum sit: aliquando negat ei locum esse oportere in curia
11   qui incenderit curiam. Nam Trebellium valde iam diligit:
oderat tum, cum ille tabulis novis adversabatur; iam fert in
oculis, postea quam ipsum Trebellium vidit sine tabulis novis salvum esse non posse. Audisse enim vos arbitror, Quirites, quod etiam videre potuistis, cotidie sponsores et creditores L. Trebelli convenire. O Fides!—hoc enim opinor
Trebellium sumpsisse cognomen—quae potest esse maior
fides quam fraudare creditores, domo profugere, propter
aes alienum ire ad arma? Ubi plausus ille in triumpho est,[14]
saepe ludis, ubi aedilitas delata summo studio bonorum?
Quis est qui hunc non casu existimet recte fecisse, nequitia
sceleste?
12   [5] Sed redeo ad amores deliciasque vestras, L. Antonium, qui vos omnis in fidem suam recepit. Negatis? Num

---

[13] *Sternkopf*: Plancus, quam †tum exiluerit† adulescens nobilis. Plancum quidem, qui *SB*: plancius videte quan decertum est
. . . pareat *[cf. 6.5]* tum exiluerit V
[14] *V*: e[s]t *Sternkopf*

---

[9] The text here is corrupt and uncertain. As printed, it em-
phasizes ironically and sarcastically how happy and vainglorious
L. Antonius is about his influential position among Antony's followers.
[10] Sentenced to exile for his role in fomenting riots that re-

Look how that young nobleman leaps for joy![9] Plancus, who was found guilty by a unanimous verdict,[10] to loud applause from you, and who somehow or other threw himself into the crowd and came back so dejected that he looked as though he had been hauled back, not returned of his own accord—Plancus is despised by Antonius, as though he were an exile. Sometimes he remarks that a man who set the senate-house on fire has no business to sit there. And for Trebellius Antonius now has great regard. He used to hate him at the time when Trebellius was opposing the cancellation of debts;[11] but now Trebellius is the apple of his eye, ever since Antonius saw that Trebellius himself cannot survive without the cancellation of debts. For I think you have heard, Men of Rome—you could have actually seen it—that Lucius Trebellius' sureties and creditors are meeting every day. Oh Faith!—I think Trebellius has taken that word as an additional element of his name—what greater faith than to defraud one's creditors, flee from home, join the army under pressure of debt? Where now is that applause at the triumph,[12] and often at the games, where is that aedileship conferred with the enthusiastic support of decent men? Can anybody doubt that his good behavior was due to chance, his criminality to a worthless character? 11

[5] But I return to your[13] favorite, your darling Lucius Antonius, who has taken you all under his wing. You say 12

sulted in the senate-house being burned down after the murder of P. Clodius in 52. He was brought back from exile in 49 by Caesar.

11 As tribune of the plebs in 47.

12 Presumably at one of Caesar's triumphs in 46.

13 Addressing the people.

quisnam est vestrum qui tribum non habeat? Certe nemo.
Atqui illum quinque et triginta tribus patronum adopta-
runt. Rursus reclamatis? Aspicite illam a sinistra equestrem statuam inauratam, in qua quid inscriptum est?
"Quinque et triginta tribus patrono." Populi Romani igitur
est patronus L. Antonius. Malam quidem illi pestem! Cla-
mori enim vestro adsentior. Non modo hic latro, quem
clientem habere nemo velit, sed quis umquam tantis opibus, tantis rebus gestis fuit qui se populi Romani victoris
13 dominique omnium gentium patronum dicere auderet? In
foro L. Antoni statuam videmus, sicut illam Q. Tremuli,
qui Hernicos devicit, ante Castoris. O impudentiam incredibilem! Tantumne sibi sumpsit, quia Mylasis myrmillo
Thraecem iugulavit, familiarem suum? Quonam modo
istum ferre possemus, si in hoc foro spectantibus vobis
depugnasset? Sed haec una statua. Altera ⟨ab⟩ equitibus
Romanis equo publico: qui item ascribunt, "patrono."
Quem umquam iste ordo patronum adoptavit? Si quemquam, debuit me. Sed me omitto: quem censorem, quem
imperatorem? Agrum eis divisit. O sordidos qui accepe-
14 runt, improbum qui dedit! Statuerunt etiam tribuni milita-
res qui in exercitu Caesaris bis fuerunt. Quis est iste ordo?
Multi fuerunt multis in legionibus per tot annos. Eis quoque divisit Semurium. Campus Martius restabat, nisi prius

---

[14] A certain type of gladiator, the standard opponent of a
myrmillo. On L. Antonius' alleged gladiatorial past cf. 3.31, n. 38.

[15] Official designation of the original order of knights. The
specific role of this order was lost later, and the term came to
be applied more broadly to wealthy citizens whose property ex-
ceeded a certain minimum qualification.

not? Is there any of you who does not have a tribe? Certainly not. Well, the thirty-five tribes chose him as their patron. Again you protest? Look at that gilt equestrian statue to the left. What does its inscription say? "The thirty-five tribes to their patron." So Lucius Antonius is patron of the Roman people. To the devil with him! I agree with your shouts. Who ever had so great a position, such a record of achievement as to dare to call himself the patron of the Roman people, conqueror and lord of all nations?—let alone this brigand whom nobody would want to have as a client. We see a statue of Lucius Antonius in the Forum, like 13
that of Quintus Tremulus, who conquered the Hernicans, in front of the Temple of Castor. Oh the unbelievable effrontery! Did he take upon himself so much because as a myrmillo he killed at Mylasa a Thracian-style gladiator,[14] one of his companions? How could we bear this man, if he had fought the contest in this Forum before your very eyes? But this is only one statue. There is another from the Roman knights with public horses:[15] they too inscribe it "to our patron." Whom did this order ever adopt as patron? If anybody, it ought to have adopted me.[16] But I leave myself out of account: what censor, what imperator has it adopted? Lucius Antonius divided land among them. How shabby were the recipients, how shameless the giver! Yet 14
another statue was put up by those who were twice military tribunes in Caesar's army. What category is this? There were many in many legions throughout all those years. For them too he divided land, the Semurian territory. The Field of Mars remained to be divided up, if he had not

[16] Because Cicero himself belonged to that class (in the broader sense) and frequently advocated policies advantageous to them.

CICERO

cum fratre fugisset. Sed haec agrorum adsignatio paulo
ante, Quirites, L. Caesaris, clarissimi viri et praestantissimi senatoris, sententia dissoluta est: huic enim adsensi
septemvirum acta sustulimus. Iacent beneficia Nuculae;
friget patronus Antonius. Nam possessores animo aequi-
ore discedent: nullam impensam fecerant; nondum in-
struxerant, partim quia non confidebant, partim quia non
15 habebant. Sed illa statua palmaris de qua, si meliora tempora essent, non possem sine risu dicere. "L. Antonio a
Iano Medio patrono." Itane? Iam Ianus Medius in L. Antoni clientela est? Quis umquam in illo Iano inventus est qui
L. Antonio mille nummum ferret expensum? [6] Sed nimis
multa de nugis: ad causam bellumque redeamus; quamquam non alienum fuit personas quasdam a vobis recog-
nosci, ut quibuscum bellum gereretur possetis taciti cogitare.

Ego autem vos hortor, Quirites, ut, etiam si melius
aliud fuit, tamen legatorum reditum [legatorum][15] exspec-
tetis animo aequo. Celeritas detracta de causa est; boni
16 tamen aliquid accessit ad causam. Cum enim legati renun-
tiarint quod certe renuntiabunt, non in vestra potestate,
non in senatus esse Antonium, quis erit tam improbus civis
qui illum civem habendum putet? Nunc enim sunt pauci
illi quidem, sed tamen plures quam re publica dignum est,

[15] del. Poggius

[17] Mark Antony's departure from Rome on 28/29 Nov. 44 was
characterized by Cicero as "flight."
[18] On the Board of Seven cf. 5.7, n. 4.
[19] Ianus Medius (the Exchange) was an archway leading into
the Forum, where bankers carried on their business.

taken to his heels with his brother.[17] However, this allocation of lands, Men of Rome, has just been annulled by
the proposal of that illustrious gentleman and outstanding
senator Lucius Caesar; we assented to his proposal and
canceled the acts of the Board of Seven.[18] Nucula's favors
are a dead letter; patron Antonius is left out in the cold. As
for the occupiers, they will leave without too much distress: they had not incurred any expenses. They had not yet
equipped their holdings, some from lack of confidence,
others from lack of money. But then there is the statue that   15
takes the prize, about which I would not be able to speak
without laughing if the times were better. "To Lucius Antonius, our patron, from the Exchange."[19] Really? Is the
Exchange now numbered among Lucius Antonius' clien-
tele? Who was ever found in that Exchange to lend Lucius
Antonius a thousand sesterces? [6] But I have dwelt too
long on trifles: let us get back to our cause and our war. All
the same, it was not irrelevant for you to pass in review certain personalities, so that in your own minds you could
think about the kind of people against whom war is being
waged.

Now I urge you, Men of Rome, to wait calmly for the
return of the envoys, even though a different course would
have been better. The cause has lost something in speed,
but the cause has gained something too. For when the en-   16
voys report, as report they surely will, that Antonius is not
in your control, nor in the senate's, who will be so wicked a
citizen as to think that this man should be considered a citizen? At present there are some, few to be sure but more

qui ita loquantur: "Ne legatos quidem exspectabimus?" Istam certe vocem simulationemque clementiae extorquebit istis res ipsa [publica].[16] Quo etiam, ut confitear vobis, Quirites, minus hodierno die contendi, minus laboravi, ut mihi senatus adsentiens tumultum decerneret, saga sumi iuberet. Malui viginti diebus post sententiam meam laudari ab omnibus quam a paucis hodie vituperari. Quapropter, Quirites, exspectate legatorum reditum et paucorum dierum molestiam devorate. Qui cum redierint, si pacem adferent, cupidum me, si bellum, providum iudicatote. An ego non provideam meis civibus, non dies noctesque de vestra libertate, de rei publicae salute cogitem? Quid enim non debeo vobis, Quirites, quem vos ⟨a s⟩e[17] ortum hominibus nobilissimis omnibus honoribus praetulistis? An ingratus sum? Quis minus? Qui partis honoribus eosdem in foro gessi labores quos petendis. Rudis in re publica? Quis ex⟨er⟩citatior?[18] Qui viginti iam ⟨an⟩nos bellum geram cum impiis civibus.

Quam ob rem, Quirites, consilio quantum potero, labore plus paene quam potero, excubabo, vigilaboque pro vobis. Etenim quis est civis, praesertim hoc gradu quo me vos esse voluistis, tam oblitus benefici vestri, tam immemor patriae, tam inimicus dignitati suae quem non excitet, non inflammet tantus vester iste consensus? Multas magnasque habui consul contiones, multis interfui: nullam umquam vidi tantam quanta nunc vestrum est. Unum sen-

17

18

16 *del. Muretus*
17 *corr. Poggius*
18 *corr. Poggius*

20 An estimate of the time needed for the envoys to return.

than befits the Republic, who say: "Are we not even going
to wait for the envoys?" The event itself will wrench that
slogan, that pretense of clemency, away from them. For
that reason, Men of Rome, to be frank with you, I put up
less of a fight today, I made less of an effort to have the senate adopt my proposal to decree a public emergency and
order the wearing of military cloaks. I preferred my proposal to be praised by everyone in twenty days' time[20] than
blamed by a few today. Therefore, Men of Rome, wait for   17
the return of the envoys and swallow a few days' inconve-
nience. When they return, if they bring peace, regard me
as overly zealous, if war, as provident. Should I not look
ahead for my fellow countrymen? Should I not be thinking
day and night about your freedom and the safety of the Republic? What debt, Men of Rome, do I not owe to you,
since you chose me, a man whose family starts with himself, for all offices ahead of the noblest citizens? Am I ungrateful? Who shows less ingratitude? When I had gained
offices, I went on working in the Forum just as when I was
seeking them. Am I a novice in public life? Who has more
experience? For I have been waging war against treacherous citizens for twenty years.

Therefore, Men of Rome, I shall be on the alert and   18
keep watch for you by means of my counsel, the best I shall
be able to offer, and by means of my labor, which will almost exceed my power. After all, is any citizen, especially
of the rank to which you have been pleased to advance me,
so forgetful of your favor, so unmindful of his native land,
so inimical to his own standing, as not to be aroused and
fired by this tremendous unanimity of yours? As consul,
I held many great public meetings; I took part in many
more: never have I seen one so large as yours today. You all

titis omnes, unum studetis, M. Antoni conatus avertere
a re publica, furorem exstinguere, opprimere audaciam.
Idem volunt omnes ordines; eodem incumbunt municipia,
coloniae, cuncta Italia. Itaque senatum bene sua sponte
19 firmum firmiorem vestra auctoritate fecistis. Venit tempus, Quirites, serius omnino quam dignum populo Romano fuit, sed tamen ita maturum ut differri iam hora non
possit. Fuit aliquis fatalis casus, ut ita dicam, quem tulimus, quoquo modo ferendus fuit: nunc si quis erit, erit voluntarius. Populum Romanum servire fas non est, quem di
immortales omnibus gentibus imperare voluerunt. Res in
extremum est adducta discrimen; de libertate decernitur.
Aut vincatis oportet, Quirites, quod profecto et pietate
vestra et tanta concordia consequemini, aut quidvis potius
quam serviatis. Aliae nationes servitutem pati possunt,
populi Romani est propria libertas.

have one sentiment, one desire: to turn Marcus Antonius' designs away from the Republic, to quench his fury, crush his audacity. All classes want the same thing; the municipalities, the colonies, all Italy are putting their shoulders to the same wheel. And so the senate, commendably firm of its own volition, has been made firmer by your backing. The time has come, Men of Rome, later than befitted the 19 Roman people, it is true, but still just at the right moment so that it cannot be deferred another hour. What may be called a fate-ordained misfortune befell us,[21] which we endured as best we could. If anything of the kind happens now, it will be of our own choice. It is against divine law for the Roman people to be enslaved, since the immortal gods willed that they rule over all nations. The ultimate crisis is upon us; freedom is at stake. Either you must be victorious, Men of Rome, as you surely will be thanks to your patriotism and your strong united will, or—anything but slavery. Other nations can endure servitude, but the birthright of the Roman people is freedom.

21 I.e. Caesar's dictatorship (cf. e.g. 3.29; 7.14; 8.32; 10.19).